We Are All Called

Four Key Births We Are Invited to Experience as Disciples of the Lord

We Are All Called

Four Key Births We Are Invited to Experience as Disciples of the Lord

Father Tom Heron

eleven twenty-four Productions, LLC

2019

IN MEMORY OF AND IN DEDICATION TO
DANIEL A. MURRAY

Priest,

Teacher,

Spiritual Guide,

Mentor,

Wordsmith,

Fellow Basketball Gym Rat,

Friend.

TABLE OF CONTENTS

FORWARD

by Mary Kay McKenna

"Once in the Kingdom of God" is how the First Penance retreat begins to share the Gospel stories of our Heavenly Father's favorite daily miracle: His forgiving, merciful love. The young penitents act out the Gospel parables of the Lost Sheep, Zaccheus, and the Lost Son. Each Gospel scene ends with "and there was much rejoicing." As pastor, Father Tom encourages parents, teachers, engaged couples, everyone to "pray and play." This is based on his experience growing up, observing his parents, who were openly expressive of their own prayerfulness and playfulness. So, as the coordinator of parish ministries at St. Matthew Parish, this mantra is the driving force behind all we do.

Fr. Tom asked me to write the forward to his book. His book is a collection of stories. Stories I heard directly from him over the 30 years we have shared our mutual life's purpose: spreading and living the Gospel of Jesus. These stories all contain some truth, often a little " Irish blarney," which he inherited from his grandfather, but mostly spun in a manner to do what he was ordained to be: *in persona Christi*, a priest in the order of Melchizedek.

This means "in the person of Jesus." Whenever a priest celebrates a sacrament, he is "in the person of Jesus" leading all to our Heavenly Father.

Fr. Tom knew in his heart and soul that terrible, yet awesome responsibility to lead those he encountered to "seek first the Kingdom of God." Seek to understand life and its rich meaning by coming to know our Heavenly Father's understanding of life, which Jesus Himself proclaimed.

As Jesus was a storyteller, Fr. Tom often says, "I love telling stories. I wake up every morning wanting to share a story." The stories frequently appear imbedded in a homily invoking a full range of emotions from laughter to tears. The story of his father's early death connected the two of us on what became a lifelong friendship, first as colleagues teaching high school and later in parish work side by side. His stories connect, healing the many, who feel disconnected in our society.

This endeavor began in earnest with his mentor Monsignor Dan Murray's early death from heart failure. The plan had originally been for Msgr. Murray to write the book in his retirement. It is hard not to imagine his presence throughout the book. Hence Fr. Tom's dedication is to his dear friend and mentor.

A sketch Fr. Tom entitled, "A Thumbnail Chronology," provided the early framework for the book, followed by an online piece written by Mike Mallowe. The positive response to that work nurtured a full attempt on my part to begin to put on paper, in a cohesive structure, the stories that needed to be told. The order took shape catalogued as Four Births: Natural, Spiritual, Vocational, and Birth Into Eternal life.

The arduous task had begun. He would write, I would write. He would edit and embellish, I would tie it together. Father sought advice from B.G. Kelley, who candidly told him to "Clean up the clutter. Simplicity breeds clarity. Show support instead of just telling statements." Kelley is an author, himself, penning *The World I Feel*, which is a book of poetry. He was also a writer for the television film *Final Shot: The Hank Gathers Story* (1992). He regularly contributes to *The Philadelphia Inquirer*, in addition to many other publications.

After two years, Fr. Tom met Kevin Haslam, a parishioner at St. Matthew and founder of eleven twenty-four Productions, the publisher of this book. Kevin's interest in bringing the book to publication fired the cause to get the job done. We spent hours with Kevin, not only telling the stories, but flushing out the connection to Gospel truth. Meaning, passion, intensity, and commitment flourished and drove all three of us to finish this great work.

Fr. Tom celebrated 40 years a priest on May 20, 2018. It is hoped that his story uplifts, encourages, touches, and moves all who read it to a deeper understanding of themselves and their relationship with Father, Son, and Holy Spirit.

Imagine, for a moment, Jesus saying to you "I love you, I heal you, I forgive you, you are precious to Me. You are passionately and profoundly loved." I am most grateful to have been an eye and ear witness, behind the scenes, dodging obstacles, facing fears and frustrations head on, challenged time and time again, but never bored.

Fr. Tom often proclaims, "I cannot thank God enough for sharing in the one priesthood of Jesus Christ." A dream fulfilled! Carpe Diem!

INTRODUCTION

"We should not fix our desires on health or sickness, wealth or poverty, success or failure a long life or a short life. For everything has a potential of calling forth in us a more loving response to our life forever with [the Blessed Trinity—Father, Son, and Holy Spirit]."

—St. Ignatius Loyola (1491 – 1556)

Legend says that when Jesus returned to heaven, the angel Gabriel asked Him if all people knew of His love for them.

"Oh, no!" said Jesus, "only a handful do."

Gabriel was shocked and asked, "How will the rest learn?"

Jesus said, "The *handful* will tell them."

"But," said Gabriel, "What if they let you down? What if they meet opposition? What if they become discouraged? Don't you have a back-up plan?"

"No," said Jesus, "I'm counting on them not to let Me down."

I want to share with you my faith life in the hope that it will shed light on your journey of faith. This journey involves a relationship with Jesus, the Holy Spirit, and our Heavenly Father.

My core identity is a disciple of Jesus, that is, a lifelong student of His way, truth, and life. Laying down my life for others is what Jesus asks of me. This is a painful experience. I need to share as honestly as possible the pains and the joys, the darkness and the light, the fatigue and the vitality, the despair and the hope of following Jesus to places where I would rather not go.

I think of three deaths I witnessed – a small 4-year-old child, Shane Famous, who died of leukemia; a wonderful, spiritual woman, named Karen Purcell, who died of cancer at 51; and my own mother, Dot, who died in 2003. Together, they give me a new and profound appreciation of the meaning of the Resurrection, the central truth of the Catholic faith.

By sharing these experiences I hope to make my own life available to others and become a witness to what, I have heard, seen with my own eyes, watched, and touched with my own hands, as it is said in 1 John 1:1.

Everything that Jesus says and does in the Gospels needs to be seen and heard from the one whose life is still among us, but often hidden.

Jesus is the most revered figure in history. His life and His teaching are imprinted deeply into the fabric of my body and soul. Yet Jesus remains a mystery.

A mystery is not something infinitely unknowable or forever incomprehensible. It is quite the contrary: something always to be further grasped and more deeply known.

I pray that the life, suffering, death, and resurrection of Jesus continue to captivate me and inspire me to plumb the depths of the central mystery of my life – the Paschal Mystery.

We live in an unbelieving age, but one that is lopsidedly spiritual. It makes a major difference whether I believe that I am made in the "image and likeness" of God or that I believe I create God in my own image and likeness.

If many are called and few are chosen, fewer still choose to be disciples of Jesus and are willing to courageously trust, radically risk, and ultimately surrender one's will to the will of the Father, like Jesus did.

As you will soon discover within the pages of this book, I inherited two gifts from my parents: playfulness and prayerfulness. That's my heritage from two Irish immigrant families, the Heron's and the Reilly's.

I wake up almost daily from my dreams, with a deep desire to tell the stories of my youth. These are the stories of my sharing in the one priesthood of Jesus Christ. By sharing these experiences, I hope to make my own life available to others and become a witness to what I have heard with my ears, seen with my eyes, watched, and touched with my hands.

I want to communicate a sense of passion and conviction during the administration of each sacrament, most especially during the celebration of the Eucharist, which is contagious and awe-inspiring. A childlike sense of wonder and animation, or as I call it, playfulness, can be illustrated by my proclivity for using props – everything from theatrical masks, to altar-servers holding up giant flashcards, to releasing a live dove on Pentecost Sunday.

In my mind, the children in the congregation – particularly the very youngest – are the truest beneficiaries of my preaching style.

Each of us, every man and woman and child, needs to accept the three roles of our faith – monk, martyr, and mystic.

These are also the touchstones of my own life as a man, as a priest, and as an unwavering force for good that is my deep desire to be a good shepherd to the flock entrusted to me as pastor.

My hope is to share my personal story in its depth, as Jesus did, in order to point out the presence of grace in my life experiences. In recalling stories of the past, I hope to shed light in a new way for you, the reader. Being attentive to my experiences is not enough. I need to shed new light, new meaning and new hope for both myself, and you, the reader.

I reflect as a touched sinner, sharing my understanding with other sinners, so that they too can recognize being touched by grace; that is, the personal, passionate, and profound love of Father, Son, and Holy Spirit.

So, I will begin with the following seven questions for you to ponder as you read these opening pages. We will explore these questions together throughout this work in hopes that you will find Gospel truth:

1. What keeps you balanced through the twists and turns of your life?

2. What motivates you?

3. What guides you?

4. What is the still point of your life?

5. How often do you <u>wonder</u> where you came from?

6. How often do you <u>wonder</u> where you are going?

7. How often do you <u>wonder</u> about the meaning and purpose of your life?

The last words spoken by the new pastor at the conclusion of his installation mass are, "For the sake of the Kingdom of God, embrace your own goodness in the eyes of God."

I have been a priest for more than 40 years, and every time I elevate the Sacred Host and the chalice containing the Precious Blood, I remember a request of my father… "Tom, I want you to be my business partner." It was a belief he taught me, that a young, impressionable son could make a difference. "Do this in memory of me."

PART I: NATURAL BIRTH

"We cannot be born enough. We are human beings for whom birth is a supremely welcome mystery."

—e.e. cummings

CHAPTER 1
The Path to Spiritual Wisdom Through Parables

"Some people's minds are like concrete; all mixed up and permanently set."

—Jesse Howard (1885 – 1983)

Jesus, during His public ministry, was considered to be a "Master Teacher," or, as His disciples refer to him: a Rabbi. He continues to masterfully teach His disciples today through parables.

A parable is an image drawn from nature or common life, captivating the listener by its vividness or strangeness and leaving the mind in suspended judgment about its precise application. Parables catch us off guard, knock us off balance, and cause us to think more actively.

Parables are poetic explanations of spiritual truths that are impossible to fully grasp. For example, the Kingdom of Heaven is far too rich to be captured by one definition. Forgiveness is impossible to explain in a few words.

Parables appeal to the imagination. I once heard Richard Rohr ask in a lecture – and I ask you to do the same right now – to imagine in your right hand that you are holding a gold thread and a dove is pulling you upward. Imagine in your left hand that you are holding a rusty chain attached to a junkyard dog. The dog is pulling you in the other direction. The choice is yours: what will you do?

Jesus conveys spiritual wisdom in many ways – the parables being one. His parables – those simple-sounding, yet amazingly profound stories – show us how the Kingdom of God is already taking shape among us. Jesus proves Himself to be our spiritual director by being "the" storyteller of all time. Jesus does not tell these stories simply to point a moral and adorn a tale. Much more than mere picturesque illustrations,

His parables question us, challenge the normal standards and securities of our lives, call for our whole-hearted response, and invite us to walk in radically different ways.

Jesus was an astute observer of the human condition. How do we know? Because St. John the Evangelist tells us so: He "did not need anyone to testify about human nature. He himself understood it well." (John 2:25). So what is in us?

To be able to hear this answer, we need to let go of some old maxims, which we hold dear. The primary one is that human beings are basically good. Without a doubt we can do good things: we can be self-sacrificing, we can serve others with a willing heart, we can be patient and kind ... In this sense we are basically good. However, the teaching of Christ pushes through this to a view of the human person, which can make us a little uncomfortable.

Jesus leaves us in no doubt that the best, the most noble, and the most impressive of us have a problem of the heart. For out of the heart – in other words, the deepest and darkest recesses of our thoughts – spring "evil thoughts, unchastity, theft, murder, adultery, greed, malice, deceit, licentiousness, envy, blasphemy, arrogance, folly." (Mark 7:21-22). We, in and of ourselves, cannot change the condition of our hearts, which Jeremiah says in his 17th chapter, leans toward self-deception. Only ongoing conversion can create in us a clean and pure heart, because through baptism we were born again of the spirit, became a new creation, and received a new heart. It is only by turning away from sin that our minds and hearts are transformed and renewed according to the 12th chapter of the Book of Romans.

Jesus' parables reveal a new world and a new way of living. They do so through language and vivid images that seem quite familiar and very ordinary, even if at times He gives His storyline unusual and extraordinary twists. Jesus tells us of two brothers, one who runs away and one who stays at home. He introduces day laborers, who work in vineyards, and managers of large estates. He brings in women searching for lost property or preparing dough for the oven. His stories present a lazy judge, a merchant hunting for precious jewels, a traveler robbed and left for dead, and servants waiting up at night for their master to return. These parables take us into the mind and heart of Jesus. They let us glimpse into His vision of the world around Him.

Through His parables, Jesus evokes a range of human experiences: things that happen to men and women frequently or at least every now and then. His stories reflect vividly how He sees our lives and cherishes the powerful and loving way God deals with us. They answer our questions: What is God like? What is God doing for us? The parables of Jesus share with us His new vision of our world and the fresh possibilities God offers us.

I remember reading a reflection on the art of teaching that can apply to Jesus, the Master Teacher. Teaching is not about filling your students' (disciples') heads with facts and information the way you fill a bucket with water. No, teaching (and learning) is about lighting a fire in the minds, hearts, and souls of your students. Jesus once said, "I have come to set the earth on fire, and how I wish it were already blazing!" (Luke 12:49).

CHAPTER 2
Grace Builds on Nature

"Our greatest happiness, our truest joy, is connection with others. Our greatest sorrow is to be cut off from them."

—Brother David Steindl-Rast, "i am through you so i" (2017)

I remember with acute awareness and fondness my first memory to this very day. My mom and dad moved from Darby, Pa., to the next town over in Delaware County, Collingdale. We moved into a corner delicatessen in the shadow of Saint Joseph's Church.

After we moved, and the business was up and running, my senses were attacked daily. To this day, when I experience the pungent smell of liverwurst or the sharp odor of Lebanon bologna, my mind's eye turns back to that beloved deli in Collingdale.

The store was on the first floor in the front of the house, and we lived above. When my dad didn't have any customers, he would come back into the kitchen area, which was behind the store, for a cup of coffee and conversation with my mom.

I was a very rambunctious little guy, so I was the great disturber of that mid-morning coffee break. My dad finally came up with a creative solution to my rambunctiousness. With his large hands, he would pick me up and place me on top of the refrigerator. Held hostage to my isolated elevation, I could do nothing but kick the refrigerator door while my dad sat at the table, a foot and a half away from me, able to somewhat enjoy his coffee after all. Dad always had a twinkle in his eye. He knew what he was doing.

Let's take a brief moment and flash forward to 1978. I think about my very first time elevating the host and the cup; changing simple, unleavened bread into the Risen Body of Christ, and transforming simple wine into the Precious Blood of our Lord. The gesture of my dad lifting me up and putting me on the refrigerator was a vivid connection for me in that moment. I realized that a simple, natural gesture that most children enjoy bridges our very souls to our Risen Lord.

This gesture is a living memory for me; a transformational moment of conversion that connects me to my dad every time I lift a baby up over the altar at a Baptism, and every time I lift up the host and chalice during the celebration of Mass. It is the constant reminder of the salvation that Jesus brought to all mankind; the Father's understanding of life that I have the privilege to proclaim.

'Let's be Business Partners'

I was born John Thomas Heron in the wee hours of the morning of Nov. 14, 1952, of strong Irish heritage. Irish was imbedded in my genes. Irishmen are fond of telling stories, some full of blarney and some full of truth. We are an intense, moody breed, and are deeply religious. My family, Irish to the core, displayed a fierce allegiance to the Catholic church, wearing green on St. Patrick's Day, and nearly genuflecting at the mere mention of Notre Dame football.

My grandfather, John Joseph Heron from Draperstown, came over to America in 1914 at just 22 years of age. He and his wife, Mary Alice Flood from Donegal, were saddened to leave their home and family. My grandfather never tired of talking about what he called, "My dear old Ireland."

The surname, Heron, is not a common one. Sometimes my grandfather spelled it with two R's, but I inherited the single-R iteration and its reference to the bird often found along coastal waterways. Perhaps that fits me best. I am small in stature with bird-like speed.

My grandfather, as well as many of my aunts and uncles, settled in small Irish "ghettos" surrounding Philadelphia with names reminiscent of the "the old country" names, such as Darby, Yeadon, and Collingdale.

My father, Jack, met my mother, Dorothy Reilly, at Baldwin Locomotive in Eddystone in 1947. She made every possible attempt to get dad's attention. It seemed to be a fruitless effort, but eventually, they agreed to a first date.

Of course, their first date was to a Notre Dame football game. They both shared a common faith that was very important to them, and they both shared that familiar Irish heritage. I have no doubt these shared interests paved the way for their eventual marriage.

They married Oct. 15, 1949, at Holy Child Church on North Broad Street in Philadelphia. A daughter, Suzanne, was born in 1950. I was born two years later, then a son, Joseph, and finally Mary in January 1957.

It may have been just another ordinary day for my dad, but for me, another life-shaping memory was formed. In July 1957, he brought me along to the warehouse to pick up the groceries. Standing on the seat, beside him, in the car (there were no car seats back then), I recall us coming to a halt at a red light at Woodlawn Avenue and Providence Road. That's when my dad turned to me and said, "Tom, I want you to be my business partner." Four-and-a-half years old, I didn't know what that meant, but enthusiastically, I responded favorably.

My dad and I shared a playful ritual when visiting the warehouse together. Standing on the rickety-wheeled flatbed cart, which had no sides to grip onto, I braced myself for dear life as dad raced me down the aisle prior to loading up the stock onto the cart.

When we returned to the deli, I wanted to keep my end of the bargain. Now that we were business partners, I wanted to help my dad. I was more of a hindrance than of help. Dad picked up on that. I still have a vivid memory of him holding my wrist and showing me how to put a can on top of another can. We would move the unsold stock forward so that would get sold first, and then place the new stock behind it.

The words, "let's be business partners," were followed up with the gesture of allowing me to help him. That's what life is all about: word and gesture. It's a sacramental phrase, because it made me believe that I was important to my dad and that I could make a difference ... I could contribute.

One month after forming this cherished partnership with my dad, my innocent life, in a vast world hardly experienced, would change forever.

Jack and Dorothy Heron's wedding day.
Oct. 15, 1949, Holy Child Church, North Philadelphia

CHAPTER 3

'Pray Hard, Dot, I'll Always Be With You'

"Those we love don't go away, they walk beside us every day. Unseen, unheard but always near, still loved, still missed and very dear."

—Source Unknown

My parents had traveled to the shore for a three-day vacation, leaving their four children with their grandparents. We all waved goodbye to my mom and dad. Little did we know, that would be the last time we would see them together.

They drove to Atlantic City (at a time way before the casinos, when Steel Pier was the only memorable attraction), checked into the hotel, unpacked, changed, went to dinner, took a walk on the boardwalk, and decided to see the movie, *The Ten Commandments*.

During the film, my dad's lungs began to retain fluid, and as a result, he could not control his coughing. Wanting to be courteous to the other patrons of the theater, he and my mom left the movie early and returned to their hotel room. Around midnight, mom called the hotel doctor, and after careful examination, the doctor called an ambulance. At the hospital, a team of doctors worked on my dad from midnight until about 2:30 p.m., the next day.

A priest came an hour earlier to anoint my dad. In his final hour, he embraced my mom, as they laughed and cried. The last words my dad spoke to his wife were, "Pray hard, Dot, I'll always be with you."

These words still echo in my heart and soul. On Monday, Aug. 26, 1957, 2:30 in the afternoon, Jack Heron was born into eternal life, at the age of 33.

The Four Births of Jack Heron	
Natural Birth	Jan. 28, 1924
Spiritual Birth (Baptism)	Feb. 12, 1924
Vocational Birth	Oct. 15, 1949
Birth Into Eternal Life	Aug. 26, 1957

The following day, I was very confused to find my aunt and uncle in my parents' bedroom. My mom came in from another bedroom, and with great emotion, said to me, "Your dad went to heaven."

As I grew to manhood and became a priest, I grew to understand that my dad had kept his dying word to my mom. Never, ever had he not been with his wife in memory or in love; his reassuring presence was always a palpable part of her life and the lives of his children.

After my father's death, my mom and her children took over running the grocery store as an extension of their family. It kept a tangible connection with my dad. My mother kept the store running despite the fact that all of her kids were under the age of 6 at the time.

My mom told this story countless times on a Sunday afternoon when we would all sit down for mashed potatoes, peas, and roast beef.

A Love That Never Left

Mom and dad's honeymoon was a two-week, restful stay on Miami Beach, which was unheard of back then. My dad was the only son of his parents. His mother, Mary, doted on him. That became a source of great conflict between my mom and dad, especially because his mother did not want him living or working too far away from her.

My dad served in the U.S. Army, but was honorably discharged due to health conditions. As a result, he was able to attend The Wharton School at the University of Pennsylvania, earning a degree in business. He worked four years at Baldwin's before suffering a heart attack at age 30. His stay at the hospital spanned almost three months, only to return home with two children (and a third on the way), a weak heart, and no job. My mom's brother was working at a steel mill in Buck's County. He was able to get my dad a job there, but my grandmother (my dad's mother) was beside herself that he would be 45 miles away from her. So, in the time before he started his new job, my grandmother went out and purchased the corner deli. That did not sit well with my mother. There was an incredible amount of tension, because my grandmother wanted to still be the primary influence in my dad's life; so much so that my grandmother really blamed my mother for my dad's death. My mom had to overcome that false and unfounded accusation. It took a couple of years for my mother's soul to be healed.

My dad was an entertainer of sorts. He engaged every person that came into the store, whether it was a child or an elderly person. My mom was shyer compared to my dad, who was extremely outgoing; yet, she was very fond of that, as well as the importance faith played in his life and influence over his own children.

While my dad was physically absent after his death, he was present in terms of memory and love. My mom was one of nine siblings, and she was 34 years old at the time of her husband's death. Everyone, from each one of her siblings to the parish priest, was encouraging her to remarry. For the most part, the encouragement was because, "Your children need a father." My mom would reflect upon this, even when we were young, during that Sunday ritual of mashed potatoes, peas, and roast beef.

"I would have to love a man in order to marry him so that my kids would have a father," she would say to us. "They don't understand that I'm still in love with your father."

That made a very deep impression on me. She talked about how they argued – it wasn't one of these lily-white marriages – but even still, she was very much in love with my dad until the day she died more than 46 years later. In some deep, spiritual way, I think their love grew, despite his physical absence.

My mom gained great strength from that remembered love, even though it only lasted seven years. This allowed her to make the decision to be on God's side of this world. Her faith and experience would triumph over any tragedy or trial. It would only be with God's help and with a devotion to the Blessed Mother. She firmly believed that God the Father would grant in the next life the promises made by His Son in the Gospels.

Clockwise from top left:
Joe Heron, Suzanne Heron, Tom Heron, Mary Heron. 1963.

CHAPTER 4
The Man of the House

"I can resist anything except temptation."

—Oscar Wilde, Lady Windermere's Fan (1892)

I came to an early understanding that natural birth is not an isolated reality. At 4-and-a-half years old, a remarkable thing was happening. Aunts, uncles, and adults in the neighborhood would say to me, "You are now the man of the house."

Like the idea of being my dad's business partner, it seemed to be a thrilling reality; it sounded good. However, it was truly an unbelievable burden, which had a de-formative effect in my life for a very long time.

I didn't fully understand the implications of being the man of the house, yet I wanted, and tried, to live that reality. Deep down, it weighed on me, confused me, exhausted me, and overburdened me. Yet, foolishly, I still tried to be "the man of the Heron household."

A Lesson Through Larceny

My mother now had to take over operation of the store. She asked me to help by placing empty Coca-Cola bottles in red, wooden crates in our basement (24 to each crate to be exact). You would get two cents for one soda bottle, so I thought it was great to be helping and "making" us some money.

Word spread in our tight-knit neighborhood that another boy was getting an allowance for taking out the trash in his household. Naturally, I went to my mother and asked for the same. She was very quick to dismiss my request. That wasn't how she was raised and it wasn't how she was going to raise me.

My mother had a rule: you could not go into the store and take anything unless you asked her permission. I had already gotten rejected on my allowance request. Sneaky and defiant, despite knowing the rules, I acted out.

Because I was up early in the morning and no one else was, I would get on a chair and unlock the door to go out into the store. Staring back at me was a boy in a glass candy case – a boy who would eventually use his wits to find a loophole in his mother's ironclad rule.

Pondering the room, I noticed that on top of the candy case were pretzel sticks. Off to the side of the candy case was another case that housed Philadelphia's famous treat, Tastykakes. Behind the candy case, there was a shelf. On top of it was a cigar box. With its top ripped off, this is where we kept loose coins.

I made it my ritual in the mornings to go out, still following my mother's rule (or so I thought), and reach my hand up, pull out two dimes, and go into the kitchen to hide them behind the refrigerator where I once sat in my playful "time out" with my father.

"If I had two dimes, what could I get?" I asked my mom when she came down in the morning.

She thought it was great, because she was teaching me a lesson on how money could be turned into goods and products.

She closed the store at 1 p.m. to go upstairs and rest for an hour. I retrieved the two dimes, unlocked the door, threw the dimes in the cigar box, grabbed the four things I calculated to be a tradeoff, and went out the kitchen door into our long backyard. My grandfather planted these bushes at the end of the yard, which I chose as my hiding spot so that I could eat all of the candy I had just "purchased."

In second grade, on the brink of my first confession, my mom found me in my bedroom, crying my eyes out. I couldn't take it anymore and finally confessed to her – before I confessed to the priest the next day – that I had been stealing from her for about two and a half years.

She told me that I had to confess that, but to let the priest know that I had already confessed to my mother, and while she forgave me, she will also be punishing me for that behavior.

It was in this guilt that I learned a very early moral and spiritual lesson through the art of larceny.

Satan has two lies he uses at different stages. Before we sink, Satan tells us that sin doesn't matter – one little sin, no one will notice. After we sin, he tells us that we are hopeless. God will abandon us. But Jesus tells us that God wants us to live free of guilt, fear and sin.

Sin is seductive. It masquerades so well that we see goodness rather than evil. Too often we are blind to our motives and ruthless in our pursuit of what we want. During the temptation of Jesus in the desert, the devil packages apparent good in three different ways, each of which has appeal. Jesus, however, sees beneath the packaging and recognizes what is at stake: His very relationship with God, a relationship in which God has absolute primacy. Jesus recognizes that to say, "yes" to the devil, means nothing less than to betray God.

None of us should have to face the wilderness alone; none of us should be thrown back on our own resources. We are all tempted; we all fail; we all sin. Sometimes we might wonder if there is an exit from the wilderness. All of us need to hear, like Jesus, the voice of the Father that recognizes us as His beloved children. When we hear that voice, the call to repent is the call to stay in the company of the One who loves us. The Gospel challenges us to change our minds about the way we think change our hearts about the Gospel we ignore, and change our ways about habits of sin. This is a lifetime task. Jesus did not overcome the temptations of Satan in the wilderness. He achieved that victory only in His death.

Sly as a Fox, Gentle as a Dove

My mother made an essential lesson of the Gospel come to life when I was 7 years old. By that time, I was helping out in the store. My mother was still holding onto it, just barely at times; the financial struggle was an ever-present reality. Near poverty was also a familiar Irish struggle in the United States.

One day, my mother closed the store early and told me to help her put some canned goods and other groceries into five shopping bags. Then, I was instructed to put them in the back seat of a neighbor's car, which she borrowed for this spiritual mission.

We got into the car and my mom began driving up the street with the headlights turned off. We parked close by the house of a family we knew; a family that desperately needed food. It was near Thanksgiving, and my mom, barely keeping her own family fed and warm, the love of her life gone, worried about this family. It was what her husband would have done and she was an extension of him.

My mom, never explaining her charity, was teaching me, her son, a lasting lesson – the kind my dad's "business partner" needed to learn.

"Tom," she said to me, "Carry one bag of groceries at a time down the alley and put them up on the back porch of this family. Don't make a big deal about it, just do it. And be quiet."

She touched my arm and brought her face close and said, "and don't let anybody catch you doing this!"

At 7 years old, I thought this was a remarkable adventure. Here we were, involved in some secret mission and I was entrusted with pulling it off! It would take a long time for the full import of that day to sink in, but when it did, I was forever grateful for the memory.

"That is the Gospel Mission," I later thought. Mom's way was to teach by example. She didn't need to discuss the theology of the Corporal and Spiritual works of Mercy. She taught them by doing them, by giving alms.

The Irish have two very distinct class divisions. One is either "shanty," and the other is "lace curtain." Most of Collingdale Irish could be classified as "shanty" with "lace curtain" ideals. I think of it as a bit like a "champagne taste" with a "beer" pocketbook.

I embodied both characteristics. While the "shanty" are wily and conniving, the "lace curtain" are upright and proper. Both are conscientious and hard working. In the words of Jesus, "be as sly as a fox, yet gentle as a dove."

Clean Like a Marine and Travel the World

This notion of being the man of the house was a theme that continued to weigh heavily on me, even before my adolescence.

My mother had to hire a woman to come in three days a week for a few hours to clean the house, do the wash, and prepare lunch for all of us, earning $8 a day for $24 a week. She worked for us for three years before informing my mother of a new job offer that would pay her almost double, $48 a week for a family in Paoli. I could tell that this was very distressful to my mother that she was going to lose this woman's services.

I made a very strong plea to this woman to stay with my mom, because this would be such a disrupting force to our family – mom especially. Despite my strongest efforts, she could not be swayed.

There were two things my mom wanted to keep her happy in life: a very clean house and travel.

After the departure of our former employee, I specifically recall at age 10, past 9 o'clock in the evening, my siblings already in bed, my mom asleep on the couch, my ambition to clean the house. I would take the kitchen chairs and put them up on the table and cleaned the house as if I were in the Marines. Oftentimes, I would work from 9 at night until 1 in the morning to clean the kitchen and the living room until it was immaculate. Dead tired, I would always make sure to be awake before my mother would awaken to see the fruits of my labor. I wanted to see the delight on her face and get a word of thanks.

We didn't own a car for about nine years. Our last one, a 1955 blue Mercury, broke down when I was just six years old. It wasn't until I was 15 that I paid $450 for our next one, a 1964 Rambler Station Wagon. I also purchased our first color television. Could you believe I paid more for that than the car? Times sure were different.

As the man of the house, I took it as my responsibility to afford these things for my family. To do this, I had two paper routes, while also cutting lawns, shoveling snow and being fiscally responsible. I paid for my own haircuts and clothing by the time I was in eighth grade in order to relieve my mother of financial burden – all of these gestures because I was named the man of the house.

I took her on cruises, as a priest chaplain, to St. Petersburg, Russia, all the Caribbean islands, the Panama Canal, Mexico, Norway, Sweden, Denmark, Holland … That was over the top, all because I never knew what it meant to be the man of the house. It did have to come to a stop at some point, though. There was some deformation that was going on, which went on until well past my mid-20s.

CHAPTER 5
A Deep Connection

"Our greatest, deepest joy is Holy Communion with family. Our greatest sorrow is to be disconnected from them."

—Anonymous

When my father was born into eternal life it seemed like most of the world expected me to grow up fast. It was as if a 4-and-a-half-year-old boy was to transform: hiding in a bush with stolen candy to hustling to save up for a mode of transportation, all in the blink of an eye.

How does one cope with the emotions and the stresses of becoming the man of the house at such a young age?

Enter John Joseph Heron: my grandfather. I never met a more prolific and hilarious human being who enjoyed the simple pleasures of life. Thoughtful, ebullient, and mesmerized by the power of language, John Heron was a poet, a workingman, a passionate defender of family, friends, Irish rights and, above all, his bone-deep Catholic faith.

He came to America from a family of 10 children in 1918, following many of his older brothers who had already arrived. He was about 22 years old at the time. Formally, he only had a fourth grade education, but in terms of observing life and learning from life experiences, he was a man of great wisdom.

An Irish friend of mine once said to me, "It is a sad Irishman that leaves a story the way he found it." If you're talking about my grandfather, you've hit the nail on the head!

John's consummate storytelling was something that he enjoyed immensely. He had these large, farmer hands, callused as can be, using them as if they were props to tell story after story about Ireland. In that very Irish way, the common denominator was that he was the hero of every story. My grandfather would tell me five stories during a visit, and in every one he was the hero of each story - getting this man out of trouble, or setting that man straight, and putting him on the right course. He believed that every story needed a hero and who better than him?

As a matter of fact, he convinced my cousins, my brother, my sisters, and me, when we were all very young, that he singlehandedly resolved the Irish Potato Famine. That was, we were convinced until we grew up and found out he was born 50 years after the fact!

At the end of every story he told, he gave his philosophy of life. With his large hands, he would stroke our heads, very firm, and say, for example, "Tommy, lad, be generous, be modest, and don't let anyone take advantage of you." That was his philosophy of life. His stories always had a point – sometimes an obvious one, other times, a subtler subtext – but, invariably, the stories revolved around John's whimsy.

Stories abound about this patriarch ... Stories, often "not to be believed" in the re-telling, yet when told and re-told in the same sequence of events, with the same precision of detail, and unsolicited by more than one family member or cousin, it was hard to discount their veracity.

There were stories of his "reckless driving" on whatever side of the road suited him, his playful needling of his wife, my grandmother, his free sense of whose property belonged to anyone and everyone, and especially if it worked for him. "Finders keepers, losers weepers," he would exclaim!

He never tired of telling stories to me, and I never grew weary of hearing them. These stories and the messages within also resonated immensely in his poetry. The stories and poetry of my grandfather prepared me for the parables of Jesus.

The poetry he wrote came from deep within that tough, enduring, Irish exterior. For the most part, John was self-taught; his formal education stopped at the fourth grade in Draperstown, Co. Derry, yet his appreciation for education was unlimited when it came to his children and grandchildren.

My grandfather possessed an unrestricted desire to know. He was especially fascinated by the natural order and the divine order and how they intersected. In the natural order, he believed everyone should have his or her hands in the soil – the earth from which we were made.

"Then the Lord God formed the man out of the dust of the ground and blew into his nostrils the breath of life, and the man became a living being." (Genesis 2:7).

He began a family history – meticulously intertwining the events of his own forbearers, especially his parents and grandparents, within the larger canvas of Irish and English history. Some of the passages are startlingly dispassionate, almost like the work of a professional historian, never repeating Irish nationalist complaints but dealing with history as it happened, treating the realities of English occupation with a mature sense of fairness and unfairness, just and unjust.

A poem he quoted by heart often, entitled, "The Irishman," reveals much about him, but even more about the influences that came to fashion and shape me, his grandson, especially after my father's death.

The Irishman
Source Unknown

"What shall we say about the Irishman?

The utterly impractical, never predictable,

Sometimes irascible, quite inexplicable Irishman.

Strange blend of shyness, pride, and conceit,

And stubborn refusal to bow to defeat.

He's spoiling and ready to argue and fight,

Yet the smile of a child fills his soul with delight.

His eyes are the quickest to well up with tears,

Yet his strength is the strongest to banish your fears.

His faith is as fierce as his devotion is grand

And there's no middle ground upon which he'll stand.

He's wild and he's gentle.

He's good and he's bad.

He's proud and he's humble.

He's happy and sad.

He's in love with the ocean, the earth, and the skies,

He's enamored with beauty wherever it lies.

He's victor and victim, a star and a clod,

But mostly he's Irish,

In love with his God."

There were two deep wounds in his heart: the loss of his Irish homeland and the loss of his son, my father. The one thing that he didn't try to be was a father to me. He was a wonderful grandfather, an uproariously funny, joyful Christ-man. That was enough.

CHAPTER 6
Playfulness and Prayerfulness

"God is happiest when His children are at play."

—The Legend of Bagger Vance (2000)

My grandfather wanted to make sure that I kept remembering that his grandson already had a father. This father of mine loved and blessed me with security. If only for the brief time we had together, an attachment was formed as "business partners." We loved each other as father and son.

This interest, this care, that Pop exhibited, was an extension of his soul, his character, that further helped me understand the mysterious way in which God works.

As far back as I can remember Pop was a great man for taking care of things. He took care of us, but he was willing to care for anybody; he was a very simple person. I wasn't afraid to straighten him out a few times, but that's what he expected: "speak up and say exactly what you need to say," were his words of wisdom. He always had a message for me.

John faced two big obstacles in his tireless efforts to take care of the family. First was the Great Depression, which made jobs as scarce as winning lottery tickets. Second was a still virulent, still thriving anti-Irish prejudice.

My cousin Kathy Gallagher recalls our grandfather's work ethic:

"Pop-Pop worked mostly as a day laborer at many different jobs and many different places when he and my grandmother were very young. Some of these jobs included a few days a week working for a plumbing supply company in Philadelphia, others in painting and cleaning jobs, and, of course, whatever grass-cutting jobs he could find. He also worked for the Pennsylvania Railroad, in a service car, one of those old contraptions where you pump the cart up and down with your arms to get around on the tracks."

Pop also worked in stores, bars, and factories. He scaled catwalks and operated boilers that could shoot out a blast powerful enough to roast a man. Whatever it was, wherever he found it, John Heron worked.

Yet, he always wore a big smile and heaved a hearty laugh. That was the constant: he displayed humor, self-deprecating, searing, on-target to those who deserved it – and God forbid you tried to "put on airs" around Pop. If he liked someone, he would tell his family, "I'd take him in; he's a good one, a real crackerjack. A fellow like this you'll have no trouble with."

One day, late in his life, I said to my grandfather, "Pop, you have big strong hands."

Pop lifted his hands up with pride and said, "That's right. Not like some dainty jackassess I know."

Then, just before I left, I said, "Pop, that's a nice hat you have," and his reply was typical.

"Do you want to take this one, Tommy? I can get another."

He was a man of prayer and playfulness, just like his son. He enjoyed a simple meal. You could see the enjoyment he got from that. If he would take us out to dinner, he would eat the scraps from everyone's plates so nothing would go to waste and stack the dishes for the waitress, always trying to be helpful to other people.

He collected stuff and exchanged it at the junkyard for money, and take other things thereafter. The trunk and back seat of his old "junker" would be filled with the treasures he collected. He would pick up papers that were dropped off on the street corners for delivery. He thought, "Boy this is great, they even tied it up for me!" That little bit of mischief kept him young and spry even in his later years.

I recall visiting the cemetery with Pop and my brother to see my dad's grave. If somebody else had flowers on their grave and they weren't around, Pop would take those flowers and place them on my dad's grave. Now you can see why it came so naturally to the not-so-innocent little Tommy-lad to steal a few dimes!

In all of his mischief, John still kept true to his spirituality. He would kneel down on the grass next to my father's grave and teach us to pray in Gaelic, Latin, and English. He knew those three languages in prayers.

He would celebrate his birthday twice every year. He's the only person I ever met who did that. As far as he was concerned, his birthdays were Dec. 25 and March 17!

He was sheer entertainment. You'd never have to watch TV in his company. He loved to engage neighbors. He would sit up on the boardwalk and encourage my brother and I to sneak into a neighboring hotel's pool, because we would stay at a hotel that didn't have one of its own. He lived life to the fullest: that is undoubtedly certain. He has influenced me positively. I took some of his bad habits, too. I don't always obey traffic patterns.

Earth and the Natural Order

My grandfather was a very strong man, physically, because he loved manual labor and gardening. He would do gardening work at his own house. Neighbors asked him to do gardening work. He would do that at our house and his two daughters' houses.

"Keep your hands in the soil," he told me. These were the defining words of his connection with the earth.

The word "earth" is derived from the Latin, *humus*. John's earthliness was the braggadocio part of him, the playfulness that he exhibited.

Humility and human are of the same origin as *humus*. To me, he was a humble, fully human being. I believe he inherited this from his hometown. You could tell where he got the poetry in him; it was from the rolling hills and natural beauty of Ireland.

He stretched the boundaries amidst the tightrope of good and evil. His belief was that you could always do good even if it meant crossing the line, as seen in his reordering of the cemetery's décor.

Pop was free from rigidity and scrupulosity, which can imprison many people. You can be too uptight or too lax. He would say that there's elbowroom in moving toward laxity, or, strict moral standards. I think that was due to his lack of formal education.

Sometimes formal education can be de-formative rather than formative. Yet, he always knew that you had to depend on God to transform all that you thought, all that you said, and all that you did. Therefore, there was a divine restraint, because he was so convinced that Father, Son, and Holy Spirit loved him, there was room for playfulness.

He was so connected to the earth and the natural order. He allowed the divine order to break in; not in a fearful way, but in a liberating way.

His joy for entertaining people continued into my adulthood. At my ordination luncheon, people were amazed to see that in one moment he sat to the side, minding his own business, and in the next, he had a crowd of 20 people around him, reciting his poem, "The Streets of Philadelphia."

I always looked forward to being with him. There was something he had … because he just enjoyed life; there was a magnetic attraction.

Artist Robert McGovern's depiction of John Joseph Heron named
The Old Man in the Winter Sky.

I took the late artist Robert McGovern out to Fair Acres, where Pop-Pop spent the final years of his life, to do a print of him – *The Old Man in the Winter Sky*. When I showed him the final copy, he gazed upon it intently and said, "I am better looking than that fellow." He's good folk, like the Irish expression says. Dementia had set in his mind, but it did not change the sparkle in his eyes or the smile on his face.

He left a favorable impression in little children's minds. When people met him, they felt more in touch with their own humanity … more relaxed about it. That was the wonderful gift that he gave. He made you feel, no matter what struggles or hardships you're facing, you can always get ahead of it, or on top of it, rather than the hardship being on top of you.

God gave him a remarkable gift. He bypassed the formative years where you transcend from the childlike playfulness and innocence to an adulthood where others may influence your actions, beliefs and core identity. That's what made him so real.

The scripture verse that I connect to him – a lesson we can all learn from the life of John Heron: "Truly I say to you, unless you are converted and become like children, you will not enter the kingdom of heaven." (Matthew 18:3).

This is not to be confused with childishness, but childlikeness. There's a big distinction. He maintained a wonderful spirit of childlikeness. I think this is because his primary teacher was the natural order of where he grew up.

My dad had that playfulness. Obviously he inherited that from his dad, my grandfather. That's something to which, early in life, I never made the connection.

When I can get into a playful mood – that happens with a lot of regularity nowadays – I feel most free – especially if I can inject playfulness when I'm giving a homily, teaching a class, or having a meeting. Everybody can connect to it. There's a magnetic connection, an attraction, to playfulness and prayerfulness that can elevate and liberate the spirit.

A good joke creates laughter. That's why laughter is a religious experience, as William James put it.

"We need not go so far as to say with the author whom I lately quoted that any persistent enthusiasm is, as such, religion, nor need we call mere laughter a religious exercise; but we must admit that any persistent enjoyment may PRODUCE the sort of religion which consists in a grateful admiration of the gift of so happy an existence..."[1]

It relaxes your mind, your heart, your body, and you don't get caught up in taking yourself too seriously and taking life too seriously.

What I have repeated in prayer, with great frequency, because it is a reminder to me is: "Lord, free me from worry and fill me with wonder." I tell a lot of people to pray those words, to "free me from fear and fill me with faith."

That's the tug-of-war on which my grandfather and father had a good grip. They would frequently tap into humor and playfulness as a way to unburden them from the heavy burdens of life: financial, political, social burdens, and stresses.

To relate it to the present day, I think that technology and an overuse of technology has the great danger of being dehumanizing, whereas, when you tap into humor and playfulness, that is what keeps you in a healthy balance and a healthy tension.

You can't be naïve about problems and issues in the world, and my grandfather wasn't, but he wouldn't get so consumed and absorbed in those things. He felt that if you were in touch with your true self, a beloved son of the Blessed Trinity in the divine order and a son loved by parents and grandparents in the natural order, you could navigate life. That childlikeness is our connection to our true selves. There's always a danger of assuming a false self, such as trying to impress people, trying to compete, trying to compare.

He died Sept. 14, 1984, during the Feast of the Triumph of the Cross.

My cousin, Kathy, put it simply, "Throughout his life, Pop-Pop continued to cut grass and work in the cemeteries and sell 50-50 tickets for the church. And love each and every one of us grandchildren."

Not a single day of his life goes by that I cease to feel that love. It could never fill the emotional void left by my father's early death, but it provided another kind of security, another fervent aspect of familial devotion and tradition.

My grandfather's influence only added to this rich family conviction that had been brought to the United States from Ireland by every member of his family. John Heron's connection with his church was a simple, and unshakable belief; that was the Irish way.

He was profoundly a man of his immigrant, struggling generation – willing to work as hard as he could to make better the fortunes, both spiritually and economically, of his children and of their children. The spiritual dimension that he helped pass on – by his actions, poems and character – became a pivotal part of everyone of his grandchildren – none more so than in little Tommy, me. He wrote a poem for me when I was just 11 years old, which would later teach me more than I realized back then:

"A little boy went into church and up the aisle he walked

He knelt down at the altar rail; to the crucifix he talked.

'Say, do you really love me, God? My mother says you do.

Then, how much do you love me God if what she says is true;

Do you love me more than a penny's worth or more than a dollar can buy;

Could it be a hundred dollars worth? I guess that's going too high.'

The little fellow listened then; He wanted to hear God's voice, and God

Just had to answer him; He had no other choice.

Oh, yes, I love you Tommy lad, what your mother says is true;

and more than all the world's great wealth is the love I have for you.

And, you know, I'd like to reach my hands And clasp you up to me.

But I can't – because of love for you, they've nailed Me to this cross-shaped tree.

So never forget I love you, boy.

May I ask one thing of you?

Because I love you, Tommy Lad,

won't you try to love me, too?'"

Later, when I discovered a faith in myself that mirrored that of my grandfather, I often thought about that poem and about the dedication to God that I had learned from his grandfather. When Pop finally died at age 94 – the beloved patriarch of a family that drew its strength and spirit from his love – I was prepared to grapple with that same divine and mysterious question that my grandfather had so eloquently posed in his poem of faith: How would I discover again and again in life the "hidden treasure" of the love of the Blessed Trinity and the "fine pearl" of my unique identity as my grandfather modeled for me?

CHAPTER 7
A Turning Point
Accompanied by Familiarity

"Tommy, lad, be steadfast, be stouthearted."

—John Joseph Heron

In February of 1989, while serving as school minister at Bishop McDevitt High School in Wyncote, Pa., I learned I was to be transferred with a new assignment to the formation faculty of St. Charles Borromeo Seminary.

While preparing for graduation on June 9, 1989, I found myself driving along Route 309 in rainy weather, planning to purchase some graduation gifts for members of a chastity group, known as Inasense, in which I was involved with dear friend and colleague Mary Kay McKenna. The students were set to graduate the following day.

Traveling together, Mrs. McKenna and I had plans to stop by school to prepare a presentation for then Archbishop Anthony Bevilacqua. He was to host a performance of the group in two weeks at the seminary.

We never arrived. A terrible car accident occurred involving a tractor-trailer. I suffered a serious ankle injury in addition to broken ribs, but no pain was greater than dealing with the reality that Mrs. McKenna had almost lost her life in the accident.

I went home after a stay in the emergency room, but Mrs. McKenna lay in a coma for three days. She did not regain consciousness for a week.

As summer rolled around, there was a turning point in my priesthood. I was enlisted as a member of the newly formed Formation Faculty, a brainchild of rector Msgr. Dan Murray at St. Charles.

To prepare for this assignment, I enrolled in the six-weeklong seminar of the Spiritual Life Institute, which took place at Seton Hall University in

New Jersey. The program featured discalced Carmelites, Father William McNamara – the institute's founder – and Mother Tessa Bielecki, who, together, fostered and taught a wildly creative approach to prayer, praying and spirituality.

The Spiritual Life Institute was founded as "a small, Roman Catholic ecumenical, monastic community of men and women who embraced a vowed life of solitude. Father McNamara founded the institute in 1960 with a mandate from the visionary Pope John XXIII," making its home in Crestone, Co., as well as Kemptville, Nova Scotia.[2]

While still recuperating, I found myself almost falling out of the chair at the conferences taught by the uproariously funny Fr. McNamara. I was absolutely hooked. More importantly, though, Fr. McNamara's style had a healing effect over my mind, body, and spirit. I could hardly wait to share this bold, fresh style with the seminarians and many friends, not only at the seminary, but also with Mrs. McKenna, a Bishop McDevitt theology teacher. She was also in need of that same healing of mind, body, and spirit.

One of Fr. McNamara's first books, *Earthly Mysticism*, engaged my soul. The Spiritual Life Institute is characterized by this idea, and "steeped in a Christian humanism" that laid the foundations for prayer in a "vibrant natural life enhanced by the Carmelite spirit."

Earthy Mysticism would be the foundational tool I would blend with lessons learned in scripture through my mentor, Msgr. Murray, in addition to Canadian Jesuit priest, philosopher and theologian Bernard Lonergan's philosophy.

Earthy Mysticism

At Fr. McNamara's workshop, I had never laughed so hard in all of my life. Standing at the podium, with a full beard, looking down his nose through the glasses he used to aid in correcting his poor vision, Fr. McNamara represented something more to me than just a master teacher. I sat in awe, hanging on to every word that resonated from Fr. McNamara's lips, as I truly thought I had met my grandfather all over again!

He talked about the idea of earthy mysticism. This was just more than four years after Pop's death, yet Fr. McNamara's approach to life and all of its challenges was so eerily familiar to that of my grandfather's.

In Fr. McNamara's own words, "Western mysticism is necessarily an earthy mysticism. The source of Christian mysticism is in the earth, in the world, in the flesh. To say this is not to speak of confinement but of contentment. This is marvelously true in two senses.

"First of all, God has revealed that he is contented to dwell in us and that he finds his delight in us when we embody him. And when we enflesh him consciously and creatively, there is no end to his delight. It is as unconfined as an active volcano.

"In a second sense, there is divine contentment in the human venture. If we are ever going to enjoy the 'passover,' then our sole content, as wayfarers and pilgrims of the Absolute, must be divine; that is to say, we must be God-centered human beings, earthy enfleshments of the Numinous."

In its most simple form, earthy mysticism tells us to be faithful to our humanity, which is the "earthy," and to allow the spirit to elevate you to be a contemporary Christ man or a contemporary Christ woman. There's always going to be a healthy tension between staying connected to your earthiness and growing in the spiritual life. Earthy mysticism keeps you centered and balanced.

Discernment

The spiritual life is simply life in the Holy Spirit. You have to be able to discern: is this of the Holy Spirit, is this of the Ego Spirit, or is this of the Evil Spirit?

No one has your fingerprints, your DNA, your voice, your eyes… Our uniqueness is remarkable, and that is the Ego Spirit. However, in order to create space for the Holy Spirit, the Ego Spirit has to die of itself. By allowing this to happen, we can grow in a healthy way.

The Evil Spirit can disguise itself as the Holy Spirit. Therefore, discernment is key. Discernment gives us the ability to stiff-arm the Evil Spirit and keep it at arm's length, so that its influences don't corrode, corrupt and disorder us.

To break it down further, discernment is an art form, a science, and a charism.

Art form is what my grandfather and Fr. McNamara exhibited in their lives. They learned how to live and observe life and human nature. They were able to see men and women who were, for example, lacking in confidence, or on the other end of the spectrum, narcissistic. The Holy Spirit tempers the Ego Spirit and can positively form it and transform it into a contemporary Christ man or woman. Your Ego Spirit is in the middle of the Holy Spirit and the Evil Spirit, and there's a tug-of-war between the two for your time and attention.

My grandfather was aware of the Evil Spirit. His superpower was to be amused by it. He wasn't threatened or intimidated by it. He engaged it in an amusing way. He didn't deny it, but it he didn't run away from it, get uptight by it, or allow it to enter in and wreak havoc in his life. What a great lesson!

My interpretation, in light of this teaching, of those pieces of advice that he gave me:

"Be generous" – help people out, and the best way you can help people out is by being in touch with your own peculiarities and idiosyncrasies.

"Be modest" – he's saying to "be humble." Modesty is an Irish phrase for humility.

"Don't let anyone take advantage of you" – trust in your fellow man or woman, but be vigilant to not be too overcome with the natural order. There's a sense of spiritual awareness that we will touch on a bit later that must be utilized to ensure you are living a life of abundance, unaffected by the actions or words of those around you.

Ultimately, art form is learning from life experience. It is observing and learning from nature and human interaction. It is that childlike curiosity.

Science is studying the lives of the saints, who were able to articulate how the influence of the Holy Spirit impacted their lives. Charism is the combination of the seven gifts and 12 fruits of the Holy Spirit.

The Seven Gifts of the Holy Spirit

- Wonder
- Piety
- Knowledge
- Counsel
- Understanding
- Fortitude
- Wisdom

The 12 Fruits of the Holy Spirit

- Charity
- Joy
- Peace
- Patience
- Kindness
- Goodness
- Generosity
- Gentleness
- Faithfulness
- Modesty
- Self-Control
- Chastity

My Four Mentors

The loss of my grandfather, and just a short time later the introduction of Fr. McNamara, is an example of a cyclical pattern that continues to play out. When you are willing to let go of many things in life, that creates the space for you to receive a new gift, or in this case, a new relationship. That takes faith.

The first required step in the spiritual life for everybody is to be attentive, to be alert, to be vigilant, to be on guard, to be awake... You cannot avoid this. That's something my grandfather had learned early on in life and was able to maintain.

In the creed, we pray that we believe in things visible and invisible. In your development in the spiritual life, you have to believe that even though it's invisible, that doesn't mean that it's unreal. This invisible thing you are pondering can be just as real as anything else.

My father died and was physically absent, but in faith, memory and love, he was really present. My grandfather died, he was physically absent, but when you're open to faith, you can maintain a relationship with that person, and you will discover a new relationship in people who influence us.

My father, with those two very dramatic experiences of the raising me up on top of the refrigerator, and asking me to be his business partner ... my grandfather with his poetry, his laughter, his earthiness ... and Msgr. Murray influencing me in an intellectual way that my father and grandfather never would have been able to ... These life forces and their character traits overlap in many other blessed souls I've encountered in my life. Fr. McNamara had the intellectual ability of Msgr. Murray and the human ability of my grandfather and my father. Those four men played a significant role in forming me.

Fr. McNamara and I developed a friendship lasting more than 25 years, until his death in March 2015.

CHAPTER 8
Weeds and Wheat

"Cheap grace is the grace we bestow on ourselves. Cheap grace is the preaching of forgiveness without requiring repentance, baptism without church discipline, Communion without confession...Cheap grace is grace without discipleship, grace without the cross, grace without Jesus Christ, living and incarnate."

—Dietrich Bonhoeffer (1906 – 1945)

Grace, or divine life and love, builds on nature. Every human being has strengths and weaknesses, whether they are physical gifts, physical deficiencies, intellectual gifts, intellectual deficiencies, emotional gifts, or emotional deficiencies. Each of these combinations are what Jesus refers to as weeds and wheat. The concept comes from a parable that Jesus teaches.

The Greek word, *zizanion*, in the parable in Matthew 13, is translated in a number of ways: tares, darnel, and consequently, weed. According to the biblical text, it had a life cycle that was like wheat. It could also easily contaminate wheat seed.

In Jesus' parable, when an enemy contaminates a wheat field with tares, or weeds, while its owner was asleep, the owner's slaves asked if they should go out to gather them up.

"He replied, 'No, if you pull up the weeds you might uproot the wheat along with them. Let them grow together until harvest; then at harvest time I will say to the harvesters, 'First collect the weeds and tie them in bundles for burning; but gather the wheat into my barn.'" (Matthew 13:29-30).

We each have vice and virtue, sin and grace, coursing through our lives. The common sense approach is, well, get rid of the weeds and live your life. This is a very young, innocent, naive approach to understanding human nature and the natural life. Early on in my life, I felt that was the right thing to do. Can we go and uproot the weeds, though?

Jesus says to us, during our lives, He will be the one who will determine the gardening of our souls. We must surrender something of immense depth and trust that we will cooperate with grace, or wheat. We must trust that we will be able to navigate the weeds of our lives without thinking that we can go in and uproot them, or change them.

We all have to live in that tension between being honest or dishonest, between being generous or greedy, between being humble or full of pride. It doesn't go away. It's a lifelong challenge. You can choose to be generous 99 times and then something comes up and you're stealing two dimes and hiding them behind a refrigerator.

The gift of faith is courageous trust in His way, not your way. Radical risk is the willingness to risk letting go of how you think things ought to be. Ultimate surrender is your call to a new understanding of this situation of your life.

What has Caused You to Sin?

"If your right eye causes you to sin, tear it out and throw it away. It is better for you to lose one of your members than to have your whole body thrown into Gehenna. And if your right hand causes you to sin, cut it off and throw it away. It is better for you to lose one of your members than to have your whole body go into Gehenna." (Matthew 5:29-30).

What Jesus is saying here is that you have to uproot the vision, or the way that you use the gift of your eyes, and do away with that vision without doing damage.

Using my hands to reach into that cigar box to steal the dimes was causing me to sin, because I was selfishly trying to secure what I wanted in life and not paying attention to the rule my mom established.

We can use our ears, eyes, words, hands, or feet to enrich life when we cooperate with God's life, which is grace; or, we can use them to disorder or disable life, such as looking at a woman and allowing lust to be a driving force, or looking at an object enviously.

How do you transform that way of looking at life so that you can live it in a healthy, generous manner, rather than a self-seeking, grasping manner?

Jesus says, "I am the way and the truth and the life. No one comes to the Father except through me." (John 14:6).

The Natural Call to Discipleship

Curiosity is the garden in which the natural call to discipleship blossoms. When I think of curiosity, I am reminded of the Elton John song, "The Greatest Discovery."

"Large hands lift him through the air

Excited eyes contain him there

The eyes of those he loves and knows

But what's this extra bed just here

"His puzzled head tipped to one side

Amazement swims in those bright green eyes

Glancing down upon this thing

That make strange sounds, strange sounds that sing"[3]

It's a song about a young boy meeting his baby brother for the first time. This childlike curiosity and innocence is exhibited through various stories about the apostles in each of the Gospels.

I too was full of curiosity as a young kid. I've always had natural curiosity and a desire to explore the meaning of life and discover new things I was always asking questions and still do to this day.

In February 1955, exploring our new neighborhood in Collingdale, amidst the hectic activities that generally take place on moving day, at two years of age, I wandered off and soon realized I was lost. Stopping dead in my tracks, I became hysterical and was taken to the police station by one of the neighbors, after various attempts to get me to say from where I had come. My dad, being alerted of my whereabouts, retrieved me from the police station. This incident began a natural and lifelong curiosity that would prove to be both a blessing and a curse!

This natural curiosity is obvious when two disciples are called to follow Jesus in the Gospel of John.

"Jesus turned and saw them following him and said to them, 'What are you looking for?' They said to him, 'Rabbi' (which translated means Teacher), 'where are you staying?' He said to them, 'Come, and you will see.' So they went and saw where he was staying, and they stayed with him that day. It was about four in the afternoon." (John 1:38-39).

Natural curiosity is the first way everybody is called.

"What is this guy about?"

When you begin to follow Him simply out of curiosity, He's going to teach an important lesson: give of yourself.

"If anyone wants to go to law with you over your tunic, hand him your cloak as well. Should anyone press you into service for one mile, go with him for two miles. Give to the one who asks of you, and do not turn your back on one who wants to borrow." (Matthew 5:40-42).

Your life will be richer if you choose to be generous and if you surrender. You won't feel like you have to protect and secure your own wellbeing. That's a tough lesson to learn. People are hesitant. It sounds good, but to put it into everyday practice is difficult.

Then, He takes it to the next level.

"You have heard that it was said, 'You shall love your neighbor and hate your enemy.' But I say to you, love your enemies, and pray for those who persecute you, that you may be children of your Heavenly Father, for he makes his sun rise on the bad and the good, and causes rain to fall on the just and the unjust. For if you love those who love you, what recompense will you have? Do not the tax collectors do the same?" (Matthew 5:43-46).

You may think, "Are you kidding me? How do you do that?" He asks us to forgive 70 times, seven times. That means balance. If you want to live according to His way, you're going to have to learn how to forgive people who make life miserable for you. Curiosity, generosity, forgiveness... it has to stop here, doesn't it? Let go of life yourself, the most precious gift the Father has given you.

There are many examples of this, even in recent history. Saint Maximilian Kolbe was a Polish Conventual Franciscan friar who volunteered to die in place of a stranger in the German death camp of Auschwitz, located in German-occupied Poland during World War II. The stranger, Franciszek Gajowniczek, as it is recorded, was one of 10 selected to be starved to death in an underground bunker. Gajowniczek cried out, "My wife! My children!" Hearing this, Kolbe volunteered to take his place. He was canonized by Pope John Paul II in October 1982, declared a Martyr of charity.[4]

Dietrich Bonhoeffer, a German pastor and founding member of the Confessing Church, took on Nazi Germany and Adolf Hitler. He was not hoodwinked by evil designs. He was able to see the evil in the Nazi regime and stood up against it. He was executed in April 1945.[5]

Word and Gesture

John the Baptist introduces us to the idea of word and gesture, a sacrament: the way of the Father, Son, and Holy Spirit communicating their life and love to you. As I said, grace is God's life and love, and grace builds on nature.

Every human being has the power to speak a creative word, a healing word, an encouraging word, a challenging word, a forgiving word … Every human being also has the power to speak a condemning word, a violent word, a destructive word … It's the Holy Spirit who guides us to speaking the positive. Our cooperation with the Holy Spirit leads us to a new understanding.

The gesture throughout the Gospels shows us a natural means to achieve supernatural effects. As John the Baptist preached (word), his gesture was baptism.

"And this is what he proclaimed: 'One mightier than I is coming after me. I am not worthy to stoop and loosen the thongs of his sandals. I have baptized you with water; he will baptize you with the Holy Spirit." (Mark 1:7-8).

John the Baptist saw Jesus for what He was: more than a man. It wasn't just a physical sighting; it was something deeper. Who gives you the vision to see Jesus' word of good news? His mission to bring about an understanding of life that reflects his Heavenly Father, and now our Heavenly Father, is His gesture of mercy. This is the medicine that heals, rather than diminishes, our lives.

Jesus acts through word and gesture in many ways: speaking in parables; touching the leper who is a social outcast. These natural means of teaching and healing are what prove to us the power of the Holy Spirit.

For me, it all relates back to the early lessons in my life. Each time I elevate the body and blood of our Risen Lord, I remember my father's gesture of lifting me up on top of the refrigerator, his word, or proposition, to become business partners, my grandfather's gesture of genuflecting at my dad's grave and his word, or prayer, in three different languages. These are the inspirations for me to use my words and my gestures to impact the lives of others.

CHAPTER 9
The Impulsive Apostles

"Ego says, 'Once everything falls into place, I'll feel peace.' Spirit says, 'Find your peace, and then everything will fall into place.'"

—Marianne Williamson

My endeavors to play basketball started at a young age, and as I grew older, my love for the sport expanded. In sixth grade, I experienced a bit of trauma. Sitting in Sister Alma Marie's class on Monday morning, I heard trucks in the schoolyard taking down the basketball backboards. So, when it came time for recess, I decided I would use my time wisely. I marched to the rectory and immediately rang the doorbell. As I was let in, I was quick to demand to see Father Andy Lavin right away. Once in his company, I needed to know why he had not consulted me in the decision to take down the backboards.

Obviously, I was too late, but this would not be my last tussle with authority when it came to the sport that I held so dearly in my heart.

This was purely a lack of impulse control. Poor Peter, the figurehead of the inner circle of the apostles, was very impulsive. This character trait is often displayed and is what makes him so relatable and human. This weakness acts as a source of encouragement to anyone who claims to be a disciple or apostle of Jesus.

A disciple is a lifelong student of Jesus, with Jesus being the Master Teacher to show us how to live life abundantly. Then, you are sent out to teach others how to live life abundantly based on your experiences of your personal relationship to Jesus. This is the key to discipleship.

There's always a paradox involved in this, which can knock would-be disciples off balance. In order to discover your true self – and that's what Jesus is trying to get you in touch with – you have to be willing to lose yourself. That means lose all of your preconceptions, all of your biases, and some of your natural inclinations.

This is the bridge from the natural order to the spiritual life. All of the apostles had to let go of something even in their initial journeys of becoming a disciple of the Lord. This happens when Peter and Andrew leave their nets, when James and John leave not only their nets, but also their father, and when Matthew leaves his tax table. We, too, have to be willing to let go and reassess. Jesus is constantly calling us to find the deeper truth in everyday experiences.

That means "conversion," which is a key word used throughout this book. Conversion is a radically new understanding of self, of life gained through your very own life experiences, and a Gospel interpretation of those very same experiences. Jesus wants us to interpret all of life's experiences, even sin, in a new understanding. Every apostle had the same desires and longings that every person holds within: the desire for security, for status, for power, for wealth, for health, for affirmation; but it's a minefield out there. How we handle and understand our desires makes a significant difference.

Security vs. Contentment

When we try to lay claim to our own security, that should be a warning sign that danger lies ahead. "I'm going to secure this parish financially," or, "I'm going to secure my life in every way," that's the paradox. If you're not willing to venture into territory that is unfamiliar, you're not going to grow in the spiritual life.

If you're paying attention, you've likely come to realize that the young Tom Heron had a little bit of an obsession with money. I've shared stories of little hands grasping two stolen dimes and hustling in the neighborhood to earn enough money to buy a car or a television. I've got one more for you…

I recall being intrigued by a vase we used to have at the house in Collingdale. As I picked it up, I heard a rattling inside that could only signify one thing: there was money in there! I squeezed my hand in to find a quarter at the bottom. "Oh boy!" I thought. However, as I lifted my hand to the top of the vase, quarter in my possession, I found that with my hand in the form of a fist, I could not be freed of the narrow bottleneck at the top of the jar.

I pulled and struggled, trying to squeeze out with all of my might, but it was no use. I let go of the quarter, unclenching my fist, and removed my hand from the vase. I decided I had to leave the quarter in the vessel and give up hope. What I didn't realize until reflecting upon the memory much later on was that I could have just flipped the jar over and dumped the quarter out.

You have to be able to identify in your own life: what is it that you're holding onto too tightly? We see something that we want, but in efforts to achieve it, we can imprison ourselves, or trap ourselves into things that can do more harm than good. If we let go of one way of achieving our desired outcome, another path could open up for us.

The apostles show us the way through both their discipleship and being universally flawed. James and John were sons of thunder. They left everything to follow Jesus. They gave up their own personal plans for His. So, when others rejected Jesus and his teachings, they were quick to spew forth rage rather than understanding.

"When the disciples James and John saw this they asked, 'Lord, do you want us to call down fire from heaven to consume them?' Jesus turned and rebuked them, and they journeyed to another village." (Luke 9:54-56).

This is not the way Jesus operates, nor does he want his disciples to operate in this manner. So, what do you do with that? You discern.

Are you going to walk the extra mile with people and are they going to come around through parables and good works, or are you going to say, "They're not ready to be receptive, so I'll shake the dust from my feet and move on. This is not to say that I'm rejecting them, but maybe in time, someone else will come along and it will be a time of fulfillment for them where they'll be ready and receptive." Jesus had the vision and patience to work in this way.

We see Peter's impulsiveness get him in trouble quite a bit, so much so that Jesus had to say to him, "Get behind me, Satan! You are an obstacle to me. You are thinking not as God does, but as human beings do." (Matthew 16:23).

I go on to think about the feeding of the 5,000 and the wedding at Cana. In both stories, a group of people is experiencing scarcity, to which Jesus transforms meagerness into abundance. That is a pattern in John's entire Gospel, and abundance is the key connector of the two stories.

Further, in the resurrection scene in chapter 21, he's cooking fish on the beach, and what was Peter doing? He was out fishing all night and he caught nothing. What does Jesus say? He says, "Lower your net," and just like that, the apostles come to shore with 153 fish.

My mom experienced this. She was always on the edge of meagerness – not making ends meet – but she believed in providential love. One Christmas, when she had no money to buy any gifts for us children, she won a 50/50 in the November prior, followed by two $500 hits on the lottery on Dec. 5 and 6. Even her luck at the casinos was remarkable. To me, that was a modern-day version of meagerness.

There are two important Greek words in scripture: *kenosis* (emptiness) and *pleroma* (fullness). We have to be willing to risk emptying ourselves out so that we can become a vessel of being full of the gifts and fruits of the Holy Spirit.

That's too risky for people. "I'd rather trust my will than surrender to the will of our Heavenly Father."

We must resist this control-freak mentality that is the air we breathe. You feel like you have to control your future – no, no – instead of controlling it, you have to be attentive to it and be receptive of how God might break in. Then, there will come a point where you are converted and change your way after getting lost. Do not let laxity, worry, or fear overcome you.

I don't like the word happiness. I often thought, "Why don't I like that word?" It seems too superficial to me. I don't ever recall my grandfather ever using that word. What I think he epitomized was contentment. He was very content. St. Paul talks about that in his gratitude for the Philippians' generosity.

"Not that I say this because of need, for I have learned, in whatever situation I find myself, to be self-sufficient. I know indeed how to live in humble circumstances; I know also how to live with abundance. In every circumstance and in all things I have learned the secret of being well fed and of going hungry, of living in abundance and of being in need." (Philippians 4:11-12).

The idea of happiness is a paradox. To be content is to live life in a healthy manner. Contentment means that you can still enjoy life in your own weeds. Instead, we live in a world of great discontent. It is one of the spiritual diseases of our time and culture. When that takes possession of us, we get disconnected from the divine order, the natural order, and the social order. As a result, isolation sets in and that's the definition of sin. At its core, sin is being a foreigner to oneself.

A lot of people say to sin is human. That is completely false. Benjamin Franklin said, "To err is human," not, "To sin is human." Every time sin impacts us, it causes us to be less than human. Jesus is asking us to simply choose to be human. He will take care of the rest.

You have to have compassion and risk not having control. It is not easy to learn whether to lead with compassion and follow it up with conviction or to lead with conviction and follow it up with compassion. That's part of the discernment process. When your life is patterned by those two traits or virtues, that diminishes the need for suffocating control, helicopter control (eg. parents trying to control the destinies of their children) and this unhealthy, individual control of all life circumstances.

Control is not a constant. It's always changing. Balance is part of the answer. Jesus is the other.

"During the fourth watch of the night, He came toward them, walking on the sea. When the disciples saw Him walking on the sea they were terrified. 'It is a ghost,' they said, and they cried out in fear. At once [Jesus] spoke to them, 'Take courage, it is I; do not be afraid.' Peter said to Him in reply, 'Lord, if it is you, command me to come to you on the water.' He said, 'Come.' Peter got out of the boat and began to walk on the water toward Jesus. But when he saw how [strong] the wind was he became frightened; and, beginning to sink, he cried out, 'Lord, save me!' Immediately Jesus stretched out his hand and caught him, and said to him, 'O you of little faith, why did you doubt?'" (Matthew 14:25-31).

Matthew is saying that when Peter is in touch with his relationship to Jesus, he too can walk on water. As soon as he takes his eye off of Jesus, he starts to fall and drown. The storms of life overwhelm him. That's a wonderful image. Jesus is telling all of us that we will have to face difficulties. We all have to face hardships, failures, and setbacks. How we respond to those experiences is crucial to reaching the goal of living life abundantly.

Winston Churchill said it best when he said, "the secret of success is to go from one failure to the next without losing your enthusiasm."

CHAPTER 10
The Purgative, Illuminative, and Unitive Ways

"I can tell you, child, that if you wish to create a new reality you must first let go of the one that no longer serves you. A glass that is already full cannot hold more water. It must be emptied first."

—Source Unknown

"Do not let your hearts be troubled." The hearts of the Greeks in the early church were troubled. Their widows were being neglected. Something new needed to happen in the administration of the church to put their hearts at rest.

The hearts of the disciples were troubled. Jesus was telling them that the time of His departure was near. Naturally, their hearts were troubled. They had left everything to follow Him. Now He was going away and they didn't understand why or where. What would become of them after He was gone?

Our hearts are troubled. The political climate in the United States is undergoing great changes. Terrorism haunts us. Workplaces are downsizing. Perhaps one of our children has fallen in with a questionable crowd, becoming more and more withdrawn, and staying out later at night. There seems to be so little time to spend with family and friends. Work seems to be taking over our lives. Health problems seem to be on the rise, regardless of age. So many people we know and love suffer from disorder, dysfunction, or disease.

Our hearts are troubled. There is never enough money left at the end of the month. With living expenses forever on the increase, how will we manage? Our relationships seem to be in trouble. We don't talk much, except to argue. We spend less time together. Little by little, addictions seem to be creeping into our lives: gambling, alcohol, drugs, smart phones, internet use.

And if this weren't enough, there are the dangers of nuclear waste and climate change. Violent crimes are happening closer to home. More and more moral and ethical dilemmas face society with the advancement of science and technology. Our hearts are troubled.

John's 14th chapter is familiar to us. We frequently hear it at funerals when our thoughts are focused on a future life in eternity, a dwelling prepared by Jesus, "up there" or "out there" somewhere with God. It is a place of complete rest, peace, and joy where we all hope to be someday.

In the meantime, while awaiting that place, our hearts are often troubled. Like Thomas, Philip, Peter, and the others, we, too, are at times feeling confused and abandoned. We are burdened by the trials, cares, and worries of our present lives. We are weighed down by our own sinfulness, laden with guilt and sadness. Our hearts are troubled as we attempt to lift ourselves and bear our burdens alone.

Addiction

Addiction is a big problem in the world, today. Addiction makes an idol out of our desires. We're addicted to money and the false security it promises. That's where the control factor comes in. "I have to secure my financial wellbeing."

The Control Paradox – The paradox is that when you are weak – when you recognize your weakness – you are strong. It takes life maturity to pick that up. It's recognizing that there is a power beyond our control to which we must surrender.

One example I can provide is of my own relationship with a close family member of mine. I understood life in a very different way than he. I was always outgoing and expressive and he was always reticent and observing life, but unwilling to share what was going on inside of him.

He had a great difficulty with expression. I think he took what is another approach to life besides addiction. Initially, I think all addicts go through a denial stage. They try to just face everything in life with a stiff upper lip.

For example, he would play football and get really hurt – tooth knocked out with a nerve exposed, getting a cleat in his chest – but, he would deny these things, or buy into the coaches telling him to just suck it up. That led to repressed feelings, thoughts, and desires. When you do that, the desires fight back with a vengeance. This can very dangerously result in a silent, internal war.

Addictive patterns of living and a stoic understanding are misguided ways to fulfill natural, human desires. What Jesus calls us to is a mystical understanding.

That's what the sacrament of baptism is: to try and orient us toward a mystical way of living, that we enter into the weeds and wheat of our lives. We don't try to control them. We acknowledge them, we don't try to repress them. We know that they can control us if we are inattentive. Every human being has to navigate all of that. Every human being needs someone as a spiritual guide to lead him or her through this dense forest of life's challenges.

Dante opens up *The Divine Comedy*, which is a great expression of life, with entering into the dark woods. The journey into our minds, our hearts, our wills, and our souls is a perilous journey for everyone.

In almost all spiritual traditions, there is a need for purification. This begins our surrender to, our connection with, and our partnership with the Holy Spirit. This process of purgation helps us order our desires in a healthy way.

Almost all spiritual traditions claim that we need to be enlightened or illuminated: that new understanding of life the way that our Heavenly Father understands life.

The apostles go through long periods of incredible misunderstanding of what Jesus is trying to teach them, by word, by parable, and by example. However, when we finally focus on our relationship with Jesus as the key – when we know Him like we know one another – then and only then can our flawed desires and misguided attempts at living life abundantly be transformed.

All of the above is commonly broken out into three "ways" of transformation: the purgative way, the illuminative way, and the unitive way.

The Purgative Way – knowing that pride can raise its head and it needs to be tempered by humility. Humility is the purifying virtue of pride. Chastity is the purifying virtue of lust. Patience is the purifying virtue of anger. Every day, we have to be vigilant in the tug-of-war between honesty and dishonesty. We can trust that God's grace will help us always choose honesty rather than dishonesty.

The Illuminative Way – we catch the subtle nuance of the wisdom of Jesus' teaching and then we make that our own. Jesus is constantly teaching us and we must be open, receptive, absorbing, assimilating, and appropriating this new understanding. The Holy Trinity is always trying to connect with us through our longings and desires. They want to reveal themselves through those natural tendencies of longing for affirmation, but they know that it can easily veer off into a misguided way.

The Unitive Way – you finally recognize that you can't do this alone. There is a radical dependence on an ongoing relationship with Father, Son, and Holy Spirit that enables you to engage the endless struggle of living life abundantly and not succumbing to despair and giving up. People can get worn out. That's why this personal relationship is what refreshes and restores you. That's what Jesus says in Matthew's 11th chapter: "Come to me, all you who labor and are burdened, and I will give you rest. Take my yoke upon you and learn from me, for I am meek and humble of heart; and you will find rest for yourselves. For my yoke is easy, and my burden light." (Matthew 11:28-30).

That's called hope. People have to get out of a childish understanding of the relationship with God. When they think that God is out to punish them, that He's going to reject them, or cause them to fail, what they are doing is clinging to an unhealthy understanding of that relationship.

The relationship with Father, Son, and Holy Spirit is meant to be fulfilling, yet accepting that you're not always going to hit the mark. In the Old Testament, sin is quite literally, "missing the mark," or, "missing the bullseye." Serious sin is shooting the arrow and not even hitting the board.

When we trust in His way, we're no longer afraid of our desires, our yearnings, and our longings. They're always going to be there, so we adopt a gentler, more accepting, and more amusing approach. That's what people like my grandfather and Fr. McNamara demonstrated. They could poke fun at this internal battle that goes on in everyone. When you can combine humility and hilarity, you have achieved a new "unitive" understanding of life. You've gotten through the childish way of thinking. Yet, we can all fall back into an adolescent thought process. Not that an adult way is the ultimate goal, but a childlike way, wonder has to be part of it, so you're not self-loathing. People get caught in self-hatred and self-loathing, or a negative way of thinking. They have this internal monologue going on, even on an unconscious level, a conditioned pattern of thinking that can really be overwhelming.

This is where we walk the tightrope of the natural life and the spiritual life. If you have a childish point of view, there's a good side and a bad side to that. The good side is the playfulness that we've previously discussed. The bad side is self-loathing and lack of understanding, or a lack of spiritual and emotional maturity. The bad or unfortunate side is a big part of being human.

You lose a loved one; in my instance, my father... the immediate thought as a human or a child is, "Why me? How could God do this to me? How could someone with infinite amounts of love cause so much pain in the world?" These are the poisonous thoughts that are out there. How do you mature past those ideas and where does all of this come from in our existence? Why do we have this inside of us?

The purgative way is what purifies these poisonous thoughts and self-inflicted wounds. Where did this type of thinking come from? That is the age-old question. Philosophers, theologians, and poets have been trying to get to the core of this since the beginning of time. From a faith perspective, it is what we call "The Fall," or Original Sin. Something happened that caused a disruption between this all-loving God's original plan for us and our receptivity/interpretation of it.

The ultimate goal of Father, Son, and Holy Spirit is to share the fullness of divinity with us so that we can become like them. In trying to understand that, pride causes us to say, "I can be like you without being dependent on you." That's where it all goes haywire and collapses. It's the misuse of the greatest gift we've received as human beings: to be free.

The snake's temptation in the book of Genesis was, "You can be God." In the world today, if anyone thinks they're God, you don't like them very much. But, He does want to share divinity with us. It's a subtle nuance. St. Irenaeus, a great father of the church, said that being fully human is being fully alive and being divine.

The greatest compliment we can receive is in the first revealed truth: "Then God said: Let us make human beings in our image, after our likeness. Let them have dominion over the fish of the sea, the birds of the air, the tame animals, all the wild animals, and all the creatures that crawl on the earth." (Genesis 1:26).

The rest of the Bible is written to convince us of that first revealed truth. In Hebrew, it is translated that you are exactly like God. Further, though, you are not the Creator, but the highest creature of the Creator.

We must accept our creature-likeness with humility to achieve the abundant life, to be full of wonder, full of trust, full of enthusiasm, full of goodness, kindness, joy, peace, forgiveness, and healing. All of that is hanging there. We can reach out and take the hand of the Holy Trinity so that they can lead us.

Sin is, "I can do it myself." As soon as that thought takes root in our minds, everything that we choose is less than what Father, Son, and Holy Spirit desires for us. They don't want us to be that.

The Frank Sinatra, "do it my way," mentality is the beginning of losing intimacy and deep union with the Trinity. It is pure isolation.

We pay a price for our uniqueness. Everyone is unique. No one has your eyes, your ears, your fingerprints ... but that uniqueness has to be in harmony with the Higher Power, the Universe, the Trinity. Sin makes us a stranger to ourselves. Sin, because of free will, causes us to think we can do it without the Trinity, and as a result, we become strangers to the Father, Son, and Holy Spirit.

So, you initiate a balancing act. You can step away to get a better perspective, but you must very quickly get in close to feel a deeper union. A cycle unfolds. That's what happens when we lose touch with abundance. Self-pity and self-indulgence kick in. As soon as you start feeling bad about yourself, that should be a flashing, red light that you're putting yourself at risk.

That close family member of mine, because he didn't share his thoughts and feelings, allowed distractions to creep in and help him deal with a lot of inner pain that he, for whatever the reason, wouldn't want to share with anybody in the family.

Accepting Help – The Unitive Way

I was sent as a pastor to St. Gabriel's Church in Norwood in the early-2000s. The church had an Alcoholics Anonymous group that met in the basement of the rectory. One of the priests that I lived with was an alcoholic, which inspired me to reach out to this group.

Matt Talbot, who died on his way to Mass in 1925, has become a role model for recovering alcoholics over the years. When Talbot took the advice of a priest during his recovery, he formed the twelve-step program.

I felt that this man from Ireland who battled alcoholism and became a champion for the cause of anybody who had to battle that struggle was an incredible figure in the church. The way you honor such a man, the way you reach out to this omnipresent addiction, is to create a shrine.

A shrine is a place to go when you know you need help and healing. I felt that creating a shrine to Matt Talbot was a way to extend help and healing to this group.

The piece was done by Norwood artist and recovering alcoholic Jim McKay and was installed in place of a confessional. How fitting! You take a closed space and open it up to the public for the very same reason: reconciliation and healing.

People from Delaware County to Philadelphia were coming out to visit this place that enabled them to face their own weakness and know that they're not alone. Inspiration breathed new life into them and gave them a healthy dependence to overcome an inordinate dependence on alcohol.

Jesus is a patient teacher. He guides us as He did those early disciples to understand that the way to God is not found in a method or a process, but in a person. Our relationship with this person, Jesus, is the key to overcoming addictive patterns of living. Jesus is the way, the truth, and the life. The dwelling place that He prepares will not be found somewhere "out there," but within believers themselves. "The Kingdom of God is already in your midst." (Luke 17:21).

We have an advantage over those first disciples who had not yet experienced the risen Christ. We know that Christ has nailed our sins and struggles to the cross and has triumphed over them so that we can live in the freedom of the Gospel.

He is saying to us, "Come to Me, all you who are tired of trying to keep up the pace of a life that is moving too fast. Come to Me all you who are burdened with carrying weapons that keep others at a distance."

Jesus is the way through our sadness and grief, our conflicts and brokenness, our fears and failures, our doubts and sins, our suffering and death. There is simply no one else to trust, nowhere else to go. St. Augustine reminded us that our hearts will be restless until they rest in God alone. Let not our hearts be troubled; may they find their rest in the One who has risen.

CHAPTER 11
Control: The Bad and the Good

"What I do, I do not understand. For I do not do what I want, but I do what I hate."

—St. Paul, Romans 7:15

My leanings were more toward the athletic rather than artistic. One day in June 1957, I noticed a resident of Collingdale was painting his garage. When he went inside to take a lunch break, I walked up his driveway, grabbed a can of paint, a pan, a roller, and a brush, and decided to help him finish painting the bottom of the garage door.

Since he hadn't come back out yet, I continued to paint the driveway, and when another neighbor came out to see what was going on, I painted her, too!

Her screeching protests brought my neighbor out of his house. He told me to put down the brush and said he needed to speak with my dad. Together, the two inspected my work and each gave me a thumbs down. So ended my painting career.

Giving can be a positive feature that can easily offset the controlling distractions, such as addictions, and unhealthy ways of life or thought, that we can easily get trapped into for a short period of time.

That same sense of thoughtfulness, those innocent attempts to help others, could also make an utter mess of things. To this very day, I still find myself learning lessons when negative results are spawned from good intentions.

The best way to help others, I've learned, is to get them to help themselves. If that's not in the mix, your attempts to help are going to cause more harm than good.

They call it the Messiah Complex. It is an occupational hazard every priest has to face throughout his priesthood. People project that onto you, but then you buy into that projection and try to fulfill it. At the end of the day, you could very well cause more harm than good. You will see very real examples of that as the story unfolds.

Inspired Control

When asked about control, I was reminded of a story that has been floating around for the past few years. The source, I am unsure of, but it stands as a strong foundation in the idea of control.

"Scientists study identical twins to learn about the influence of genes on our characteristics. In a study on alcoholism, the scientists were particularly interested in a pair of identical twin sons with an alcoholic father, where one of the twins was an alcoholic and the other twin was not. They interviewed them both, hoping for insight as to why they ended up so different, despite their identical genes and their presumably similar environments.

"The alcoholic son told them, 'Well, I grew up with an alcoholic father, as you know. Alcohol was in the house all the time. I saw my dad drinking. So I guess it was natural enough that I became an alcoholic, too.'

"The son who was not an alcoholic said, 'Well, I grew up with an alcoholic father, as you know. Alcohol was in the house all the time. I saw my dad drinking, and I saw what it did to him and to my family. So I guess it was natural enough that I swore I would never be like that, and so I don't drink!'"

I grew up in an emotionally chaotic family where being attuned to the feelings and moods of my mom, my two sisters, and my brother was vital to day-to-day survival.

When I was young, I was a first-class, competitive overachiever. Everything from sibling rivalry to sports became a referendum on my worth as a person.

I was intense as a teacher, player, and coach. Relaxing was a waste of time. What is the next mountain to climb and conquer?

I needed to learn to allow good relationships to increase my sense of wellbeing and robust physical health.

Hypersensitive to the behaviors, intentions and emotions of others, what allowed me to thrive in childhood also made me vulnerable to people's fears and anxieties. Anxiety is contagious through undifferentiated mirror imitation.

I have no doubt in my mind that my dad's poor physical health stirred in me the desire to do everything I can in terms of exercise, proper eating habits, rest, and relaxation, so that I can live life on the physical level to my fullest potential.

I know that my dad having a weak heart physically motivated me to live life by exercising. I go overboard even to this day at 66 years old, waking up at 4:30 each morning, praying, hitting the stationary bike, stretching and strengthening my muscles, shooting hoops, and swimming. To me, it's a healthy addiction.

I know that I unconsciously wanted to try to honor him, but that motivation also got out of whack. There's no question about that. Sometimes you have to stretch out really far in your motivation and then you come to a new understanding when you're way out there. So, you try to balance it by bringing it back in to your current reality. That understanding for me is that grace isn't magical. It needs a good, natural receptacle – a healthy body – that will allow it to do its work. The Gospel calls us to live life abundantly: to be physically, intellectually, emotionally, socially, and spiritually alive.

Jesus the Man, Jesus as God

There are two genealogies found between the Gospels of Matthew and Luke. They are found in the beginning chapters of both Gospels and go in different directions. The purpose of a genealogy is to say everyone has a specific role to play in the plan of salvation history. That's where discernment comes in to be able to fulfill that plan.

Again, it's not predestination, which people sometimes confuse, too. It is something where you have the freedom to go down a path and self-destruct. That is not God's plan by any means, but that doesn't mean you can't go there. How do you navigate all of that? That's the lesson we must take from sin: that we shouldn't give up on ourselves, because He doesn't give up on us. We have to keep working at it.

Everybody needs a Moses figure in his or her life. That means someone who can lead them through the weaknesses, brokenness, and darkness that inevitably will challenge us in maintaining a healthy, natural order. In St. Matthew's entire Gospel, Jesus becomes the new Moses.

In Mark's entire Gospel, Jesus is a Messiah, or an anointed one, but he is a suffering, servant Messiah. To unpack and explore the meaning of that, He suffered for our sake innocently so that we, too, as His disciples, will be called to suffer like Him in love to try to eliminate the suffering that is rooted in sin in the world. This is the transition from the natural order to the spiritual order.

In Luke's Gospel, healing is the absolute dominant force. People believe Luke was a physician. The healing of the Good Samaritan is unique to Luke. The healing of the prodigal sons is unique to Luke. It centers around the theme of being lost and being found.

John's Gospel shows an unlimited ability to grow so that we can be a Christ-man or Christ-woman. Transcendence is the emphasis. Abundance is the key in John's Gospel. Jesus came so that we may have life and have it abundantly in the natural order and then even more abundantly in the spiritual order.

In our culture, today, the word that would be used for Moses would be mentor. You cannot navigate the spiritual life alone. Everyone needs a mentor or specialist from time to time if they are serious about growing in the spiritual life.

A new lawyer needs a seasoned lawyer to help. A teacher needs a Master Teacher. A priest needs other priests. Doing it alone makes it more complicated and oppressive. You put an undue pressure on yourself. Everybody can look back and say this person played a mentoring role in my life at a certain time.

When you have surgery, proper medical procedure requires that you consult with many people. Physicians tell you why you need the surgery. Surgeons tell you what will be done. Nurses check your medical history and tell you what you may eat before the operation. Physical therapists tell you what sort of activity you will be able to pursue after the surgery and the exercises you must do to recover. The financial and insurance representatives of the hospital make certain that someone is paying the bill! Each professional is a specialist who does one specific thing to take care of you.

Specialization may seem very modern, but it has been with us for a long time.

In chapter six of Acts of the Apostles, we see the first specialists in the history of the church. The apostles wanted to see justice done in the distribution of food. They knew that Jesus had commanded them to bear witness to Him at His ascension, so they appointed seven men to serve the Greek-speaking members of the community. So "the Twelve called together the community of the disciples and said, 'It is not right for us to neglect the word of God to serve at table.'" (Acts 6:2). The apostles established two specialized ministries. They seemed to say, "We will pray and preach while these seven men will take care of works of justice and mercy."

Some believe Christians should be mostly concerned with prayer, and others believe it is just as important to care for the poor and the needy. Human beings tend to divide the world in two: on one side are the things of the spirit – prayers and Church, and on the other side are the things of the real world – food and shelter.

Even the apostles Thomas and Philip in chapter 14 of John's Gospel appear confused about the physical and spiritual, and they want Jesus to clearly spell out where He is going and how they can get there.

Jesus came, suffered and died, and then rose from the dead to show us that what looks like two worlds is really one. The Son of God united the world of the spirit and the world of flesh when He took flesh in the womb of the Virgin Mary. He united the world of the spirit and the world of flesh and blood when He gave His flesh as real food and His blood as real drink. Jesus often used material images to teach us spiritual truths. He told His disciples: "In My Father's house there are many dwelling places." (John 14:2). In fact, St. John's Gospel is filled with signs that Jesus worked in order to reveal His glory.

It would be much easier if all we had to do were pray. It would be much easier if all we had to do were to be nice to each other – those works of justice and mercy. If we are to be true to Jesus' message, it has to be both prayer and works. The praise of God is in feeding the hungry and offering prayers and supplication. The praise of God is in welcoming the stranger and not neglecting the Word. The praise of God is in clothing the naked and praying over them. For those who believe in Jesus will do greater deeds than He did, because Jesus intercedes for us.

Our hearts need not be troubled. When we go to the table of the Eucharist, we join together with Jesus in the greatest prayer of praise, and we are strengthened to go forth to do the works that Jesus did. He gives us Himself – body, blood, soul, and divinity – that we might continue to make Him visible in our world today.

Without wisdom, people perish. You need to have internal vision to see what's going on in your mind, heart, and soul. You need to have an outer vision, too. Even in Matthew's Gospel, a very telling phrase pops up: "Jesus looked out at the crowd."[6] What this means is, Jesus saw the individuals in the crowd physically, socially, and spiritually. Vision has all those levels of meaning to it.

The Greek word represented in the text means, "penetrating gaze." Jesus had the ability to see around you and see through you. You couldn't pull the wool over his eyes. He knew human nature so well that he wasn't going to be buffaloed. He wants us to have that quality, too, not only in our looking at other people, but also looking at ourselves.

Even now, what would be considered at first glance a very noble gesture, in the world today can be looked at with great suspicion. "Is this the beginning of grooming? Is there a hidden agenda?" People sometimes see evil in anything and everything. They're so cynical and so jaded by life that they get a warped view of things. How do you avoid that pitfall or that way of seeing?

The sin against the Holy Spirit is you have eyes to see, but fail to see. You have ears to hear, but fail to hear. That's the natural order. You have a heart to understand, and you fail to understand.

Every philosopher, theologian, and biblical scholar has faced the conundrum: how does this person, Jesus, have two natures, and how do they blend and mesh? That's a mystery. People keep trying to articulate it. That's why a differentiation has been created of low Christology and high Christology.

Some people find those categories not good and misleading, but without question, Mark, Matthew and Luke are low Christology and John is very high Christology. John really is emphasizing the divinity over and over again. He was the last to write his Gospel. There was a need to try and put a balance between divinity and humanity. On the other hand, Mark wants to stay true to the fact that Jesus is the anointed one, the Messiah. Matthew and Luke are thinking of a hero or conquering Messiah. That was the mindset at the time. Mark had to teach them, no, Jesus is a suffering, servant Messiah, and He is very good.

CHAPTER 12
Discerning the Gifts and Fruits of the Holy Spirit

"Be patient toward all that is unsolved in your life. And try to love the questions themselves."

—Rainer Maria Rilke (1875 – 1926)

With birth, no one knows how long we have in life. You try to nurture, protect, and develop all of the gifts and talents that a human being can possess, but there's always a deadline. We don't have a choice in how or when that happens. So, what we are called to do is live life abundantly on all levels: physically, intellectually, emotionally, socially, and spiritually. That's what makes you a full and complete human being.

Death ends a physical life, but it doesn't end a relationship. It comes full circle. In death, life changes, but is not ended. I credit my mother for teaching me that most important life lesson. She was still deeply in love with her husband, with whom she only had the opportunity to share seven years of physical life.

We stay connected to those who have gone before us through faith, memory, and love. Any one of those is a good, connecting link, but when you have all three, a bond is sealed and deepened, even though there is a physical absence. Almost every Mass of Christian Burial that I celebrate, I talk about the importance of faith as living memory. It does not serve as just memory of the past, because you can bring those past events into the present moment. They sustain you.

My mom was a shining example of our belief in the Resurrection. We are born in this life so that we can share in the life thereafter. As you will learn as this story unfolds, this is the reason why I refer to death as "birth into eternal life." It's a more positive understanding of something that is without doubt filled with loss, sadness, and grief. When you have faith and a remembered love, you can allow that loss to strengthen you and enable you to continue to live life fully and abundantly without allowing it to cause you to give up on your own life. Unfortunately, that is a tragedy that many people don't learn. They become completely inconsolable, and they get lost in the darkness of their grief and their sadness … listening to the Ego Spirit and the Evil Spirit. They get buried alive.

The Gospels talk about "little faith," "weak faith," and "great faith." Every person who is a disciple of Jesus bounces around between those three types of faith.

Little faith always has to do with a distraction that moves our focus off of Jesus. Peter is a shining example of getting distracted. Jesus tells Peter he has little faith when he got distracted while walking out on the water. In loss, distractions lead us to display self-pity rather than facing our grief and sadness on the way to healing.

Weak faith is a righteous understanding of life that is harsh. The apostles often told Jesus to obliterate or do away with those who were not with Him. People of weak faith cannot tolerate paradox, ambiguity, their own weaknesses, or their own brokenness. Righteousness is when you must have everything right, but you deny that you're not right. You can give great commentary on everybody out there who is wrong, but that gives you false holiness. Weak faith can't deal with the daily tension of weeds and wheat.

Jesus is patient and tolerant with our little and weak faith.

Great faith doesn't allow any obstacle to overcome your desire to getting to Jesus. In the Gospels, a Syrophenician woman begs Jesus to exorcise a demon out of her daughter. First, Jesus ignores her. As she persists, the apostles ask Jesus to cast her away. Then, she's ridiculed and compared to a dog. She had overcome stone silence, social rejection, and name calling, but she had "great faith," and for that, Jesus healed her daughter.

My mother demonstrated great faith. Was she still sad? Of course she was, but the reason she demonstrated great faith was because she was connected to the faith, memory, and love of her husband, which carried on until her death decades later.

The darkness of grief, sadness, and loss can blind us to faith, memory, and love. Many people, because of their disconnect from faith, memory, and love, become bitter and depressed for extended periods of time, and just live out life without meaning or purpose. Everybody has dark memories. My mom and my grandfather demonstrated to me that faith and love were key ways to heal blindness caused by darkness.

The Pious Practice of Prayer

The inkling of my thirst for holiness lived deep inside my soul since childhood. As a 5-year-old child, I could recognize that something was going on as I sat beside my mother in the pew at mass. Waiting for her to come back from receiving Holy Communion, I saw the mystery unfold before my very eyes. It was special. She had a peaceful, content, even radiant look on her face that I never saw when she was doing anything else. I wanted to be a part of that. I wanted to find out what that mystery was.

As she performed the pious practice of putting her face in her hands and praying, I tried to look through her fingers and through her hands.

This childlike wonder was strong, but it could not grasp the experience of being uplifted and transformed by receiving Holy Communion. My mother's deep, prayerful countenance communicated a close encounter with the Risen Lord in a way for which I hungered.

Years later, I recognized she was entering into the deep experience of Holy Communion. Just like lifting up the chalice and the host, that idea gives me a way to meditate on how God's life is breaking into our ordinary, everyday lives and how it has an enriching effect on how we live.

My mother taught me that you can allow the pain of physical absence to be a stepping stone rather than an obstacle to real, spiritual presence. She missed her husband deeply, but she remained connected to him through faith, memory, and love. They were the variables that enabled her to transform his physical absence into a continued, deep, abiding, present love. I call it "felt absence." This paradox is a part of learning. If you don't understand it, you're going to get caught in bitterness, resentment, and self-pity. You will never get a complete and total answer, but you know that you can probe deeper and come up with a newer, richer, and fuller understanding of something more than yourself.

Life enables you to learn to love the questions, themselves. We live in a world that loves instant and absolute answers, yet we claim that everything is relative. Einstein had it right that all things in the natural order are relative. In the relativity, everyone must discover a deeper understanding of divine truth. Ongoing search is your rudder, guiding you through the lifelong commitment to this process of constant discovery.

As you are on that journey, it is crucial to have the ability to let go of former patterns of thinking.

The Lesson in Living Your Natural Birth

How do we discern the Risen Lord's presence, the Father's will, and the Holy Spirit's seven gifts and 12 fruits in our daily lives? There are four natural qualities that can help us make clearer decisions and bring us closer to our spiritual birth. Those qualities are simplicity, spontaneity, playfulness, and creativity.

Simplicity is one-fold. Do not hide your issues or make them complex. The prophet Isaiah says, "a child will lead us." The wisdom in his words is that people who maintain childlike characteristics have great potential to be good mentors, leaders, or guides. Even Dante's *Divine Comedy* shows a need for a guide to take the protagonist through the various stages of Hell.

Spontaneity means you are full of wonder, eager to learn, curious, and studious.

In a backyard in Ambler, I remember vividly, pitching a ball to Mrs. McKenna's 3-year-old son, Pierce. He owned a big, yellow, plastic bat and a ball. Pierce told me my role. I was to throw the ball and he would try and hit the ball with the bat. That sounded like fun. He swung at the first pitch and hit the ball, squealing with delight after impact.

"Mommy, I did it! I hit the ball," he said to his mother, who was standing in the kitchen. Joy radiated from his soul to his 3-year-old old face. It was an experience of abundant grace and wonder that I will never forget.

Playfulness combines two unskippable virtues: humility and hilarity.

I give children going through their First Holy Community this prayer as penance: "Lord, help me to be a peacemaker, rather than a no good, stinking, rotten troublemaker."

They get such a kick out of that, because they know when they're troublemakers.

What I'm trying to teach them is the combination of humility and hilarity.

When you can laugh at yourself, you've made a significant step and leap forward in the spiritual life. When you take yourself too seriously, then you start grasping for control of everything. That's why a sense of humor is a vital part of transforming into the spiritual life. That's what my leaders, mentors, and guides, Fr. McNamara and my grandfather, taught me.

God laughs at us when we misuse the precious gift of freedom that He's given to us. We have it! It's right there for our enjoyment and we seem to find ourselves messing up big time. It's a constant battle, which can be overcome by exhibiting childlike wonder.

On Ash Wednesday 2010, I celebrated mass at St. John Neumann in Bryn Mawr for the schoolchildren. After mass, I visited the third grade and asked the students what sacrifices they were going to make during the season of Lent. One young, engaging fellow informed me that he was giving up cake for Lent.

I said, "And you will be able to do this for 40 days?"

He looked a little puzzled, but in a flash, responded by saying, "But, I can still have cookies, Father!"

Keep things simple, have the wonder of spontaneity, combine humanity and hilarity, and you can ease the struggle of missing the mark.

Creativity breeds from God's message, "I made you in my image, after my likeness, and you are very good."

Words denote not only what is present, but also what is absent; not only what is near, but also what is far; not only the past, but also the future; not only the factual, but also the possible. Words denote the ideal, the ought-to-be for which we keep on striving, though we never attain.

So, we come to live, not as the infant in a world of immediate experience, but in a far vaster world that is brought to us through the memories of other men, through the common sense of the community, through the pages of literature, through the labors of scholars, through the investigations of scientists, through the experience of saints, and through the meditations of philosophers and theologians.

The humanistic philosopher Erich Fromm rounds out the idea of creativity best when he says, "Creativity requires the courage to let go of certainties."

So, the question is: who gets to write your life story? This is a question that haunts most people. The freedom and creativity to make meaning out of our life experiences is one of the deepest cravings of the soul. This freedom, according to Victor Frankl, is the essence of life, itself.

PART II: SPIRITUAL BIRTH

"The Blessed Trinity might be invisible to us at times, but with the eyes of a child and the constancy of a mature believer, we pledge ourselves to remain faithful to the dream of Jesus of Nazareth, realizing that perhaps the maddest thing of all is to see life as it is and not as it should be."

—Paraphrased from a funeral homily

CHAPTER 13
Be a Hero, Deny Oneself, and Follow Christ

"Jesus came and touched them, saying, "Rise, and do not be afraid." And when the disciples raised their eyes, they saw no one else but Jesus alone."

—Matthew 17:7-8

We yearn for messages that go beyond information to meaning. For the people of Israel, the fullest communication and the deepest instruction of all was the body of literature they had come to recognize as the Torah, which, in Hebrew, means to guide/teach.

Who are we? What is life about? What does it mean to do the right thing? The answers to these questions were contained in the Law and the Prophets, and these components were personified, especially in Moses and Elijah.

Every year on Ash Wednesday, we approach the altar and are challenged by the words: "Turn away from sin, remember you are dust and to dust you will return, be faithful to the Gospel." The ashes are a symbol of our mortality. The cross formed on each of our foreheads is our reminder of the sacrifice Jesus made on our behalf.

The 17th chapter of Matthew's Gospel begins with the story of the transfiguration of Jesus, which provides us with a symbol our transformation, of what awaits us in heaven as long as we are faithful to what Jesus asks us to do in this life. Just as both the ashes and the cross were realities in Jesus' life, so both are realities in our own.

The story of Jesus is well known to us. It displays the might of the powerful, political, and religious institution plotted against Him. Nails were driven into His hands and feet. A sword pierced His side. He was buried in a borrowed grave. Just when His enemies thought they had laid this carpenter to rest forever, just when they thought they had triumphed over His kingdom of love and compassion, just when they were feeling comfortable with their treachery, a stone mysteriously moved from in front of the grave. Jesus would not be defeated. His love is stronger than any army. His spirit is alive today. This unique man stepped forward to conquer the forces of evil – sin and death.

This Jesus, transfigured, risen, but with the print of the nails still visible, asks us to do three things: be a hero, practice self-denial, and follow Him.

Be a Hero

You know that on one occasion in His public ministry, Jesus miraculously fed more than 5,000 men and an equal amount of women and children. He cured countless people of various diseases and yet when the chips were down, these thousands were reduced to only 12 apostles and six or seven women. Obviously, not everyone who heard Him speak or saw His miracles was willing to pay the price of discipleship. Following Jesus was not for the faint of heart. It is a call to the heroic.

Practice Self-denial

Being heroic in life means opening up a new frontier. It requires men and women to lay aside their own priorities in life and immerse themselves in Jesus' priorities. It means going where few have gone before.

We all practice self-denial during Lent. We fast from candy, cake, or ice cream. We abstain from wine, beer, or liquor. We get up early to go to Mass. We say a few more prayers. But do we fast from gossip? Do we abandon pornography? Do we stop ourselves from cursing, swearing, or losing our temper?

These fasts are the real dying we must do. Self-denial is the willingness to give up what is most precious to us so that another can gain. Abraham was willing to give up his son. God gave up His Son.

Follow Me

What does it mean? It means to live as simply as Jesus. It means to fill your heart with as much love as Jesus bestowed upon his brothers and sisters. It means to use His example to forgive others.

If we do these three things: answer God's call to be a hero, practice self-denial, and follow in Jesus' footsteps, then we will experience a transformation in our lives here and now, which will be a foretaste of the transformation that awaits us in eternal life.

CHAPTER 14
An Untimely Death, an Inner Struggle

"Despair is suffering that fails to teach."

–Fr. Thomas Keating

Death frightened me. Even as a teenager, I couldn't grasp why my dad had to die at such a young age. I knew he died because of a heart attack, but it still seemed unfair. Although I kept myself busy with my role as man of the house and my unconditional love for basketball, I still found myself pondering questions that remained unanswered about the divine.

Yet again, I was reminded of my father's death when two more untimely deaths occurred toward the end of my days in high school.

My cousin, Joanne Benine, 25 at the time, just married, went to the doctor thinking she was going to hear wonderful news. She thought she might be pregnant. Instead, horrifying news was delivered to her: she was losing a battle with leukemia. She died on Feb. 14, 1970.

Why would God take such a kind, generous young woman with so much potential in life? Because she would come out with regularity to help my mom, that made it all the more painful for me to think about. I had a very favorable opinion of anybody who helped my mom.

My uncle, Jerry Reilly, came to take care of my siblings and me when my mom went in for her hysterectomy. I remember watching television and movies with him and he'd be in a fit of laughter. He, too, had a weak heart, like my dad, but died 10 years later, at the age of 43.

The impact of the deaths of my dad, my cousin, and my uncle confused me. I asked myself, "What is the meaning of life and the meaning of death?"

At that time, I understood what was called a mystery. When you're baptized, you're immersed into the life of Jesus, the suffering of Jesus, the death of Jesus, and the promise of eternal life. Up until and through my uncle's death, these were all just words to me. They didn't have any real meaning, but yet I wanted to know what it all meant.

I spent a lot of time trying to find that answer and still, to this day, come up with an unsatisfactory answer to the events of those three people dying. How does this fit into the whole scheme of living your life in a fruitful, abundant way?

After Uncle Jerry's Mass of Christian Burial at St. Martin of Tours Church on Roosevelt Boulevard in Philadelphia in June 1970, I drove to St. Charles Borromeo Seminary in Wynnewood to be interviewed for admission. I had already been accepted to Mount St. Mary's University in Emmitsburg, Md., in April, and had sent in a room deposit – a whopping $50 fee. I was interested in playing basketball there. Something inside of me told me I had to give the seminary a chance.

Monsignor Vince Burns, a member of the admission committee welcomed me and brought me to the interview room. I shook hands with Father Henry Deagnan, Father Frank Loughran, Bishop Tom Welsh, and Father Jim McBride before sitting down. They presented several questions about my family, education, health, and interests. One thing I told them I would like to experience for certain is to establish in my life a faith reflective of the faith of my mother.

Near the conclusion of the interview, the bishop asked, "Tom, why do you want to be a priest?"

I paused, looked at each priest, and then made eye contact with the bishop.

"I do not know if I want to be a priest," I replied. "What I do know is I have many unanswered questions about faith, God, suffering, evil, and the meaning of life, that I raised during my four years of high school to several priest-teachers, but never received satisfactory answers. I hope that I find someone at the seminary who will be able to answer these questions."

Death has a way of giving you a new perspective on life. I definitely struggled with, "What does God want me to do with my life?" I felt that was a very real question. I needed someone to guide me so that I could do what I believed God was calling me to do. In observing my friends, they just seemed disinterested in that question. They were OK with just drifting along and allowing things to fall into place. I couldn't accept that kind of approach. I guess I had some sense that if God does love everybody, He is calling everybody to live life in a specific way. I still believe that everybody is called. Whether they listen to that call or respond to that call is a whole different question.

Bishop Welsh said, "I am confident there is someone on the faculty who will be able to answer your questions. Whether you stay here for a year or get ordained, I hope you get your answer satisfactorily answered. Then, you can make a decision on what you're going to do with your life."

One of the priests led me out and gave me the confidence that I had a great interview. It even made me chuckle when the priest who led me out complimented me on the fact that he noticed how dry my hands were when we greeted each other and said our goodbyes – a sign that I was cool, calm, and collected throughout the process.

A week later, I received a letter of acceptance to St. Charles Borromeo Seminary, along with a list of all the items I was expected to bring. Now, a decision had to be made. Do I delay entrance into St. Charles and go to college, or do I inform "The Mount," as it is known, that I would not be coming?

I had a fear that basketball, although it was a strong influence in my life, could have been a distraction to keep me away from asking the questions and getting to the answers of something that was more important. I recognized basketball as a distraction. I would put myself fully into that and probably push off this other thing.

Even though I applied to the seminary, I wasn't certain that it was what I was called to do. I knew that could be a place where questions could be explored in more depth than in any other place that I had found. So, as you likely assumed, I did decide in favor of the seminary. I did not buy a black suit, though. I had a dark blue suit from my senior year in high school and that is the one I used.

I waited until late August to inform my two sisters, Sue and Mary, my brother, Joe, my friends, and pastor, Father Andy Lavin, of my decision. On Tuesday, Sept. 8, 1970, I packed the car with my meager belongings, and along with my mother and siblings, I drove to the seminary for Mass and orientation. After lunch, I went up to my room, changed, and found the gym in the basement of the seminary and shot a basketball, alone, for a while, then took a swim and returned to my dorm room to prepare for the opening retreat given by Father Leo VanOverbreck. Still, what occupied my mind were the burning questions … "Who will answer my questions and when will I find that person?"

The retreat lasted three days. The retreat master was lively and challenging. He kept our attention, which even suggested there was so much I admittedly did not understand.

CHAPTER 15
A New Mentor Rises

"A life is not important except the impact it has on other lives."

—Jackie Robinson (1919 – 1972)

On Sunday, Sept. 13, 1970, beginning with a long procession, both the college and theology division attended mass together in St. Martin's Chapel. The 36 new men, dressed in black suits, white shirts and black ties, led the procession, followed by second, third, and fourth college seminarians. Then, the deacons in cassock and surplus and stoles followed seminarians that were in first, second, and third theology.

As I watched them pass, I wondered if I would be here as a deacon in seven years. One man, who had entered with me three days earlier, already decided to leave the seminary.

On Monday morning, after Morning Prayer, Mass, and breakfast, I attended my first college class with Joe Grady, who taught communications. The days were full of activity: chapel, meals, classes, study, and recreation. On Thursdays, there were no classes. Seminarians were given field education assignments, except for those in first college. So, Thursdays were a free day, unless you wanted to volunteer to help the children from St. Katherine School for Disabled Children at the pool in the morning. Joe Doyle, a seminarian in his senior year (fourth college, as it is known in the seminary), asked me if I would help out.

I said, "Of course!"

After lunch, I studied for a few hours, then decided to go to the gym, where there was already someone shooting them up.

"Can I shoot with you?" I asked. "My name is Tom Heron and I am new here."

The stranger replied, "I am Father Dan Murray and I, too, am new … to the faculty."

"What do you teach?" I asked.

"Sacred Scripture," replied Fr. Murray.

We began taking turns shooting the ball. After a game of one-on-one, Fr. Murray said he had to go. Standing on the steps of the gym we talked for 10 more minutes. I remember distinctly when Fr. Murray asked how my classes were coming along.

"Fine, except for Latin," I blurted out.

"Study harder," Fr. Murray encouraged.

A connection had been made, but little did I know then that Fr. Murray would be the person who would answer many of my burning questions over the next 44 years.

He found out that I was a cousin to two priests, one ordained with him and one ordained ahead of him. I think, because he knew that I was related to those two, he took a little bit more of an interest in me.

In my first year, we had a class in liturgical music. Very similar to my skills in the art of painting, I had a very underdeveloped musical background. I had no interest in it. One Saturday afternoon, I was eating lunch and heard rumblings of a basketball game being played at 1:30 p.m. My liturgical music class was at 2. So, what did I do? I cut that class to go play basketball. This, I thought, was far more important than going to that class.

The dean of the college division who was in charge of discipline called me in to his office and told me I had study hall for a month. There were two other guys who cut classes and they were really devastated by that, but I felt it was a fine tradeoff. I stood by my decision, because I would've rather played that basketball game than go to music class.

Dan Murray heard about that and called the three of us in. He couldn't believe how casual I was to accept the punishment. I knew that if I had to do it over again, I would do it again. So, I wasn't learning responsibility according to the dean at the time.

After mass one morning, I remember going back to him in the sacristy on the lower side of the seminary and asked, "You really believe what you said about the Gospel?" This was the sort of relationship we had: an open-door policy of sorts.

He lived in the faculty wing. They were building a new dormitory up in the theologian division. He moved up to the fourth floor of the new dormitory.

I would go up to visit him at night and bring a Bible that I still have, and say, "Listen, I want you to teach me everything you know about sacred scripture."

He said, "Put the Bible down and we'll talk."

I would talk about growing up in Collingdale and discuss the memory of my mom.

Not only did he answer my questions, but he also directed my inquiring mind and heart to consider countless other questions along the way. He would get an index card and write three questions on it. The next time we would meet, we would discuss those three questions and learn something about sacred scripture. Three years later, we still never opened the Bible I would bring up. I would spend more time, each week, reflecting on his set of three questions than I spent studying for any of my classes.

I finally found the course, curriculum, and teacher for which I so eagerly sought. That shows how important Fr. Murray was to my spiritual development.

(Center) Cardinal Ratzinger (Pope Benedict) with (L-R) Gerry Wild, Fr. Tom Heron, Fr. Dan Murray, and Jeff Bond. July 1984.

The Questions

Beginning in 1971 when I started to meet with Fr. Murray for spiritual direction, rather than answering my questions, he began by questioning me. Six of the most important questions come to mind when I remember our meetings.

1. What is your vision of life?
2. What is your understanding of the Blessed Trinity?
3. Do you have a reflective approach to living?
4. How do you pray?
5. Do you possess a reverential approach to all of creation?
6. Do you expect to discover Divine Love daily? Where?

Fr. Murray was a keenly observant man. His talent for noticing became the cornerstone of his approach to the spiritual life, along with his understanding of sacred scripture and the philosophy of Bernard Lonergan.

It is now July 1973. I am coming home from the New Jersey shore, driving across the Walt Whitman Bridge with Fr. Murray. During our conversation, he said something to me that would change everything.

"You have a lot of life in you," Fr. Murray proclaimed, "but it needs to be disciplined and channeled."

It was that very moment when I suddenly experienced an intensely powerful desire to have a spiritual father/son relationship that would not trespass my relationship with my natural father.

My father's voice rang through my consciousness, "I want you to be my business partner!"

The memory of the simple gesture – guiding my small hand, placing one can on a shelf at a time, labels facing forward – intuitively let me believe I could make a difference. I could make a contribution that would help not only my dad in the family corner deli, but also have some impact for those I would serve in my duties as a priest.

I had found the answer to something deep in my heart, soul, and mind, for which I had yearned from the time I sat next to my mother in the pew, curious about the mystery of her faith; her pious practice of prayer.

Fr. Murray was the priest that was willing to not only engage my questions about life, but to give me questions that I needed to consider about life. This tremendous, gracious act continued over the course of the next 44 years.

CHAPTER 16
A Biblical, Philosophical, and Lived Reality

"Ignorance is the parent of fear."

–Herman Melville, Moby-Dick (1851)

Education was a very important part of my mom and dad's lives. They wanted to make sure that all of their children received a good, Catholic education. I was sent to kindergarten as a 4-and-a-half year old. Neighbors said it would be better to get me out of the house. So, I went to both morning and afternoon kindergarten. Double trouble!

Like many others in the neighborhood, I attended Monsignor Bonner High School, graduating in June 1970 with a class of 640 boys. I was the only one to enter the seminary.

My time there was spent trying to fulfill that deep yearning to know, understand, and appropriate the experiences of my life to find meaning, significance, and purpose. I needed to connect my story with the greatest story ever told: Jesus of Nazareth.

Fr. Murray was always trying to get me to a deeper understanding. I wanted him to explain to me how you come to a deeper understanding of the New Testament and the person of Jesus.

His response was, "You have to understand yourself before you can even begin to understand who Jesus is and what he's about."

So, his early and strong emphasis was on self-understanding. He based that on a mentor of his, Bernard Lonergan, who wrote a book in 1957 called *Insight: A Study of Human Understanding*. One of the key components to Lonergan's teachings that Fr. Murray appropriated, and even on which he based an entire elective course that he taught, was the necessary precondition to understanding the New Testament and the life of Jesus: a cognitional structure that every human being's brain should follow.

Lonergan bases his understanding on the teachings of St. Thomas Aquinas, St. Augustine, Plato, and Aristotle. I'd say you're in pretty good company as you're developing that.

How is the human mind structured? Everybody comes to understand through being attentive or inattentive to his or her experience. That's the first step. Then, you have to come to understand your attentive experience in an intelligent way. That will lead you to being able to make reasonable judgments, and then authentic decisions. It's attentiveness to your experience, intelligently understanding your attentive experience, reasonably making judgments about your intelligent understanding of your attentive experience, so that you can make authentic decisions.

The brain does that at a rapid pace. The more you're aware of those steps, the more you can have a deeper grasp of what life is and come to intelligent understanding and authentic decision making.

This cognitive structure receives support from Lonergan's three steps of conversion. First, we must go through an intellectual conversion, which can lead us to a moral conversion that may result in a religious conversion, thereafter. The order in which these conversions are supposed to occur causes chaos and paradox in Christian minds.

When a person does not follow these steps in the correct order, he or she may come to experience, and go right to, judgment without understanding. Everybody's life experience is unique.

Fr. Murray would always tell me, "I cannot influence your life experience, but I can help you come to understand your experience in an intelligent way. I shouldn't make decisions for you, but I can help you make reasonable judgments so you can make reasonable decisions."

A mentor can really only work in the realm of steps 2 and 3 by raising the right questions to help people come to an intelligent understanding of their lives. This probes us to ask the right questions so that judgments can help us make a reasonable decision. It's a wonderful paradigm for people to develop.

I was continually frustrated by Fr. Murray's method. Here's the student trying to tell the teacher how to teach. I was so determined to get him to not allow me to be off track.

I would demand of my spiritual mentor, "Let's read a text of scripture and you show me how I can come to understand what is being said there!"

There was always that frustration, which was put on the backburner. Yet, every time I walked up those stairs to Room 417, where he resided, I convinced myself I would not let him distract me. No, not this time; but, what happened? Time and again, he would guide me, not the way I wanted to be guided, but the way I needed to be guided. This was my mountaintop experience. Slowly and painfully, my horizon was expanded.

He was completely convinced of this idea that you cannot ignore self-understanding. In his mind, it was an unskippable step in coming to a spiritual understanding of oneself. I was frustrated, because I wanted the spiritual understanding.

That eventually came, but it came in his methodology of saying, "Let's get you connected to how your mind works. Let's get you connected to how your emotions work, and how they can be a gift for you and others, rather than an ongoing frustration."

I still had a quick fuse, where I could get frustrated and angry. He was trying to teach me how to rein that in so that it did not become an obstacle for me to live my life. It can actually be an aid in living life.

He was constantly trying to get me to keep reflecting on what's going on inside of my mind, body, and soul, and asked me to think about how I was able to take those frustrations, thoughts, and emotions, and express them in a creative and helpful way, rather than in a harmful or debilitating way.

Who would ever think that you need intellectual conversion before you achieve moral and religious conversion? That almost sounds reverse. Again, most people have it backward. Most people are baptized into Christianity, receive First Holy Communion, and then confirmation, which they think completes their religious training, thus finishing a religious conversion.

This, we think, helps with moral conversion. We are trying to prove the answers based on ideas and facts that we do not fully understand. This is inductive reasoning, where we are presented a conclusion or hypothesis, and work our way backward to make a statement or a judgment.

However, if we take a deductive approach, or an approach where we work from the top down, we can follow the steps to conversion properly: first, understand yourself and your own life experiences; second, develop your morals based on the circumstances around you; and finally, take your understanding of yourself and the morals that you've developed to relate them to the life and teachings of Jesus. Now, we can fluidly weave the intellectual with the moral, the moral with the religious, the religious with the moral, and the moral back to the intellectual. We are constantly being converted!

That chain of conversion is the difference between blind faith and authentic faith. Now, you're educated. You have a reason behind your religion, as opposed to, "This is the way it's been, the way I was told."

Even in the Gospel, there are three would-be disciples of Jesus. The first one is naïve.

"Lord, I'll follow you wherever you go," he says.

Jesus just looks at him and says, "I have nowhere to lay my head."

What he's saying is, "You're very naïve. You're innocent and naïve." Jesus doesn't want would-be disciples to be innocent and naïve. So, he puts him in his place. Innocence and naivety won't take you very far on this spiritual journey. What happens is your words do not match up with your commitment and your understanding of what will be involved in following in Jesus' footsteps ... in following in His way.

CHAPTER 17
The Biblical Notion of Conversion

"If anyone wishes to be first, he shall be the last of all and the servant of all."

—Mark 9:35

The opening line of Mark sets a theme of hope that runs throughout his Gospel. "A beginning of the Good News of Jesus Christ, Son of God." The key word in this sentence is the very first one: αρχή, which means, "a beginning." Mark is telling us that the message contained in the Gospel is merely the beginning of something. The final consummation is yet to come.[7]

Most scholars of Mark's Gospel[8-10] believe that the evangelist is addressing a crisis in his community: a crisis of hope. The message proclaimed by Jesus in Mark 1:15 is the antidote to this crisis. "The time has been fulfilled, the reign of God is at hand, be converted and believe in the Gospel."

There are four key elements in this programmatic sentence by which Jesus begins his public ministry. The first element is the idea of time. Mark is not speaking of chronological time. Rather, he speaks of kairological time,[11] that is, a time pregnant with meaning, creative time, the time indicated by the prophets when they said, "In days to come..." Jesus proclaims that this is in the process of being fulfilled in his person and ministry.

The second element states that the Kingdom of God is close at hand, if not somehow present in the person of Jesus. The Kingdom of God, *malkuth Yahweh*,[12] is a symbol for the Father's understanding of life. This understanding was gradually revealed throughout the period we know as the Old Testament. It is now being revealed in a definite way in the person and message of Jesus.

The third element is conversion, *metanoia*.[13] I will treat more fully the New Testament meaning of conversion later. Suffice it to say, here, that conversion is not to be restricted to the areas of religious or spiritual conduct. Jesus is after a change of heart, a turning of one's self inside-out.

Finally, the fourth element is "believe in the Gospel." The verb, *pistuein*, and the noun, *pistis*,[14] always indicate faith in someone. This faith brings with it an attitude of confidence, fearlessness, courage, and perseverance in the face of life experiences that may be to the contrary.

It is immediately after this programmatic sentence that Jesus calls four men into the service of discipleship. The passage is Mark 1:16-20. This is one of three passages in which Mark has a theology of discipleship:

Mark 1:16-20

"And he made his way along the Sea of Galilee, and he observed Simon and his brothers casting their nets into the sea; they were fishermen. Jesus said to them, 'Come after me; I will make you fishers of men.' They immediately abandoned their nets and became his followers. Proceeding a little further along, he caught sight of James, Zebedee's son, and his brother John. They too were in their boats putting their nets in order. He summoned them on the spot. They abandoned their father Zebedee, who was in the boat with the hired men, and went off in his company."

Mark 2:13-14

"Another time, while he went walking along the lakeside, people kept coming to him in crowds and he taught them. As he moved on he saw Levi, the son of Alphaeus at his tax collector's post and he said to him, 'Follow me.' Levi got up and became his follower."

Mark 10:17-22

"As he was setting out on a journey a man came running up, knelt down before him and asked, 'Good Teacher, what must I do to share in everlasting life?' Jesus answered, 'Why do you call me good? No one is good but God alone. You know the commandments: You shall not kill; You shall not commit adultery; you shall not steal; You shall not bear false witness; You shall not defraud; Honor your father and your mother.' He replied, 'Teacher, I have kept all these since my childhood.' Then Jesus looked at him with love and told him, 'There is one thing more you must do. Go and sell what you have and give to the poor; you will then have treasure in heaven. After that, come and follow me.' At these words the man's face fell. He went away sad, for he had many possessions."

The following structure is revealed in each narrative:[15]

1. Jesus is along the Sea or on the road when the call takes place.
2. Jesus saw or looked upon those he called.
3. Jesus spoke.
4. His words were: "Come after me," or "Follow me."
5. Following Jesus involves abandoning old ties.

The points in the structure give us some understanding of what is involved in being a disciple of Jesus. Discipleship begins when Jesus issues the invitation to follow Him. The initiative is Jesus'. He is the one who calls and the call comes after He has seen the prospective disciple or looked him in the eye. Fishermen are called, tax collectors are called, rich and poor are called. They are to follow Jesus. Before doing this; however, they must leave something ... someone. Simon and Andrew abandon their nets; James and John abandon their father; Levi abandons his tax table. The point is that there can be no hindrance to the following of Jesus. There is something total about it. The passage about the call of the rich man, (Mark 10:17-22), reveals something else. Following Jesus involves more than keeping the Commandments. "Teacher, I have kept all these since my childhood." Mark tells us of Jesus' pleasure in this man's response. He "looked at him with love." Yet, this faithfulness to God's Commandments wasn't enough. "There is one thing more you must do."

"Go sell what you have and give to the poor ... after that, come and follow me." The rich man is asked to abandon his riches. This, he cannot do, and the result is that he 'went away sad." He could not follow Jesus.

Mark is telling us that the Kingdom of God affects people; it dislodges them from their native environment. It is a call to a "forced departure" from professional and personal pursuits. Everyone called must sever ties with the past and put on a new way of life. Life in the kingdom is gained only at the price of conversion, change, and breaking loose from a familiar lifestyle.

The passages examined above indicate that following Jesus involves abandoning fishing nets, tax tables, parents. Three other passages in Mark reveal how Jesus further clarifies what discipleship involves. These passages will show that discipleship involves struggle and provokes opposition. In these passages, Jesus will speak of abandoning something within ourselves"

Mark 8:34-38

"He summoned the crowd with his disciples and said to them: 'If a man wishes to come after me, he must deny his very self, take up his cross, and follow in my steps. Whoever would preserve his life will lose it, but whoever loses his life for my sake and the Gospel's will preserve it. What profit does a man show who gains the whole world and destroys himself in the process? What can a man offer in exchange for his life? If anyone in this faithless and corrupt age is ashamed of me and my doctrine, the Son of Man will be ashamed of him when he comes with the holy angels in his Father's glory.'"

For Mark, conversion/discipleship is not an event that occurs abruptly, that is, once, in the life of the true disciple. Denying self, taking up one's cross involves a prolonged process that is slow and gradual. Jesus' linking conversion to the cross forces the disciple to ask some questions. Basic among them is what does it mean concretely for me – a would-be disciple – to take up the cross? Jesus teaches that it definitely involves participating in his suffering and death. In other words, there may be no worldly advantage to this call. Self-denial and privation do not come easy. The true disciple cannot ask, "what is in it for me?" Later, I will attempt to show how this "law of the cross" was lived out in the life of Dorothy Day, with whom I spent some time after I was ordained into priesthood.

Mark 9:33-37

"They returned to Capernaum and Jesus, once inside the house, began to ask them, 'What were you discussing on the way home?' At this they fell silent, for on the way they had been arguing about who was the most important. So he sat down and he called the Twelve around him and said, 'If anyone wishes to rank first, he must remain the last one of all and the servant of all.' Then he took a little child, stood him in their midst, and putting his arms around him, said to them, 'Whoever welcomes me welcomes, not me, but him who sent me.'"

That Jesus uses a child to teach the disciples a lesson is most significant. In the Jewish world of the New Testament, the child was always regarded as a prototype of insignificance, dependence, unimportance, and helplessness.[16] The child was looked upon as one who deserved no attention, who had nothing to offer, and therefore, could make no claims. Jesus is teaching that to let go of arrogant self-assurance, and admit dependence and helplessness is the call of every disciple. To continue to be preoccupied with status and honor and power is to be unconverted, hardhearted, blind. Rather than seeking honor, status, and power the disciples must seek to make themselves the least significant of all if they hope to be part of the Kingdom of God. Retaining childlike qualities such as playfulness, wonder, trust, adventure, and newness is essential if conversion and discipleship are to be authentic. Later, I will demonstrate how Day possessed these childlike qualities throughout her life.

Mark 10:35-45

"Zebedee's sons, James and John, approached him. 'Teacher,' they said, 'We want you to grant our request.' 'What is it?' he asked. They replied, 'See to it that we sit, one at your right and the other at your left, when you come into your glory.' Jesus told them, 'You do not know what you are asking. Can you drink the cup I shall drink or be baptized in the same bath of pain as I?' 'We can,' they told him. Jesus said in response, 'From the cup I drink of you shall drink; the bath I am immersed in you shall share. But as for sitting at my right or my left, that is not mine to give; it is for those to whom it has been reserved.' The other ten, on hearing this, became indignant at James and John. Jesus called them together and said to them: 'You know how among the Gentiles those who seem to exercise authority lord it over them; their great ones make their importance felt. It cannot be like that with you. Anyone among you who aspires to greatness must serve the rest; whoever wants to rank first among you must serve the needs of all. The Son of Man has not come to be served but to serve – to give his life in ransom for the many.'"

In this teaching, Jesus required that the genuine disciple renounce all honors and ambition and seek instead to be the servant of all. In this passage, the disciples are presented in an unfavorable light. They are guilty of ambition and jealousy. When James and John seek preferential treatment, the remaining disciples become indignant. Jesus once again clears the air. He responds to their petty bickering by stating that they are to take their cue from him and not from secular rulers when it comes to the exercise of authority. Lording it over people or acting "high and mighty" was never Jesus' style. He strove to be the servant of all. Genuine disciples should settle for nothing less for themselves. To be baptized is to drink the cup. This means involving yourself in the conversion process in a fundamental and radical way.[17] Once again, Day comes to mind as a living example of a genuine disciple who freely drank from the cup.

CHAPTER 18
The Philosophical Notion of Conversion

"The devout Christian of the future will either be a 'mystic,' one who has experienced 'something,' or he will cease to be anything at all."

—Karl Rahner, "Christian Living Formerly and Today,"
Theological Investigations, volume 7 (1971)

In chapter 16, we met Bernard Lonergan. I believe he is the philosopher/theologian who best captures the New Testament notion of conversion. In his article, "Theology in its New Context," Lonergan has this to say about conversion:

"Fundamental to religious living is conversion. It is a topic little studied in traditional theology since there remains very little of it when one reaches the universal, the abstract, the static. For conversion occurs in the lives of the individuals. It is not merely a change or even a development; rather, it is a radical transformation on which follows, on all levels of living, an interlocked series of changes and developments. What hitherto was unnoticed becomes vivid and present. What has been of no concern becomes a matter of high import. So great a change in one's apprehensions and one's values accompanies no less a change in oneself, in one's relations to other persons, and in one's relations to God."[18]

The word "conversion" has always presented a problem to Roman Catholics. They often think of it as an experience available to non-Catholics, agnostics or atheists who wish to become Catholic. In Lonergan's explanation; however, conversion is available to, and needed by, Catholics as well as anyone else. Conversion is more than the Protestant acceptance of Jesus as personal Savior. It is also more than what Christians mean by "being born again."

Lonergan's idea of conversion is broader and deeper than the commonly understood notion of conversion. His idea of conversion involves what he calls "horizon-expansion." According to Lonergan, horizon, literally is the line where earth and sky seem to meet, a dividing point between what is seen and unseen, what is accessible and what is not. It is what circumscribes the limits of a person's interest and knowledge; beyond it are matters that the person neither knows nor cares about.[19]

There are two types of horizon, relative and basic. Relative horizon is a person's present horizon development, which is dependent on his psychological, educational, sociological, and cultural development. This relative horizon varies, first of all, with the present condition of the human sciences, and secondly, with the person's comprehension of them. Basic horizon is a person's stance in life relative to his differentiation of what Lonergan calls four basic conversions, namely, intellectual, moral, religious, and Christian.

Let me briefly indicate what Lonergan means by each of these conversions:

At the heart of all intellectual process is the unrestricted desire to know everything, the drive to eternally question (Lonergan's Insight, Philosophical Library, 1970 is the most complete treatment of intellectual). Intellectual conversion involves the elimination of a myth concerning reality, objectivity and human knowledge. The myth is that knowing is like looking; that objectivity is merely seeing what is there to be seen and not seeing what is not there; that the real is only that which is out there now to be looked at. The myth overlooks the distinction between the world of immediacy and the world mediated by meaning. The achievement of intellectual conversion allows a person to make intelligence and reasonableness the major concerns of his life. It makes the individual open to whatever intelligence and reasonableness may impose on him. The individual is thus beyond the realm of any limited horizon to worlds of meaning.

Moral conversion is a change in the criterion a person uses in making decisions and choices.[20] The change is from "what gives pleasure," or "I do it to satisfy my parents, teachers, peers, etc.," to a question of values. The morally converted person realizes that it is up to him to decide for himself what he is to make of himself. This decision is what can be called his existential moment. It is the discovery of the fact that he is free and responsible for himself and with respect to his community. Moral conversion consists in opting for values, for what is truly good and worthwhile. When one discovers such freedom, he achieves what Lonergan calls real self-transcendence. This is only the first step in a lifelong process of choosing the good and the valuable. Moral conversion comes only when a person falls in love, when his being is being in love.

Religious conversion is being grasped by someone; it is an other-worldly falling in love (Lonergan, op. cit.). The facts of good and evil, of progress and decline, give rise to questions about the character of the universe such as: Is life worthwhile? Does history have its source in a moral being? Is there a God? Is this God a loving God? If these questions are answered in the negative, you have atheism. The positive answers to these questions, however, have been worked out in the many theistic religions of the world. The religiously converted person surrenders himself totally and permanently to mystery. He is in love with "God." This "being in love" abolishes the horizon in which he formerly knew reality and made decisions. Such a "being in love" is what Rudolph Otto describes as the experience of the holy, *mysterium tremens et foscinans*.[21]

Christian conversion is a specific type of religious conversion. (the idea was first developed by D. Tracy in a talk he gave at the Lonergan Symposium at Boston College in 1972. The talk is unpublished.) It is what St. Paul talks about in 2 Corinthians 5:14-17:

"The love of Christ impels us who have reached the conviction that since one died for all, all died. He died for all so that those who live might live no longer for themselves, but for him who for their sakes died and was raised up. Because of this we no longer look on anyone in terms of mere human judgment. If at one time we so regarded Christ, we no longer know him by this standard. This means that if anyone is in Christ, he is a new creation. The old order has passed away; now all is new."

Christian conversion allows a person to affirm that life has ultimate meaning. It also allows a person to encounter Jesus and make him and his values the center of his life. It is an intensely personal reality. No one can experience it for anyone else. It is that personal.

By way of concluding this chapter, let me say that conversion is obviously a process, a prolonged process that is slow and gradual. It is more than a mere development. It is a radical transformation.

CHAPTER 19
How Conversion Works

"All the forces in the world are not so powerful as an idea whose time has come."

—Victor Hugo (paraphrased from a French translation)

In chapter 17, I offered an explanation of what Jesus' call to conversion/discipleship involved. In chapter 18, I discussed Lonergan's definition of conversion and the four levels that he so carefully delineates for his readers. In this chapter, I would like to attempt to explain how the process of conversion works. The principal source for this analysis will be Sallie McFague's article entitled "Conversion: Life on the Edge of the Raft."[22]

McFague describes the process of conversion as passing through three distinct, yet related, stages of life. She labels these stages: orientation, disorientation, reorientation.

By orientation, she means the worldview or horizon the person had before conversion occurred. Perhaps, the best way to understand what McFague means by orientation is to utilize Lonergan's notion of relative horizon. Earlier, I defined relative horizon as a person's present horizon development, which is dependent on his psychological, educational, sociological, and cultural development (Tracy, op. cit.). Within anyone's relative horizon it is necessary to distinguish between the world of immediacy and mediacy. The point is that meaning or orientation in life is communicated to each one of us by both of these worlds. When I speak of the world of immediacy, I am thinking of the world of the infant, primarily, of what is felt, touched, grasped. It is the world of experience without insight. It is the world of pleasure, pain, hunger, thirst, food, drink, sex, sleep. In a word, a world in which meaning is communicated solely through the senses (Lonergan, op. cit.). This is the most complete treatment of the worlds of meaning that I have found.

Beyond the world of immediacy, lies the world mediated by meaning. As the infant learns to speak, read, walk, etc., he moves out of the world of his immediate surroundings to a far larger world than the nursery or home. This larger world is revealed through the memories of other men, the common sense of the community, the pages of literature, the labors of scholars, the investigation of scientists, the experience of Saints, the works of artists and the writings of philosophers and theologians. All of these influences constitute a person's orientation in life. They form the person to be who he is before conversion takes place.

However, it is important to recognize that while the meaning communicated by each of these factors can exercise a positive formational influence on the person, meaning can also go astray. There is myth as well as science, fiction as well as fact, deceit as well as honesty, error as well as truth, fantasy as well as reality. Lost meaning exercises a negative formational influence on the person. This happens before conversion takes place. The world mediated by meaning then provides both a security and insecurity. It further provides positively formational as well as negatively deformational factors that constitute a person's orientation in life.[23]

The second stage in McFague's process of conversion is called disorientation. Disorientation is the critical moment in the process of conversion. I think Lonergan's analysis of "horizon shift" best describes what McFague means by disorientation. In the process of asking questions, Lonergan says that three distinct realities appear (Tracy, op. cit.):

1. **the known** – the range of questions a person can raise and answer in his present state of development

2. **the known unknown** – the range of questions which a person can raise, can find significant, and can find possible ways of solving, but which he cannot yet answer.

3. **the unknown unknown** – the range of questions that a person does not and cannot in fact raise inasmuch as such questions lack significance for him; they are literally meaningless to him.

Horizon can be described as the limit or boundary between the known, unknown, and the unknown unknown. What lies beyond a person=s present horizon does not consist of unknown answers but of questions that are meaningless and irrelevant to him.

The problem is how is a person to know that his horizon is limited. The problem is very complex because a person cannot have within his present horizon a clear picture of its boundaries and limitations until he in fact surpasses it.

Lonergan suggests a person's horizon begins to shift in what he calls moments of heightened awareness. It is in such moments that a person begins to questions meanings and values that before he had taken for granted. In other words, there comes a moment in a person's life when he raises questions that disorient his basic orientation. For instance, such disorientation occurs when the adolescent begins to question parental authority and/or values. Disorientation also sets in when the young adult begins to question the Church's teaching in the area of sexual morality, namely, pre-marital sex, artificial means of birth control and abortion.

Questions raised in these specific areas of sexual morality disrupt his entire identification with the church. My years of pastoral practice reinforce the truth of this. A person whose entire present orientation, interest, or concern has been challenged on a basic, existential level can experience disorientation. Here, such moods as boredom and angst set in, and the person begins to question the very meaning of his existence. Quite specifically, the person asks such questions as: Do I love myself? Can I love another person? Can another person love me? (Tracy, op. cit.).

St. Paul experienced disorientation in that moment usually referred to as the Damascus experience.[24] That experience put in question the orientation in life that was his as a Jew, a Pharisee, a strong, independent self-willed individual. Augustine experienced disorientation in that moment when an inner voice told him "*Tolle et lege.*" From that moment on his prodigal ways were called into question.[25]

In such moments of disorientation, a person is confronted with three possible options. First, he can be frozen in his disorientation, and choose to live out his life in quiet desperation. Secondly, he can clearly see that his life orientation is basically threatened by this moment of crisis, and spontaneously, ingeniously, even subconsciously resists the demands for change. Such a person refuses authentic living. Thirdly, he can see that this moment of crisis or disorientation is in reality a *kairos*, an opportunity for change. He understands that the achievement of a new horizon by means of conversion or reorientation is a possibility.

The third state in McFague's process of conversion is reorientation. Such a reorientation is not without its painful moments. It is fraught with doubt, ambiguity, and discomfort. It involves risks and demands courage. The person who chooses reorientation as his response to that moment of crisis (disorientation) chooses in reality a new way of life. He sets out on a life-long journey in which he continually discovers new and great horizons. Entire universes of meaning open up to the person, as a childlike sense of wonder returns.

He is involved in a radical transformation. New energies are released and he experiences fundamental changes on all levels of his living. He begins to notice things that before went undetected. Questions and issues once considered irrelevant become vital. Questions and issues that were so pressing in his old way of life are now insignificant. Such a person discovers that not only is he changing but that his relationship with others and the world is also changing.[26]

On this new way of life, the reoriented person discovers that he has fallen in love. Such a falling in love is the fulfillment of the human capacity for self-transcendence. It abolishes his former horizon in which all his choosing and knowing were done. In this new "love-horizon" his values are transvalued.

He soon discovers that this being in love is not something abstract. It is a conscious dynamic state of being in love with God that manifests itself in action. The self-transcendence, which he is in the process of achieving is always precarious. Human authenticity is never a pure, serene, and secure possession. Inauthenticity always lurks as a possibility. Every advance in authentic living only brings to light the need for further advances. What sustains the authentic living of any person, is the realization that such living involves not just simply the conversion of his person, but also a conversion to three persons, Father, Son, Spirit.

I want to conclude this chapter with a lengthy quote from Lonergan, which summarizes well the reality of being in love with God:

"But this being in Christ Jesus may be the being of substance or of subject. Inasmuch as it is just the being of substance, it is known only through faith, through affirming true propositions, meditating on them, concluding from them, making resolutions on the basis of them, winning over our psyches, our sensitive souls, to carrying out the resolutions through the cultivation of pious imagination and pious affects, and multiplying individual effort and strength through liturgical union. Inasmuch as it is just the being of substance, it is being in love with God without awareness of being in love. Without any experience of just how and why, one is in the state of grace or one recovers it, one leaves all things to follow Christ, one binds oneself by vows of poverty, chastity and obedience, one gets through one's daily heavy dose or prayer, one longs for the priesthood and later lives by it. Quietly, imperceptibly there goes forward the transformation operated by the Kurios, but the delicacy, the gentleness, the deftness of his continual operation in us hides the operation from us.

"But inasmuch as being in Christ Jesus is the being of subject, the hand of the Lord ceases to be hidden. In ways you all have experienced, in ways some have experienced more frequently or more intensely than others, in ways you still have to experience, and in ways none of us in this life will ever experience, the substance in Christ Jesus becomes the subject in Christ Jesus. For the love of God, being in love with God, can be as full and as dominant, as overwhelming and as lasting, an experience as human love.

"Being in Christ Jesus is not tied down to place or time, culture or epoch. It is catholic with the catholicity of the Spirit of the Lord. Neither is it an abstraction that dwells apart from every place and time, every culture and epoch. It is identical with personal living, and personal living is always here and now, in a contemporary world of immediacy, a contemporary world mediated by meaning, a contemporary world not only mediated but also constituted by meaning." (Lonergan, op. cit.).

Lonergan is stating that "being in Christ Jesus" is of two kinds: namely, substance and subject. The New Testament call to conversion is the call to move from substance to subject. Life in Christ Jesus as substance is being in love with God without being aware of it. The ongoing process of denying self, taking up the cross, becoming like a child, choosing to serve rather than to be served is what leads to a "being in love" with God which is that of a critical subject.

The "critical subject" conversion is then a process and is rooted in an event, which was referred to in earlier chapters as a moment of heightened awareness. The main emphasis of an ongoing conversion is not so much the event, as the discernment of the process. It is possible to deny one's self, take up one's cross, become like a child, choose to serve, without being aware that in doing all this one is being grasped by the hand of God's love.

This state of "being in love" is that of the substance rather than of the critical subject. New Testament conversion is a call to be in love with God as critical subject.

CHAPTER 20
A Shining Example

"Our Faith is stronger than death, our philosophy is firmer than flesh, and the spread of the Kingdom of God upon the earth is more sublime and more compelling."

—Dorothy Day (1897 – 1980)

In this chapter, I want to go into further depth of Dorothy Day's conversion. She truly exemplifies the understanding of conversion/discipleship as developed in the New Testament and in Lonergan's theory. Day was a holy woman, a genuine disciple in love with God, a critical subject.

I came into contact with both Lonergan and Day through Fr. Murray. Lonergan was a teacher at the Gregorian University where Fr. Murray attended in 1961. At that point, Lonergan had already written *Insight*.

I met Lonergan at Boston College. It was a fascinating experience in that people would go out to dinner with him and throw question after question at him and he'd say, "Can you let me eat my steak?" He didn't want to be just looked upon as this brilliant mind. There were still relative things that were important to him, such as having a meal.

It was a great experience to be in a room with him giving a lecture and responding to questions that people had for him. I'm very grateful for having had that experience of meeting him. It was a simple, little exchange. There was a crowd coming up and thanking him for what he had done. So, it wasn't anything of great length, but to be exposed to him and listen to him was a great experience.

As already discussed in depth, Lonergan believed that everyone had to undergo multiple conversions: intellectual (how you come to know what you know), moral (to change how you live the way you live), and religious conversion (applying your experiences and morals to the life and way of Jesus Christ). When people bypass the intellectual and moral conversions, a great deal of confusion rises in the spiritual realm. Many students of religious conversion haven't put enough time into coming to understand who they are; the self-understanding that would evoke Gospel behavior that would enable you to be more receptive again and again to God's ways rather than our own ways.

I read Day's autobiography, *The Long Loneliness*, and then I went up and lived with her for five days in the Lower East Side of Manhattan. My experience of meeting her was brief, like my experience with Lonergan. I was ordained in 1978, went up there in 1979, and she died in 1980. Even back in 1979, she, more than any other person, lived the Gospel from a "basic horizon" perspective. I admired that. I was inspired by her lifestyle. *The Long Loneliness* is about her conversion, because she wasn't born or raised that way. Her life is a prime example of an extreme. She had come from not living a spiritual youth, whereas some people are born into Christianity and become far more lost than someone who converted. It was the birth of her daughter that brought about this conversion.

As I stated earlier, conversion is a process that is slow and gradual. In point of fact, conversion is a lifelong process of achieving real self-transcendence in a radical way. The title of her book suggests that conversion was, for her, a lifelong work of art. It didn't come easy. At great expense – physical, psychological, spiritual – she radically transformed her life.

My purpose, then, will be to apply the combined New Testament and Bernard Lonergan notions of conversion to Day's life. I will also utilize the three stages of conversion, as developed by McFague, namely, orientation, disorientation, and reorientation, as a framework to trace her personal conversion.

Orientation

Day was born on Nov. 8, 1897, at Bath Beach, Brooklyn, the third child in a family of five children. Both her parents came from small Episcopalian stock. Her father worked as a newspaperman. His working hours were unpredictable, keeping him away from the home most of those times when the children would be up and around. This meant that Day's relationship with her father was always somewhat remote. The unifying and stabilizing presence in the family was the mother. The young Day remembers vividly her childhood days of sitting around the kitchen table with her sister and brothers as her mother talked about "When I was a little girl."[27] Like most children, Day loved to hear these stories from her parents' past. It gave her a sense of continuity.

Anyone reading her autobiography realizes that with all the family tensions, Day had many fond and happy memories of her childhood. Her family lived a kind of vagabond existence traveling from coast to coast. Daniel Berrigan puts it well:

"An American woman, come of an American Family: a touch – no more – of Eugene O'Neill or Arthur Miller. In Dorothy's childhood, Day senior roamed the country, East Coast to West, someone called a 'newsman' perpetually on the spoor of something called a 'story.' Whatever that elusive something was, it was to make their fortune at last. It was the quintessential American dream; the children were caught up in it – a hit and miss education, fat days and lean, life on the road. And amidst it all, drinking it in, this wide-eyed, intensely observant child.

"It was a good family, recalled with affection. The parents never dull or demeaning; warm at the center, a bit chilly at the edge. And there was an infant brother whom she loved boundlessly. All considered, here was a lucky start; she tasted love, a first taste of nature."[28]

When she was 6, the family moved to California. However, the San Francisco earthquake of April 1906 brought to an abrupt end this West Coast venture. The earthquake threw the Day family out of their complacent happiness and into a world of catastrophe. Only 8 years old at the time, she remembered not so much the sorrow of the disaster as the joy she experienced in sharing "whatever we had with others after the earthquake." (Day, op. cit.). Already one can see the beginnings of the kind of sharing that would be characteristic of her adult life at the *Catholic Worker*.

Although she had three brothers and a sister, she wasn't a good mixer. Many hours alone playing with dolls, working in a small garden, and reading were the seed ground for the love of solitude and contemplation that were so much a part of her later life. She loved books. Many new worlds of meaning were mediated to her through her reading the works of London, Dickens, Scott, Stevenson, Cooper, Poe and Hugo. Once again, Berrigan captures this influence in her life very well:

"The girl loved books, too; she read like a demon all through her youth: early on, romances, the Bible, Shakespeare, classics and later, Jack London, Kropotkin, Upton Sinclair, Dostoevsky and Tolstoy, Frank Harris on the Haymarket anarchists, Eugene Debs." (Berrigan, op. cit.).

Amidst all the joys and happiness she experienced in her youth, her childhood days were not without moods of sadness and uncertainty. She recalls quite vividly that her parents did nothing to offer distraction or entertainment when such moods set in. Thus, at an early age, she began to learn the discipline of facing her moods and the asceticism of overcoming them.

Day did not have much of a formal religious upbringing. While religion in the Day home was politely acknowledged, it definitely assumed a low profile. The parents were not regular churchgoers. Yet, the young Day was occasionally taken to church services by friends (neighbors), where she was thoroughly distracted. She did not search for God as a child. She took Him for granted.

Nevertheless, very early on she had a sense of right and wrong, good and evil. She recalls:

"Very early we had a sense of right and wrong, good and evil. My conscience was very active. There were ethical concepts and religious concepts. To steal cucumbers from Miss Lynch=s garden or Cropsey Avenue was wrong. It was also wrong to take money from my mother, without her knowledge, for a soda. What a sense of property rights we had as children! Mine and yours! It begins in us as infants. AThis is mine.@ When we are very young just taking makes it mine. Possession is nine points of the law. As infants squabbling in the nursery we were strong in this possessive sense. In the nursery might made right. We had not reached the age of reason. But at the age of four I knew it was wrong to steal." (Day, op. cit.).

Disorientation

Her high school years were uneventful, except for the fact that she excelled academically. She was sixteen when she graduated and was awarded a partial scholarship to the University of Illinois. Here her world began to expand. Here too she began to lead the Hound of Heaven on a great chase. A great sense of independence took possession of her. The idea of earning her own living, by her own work, thrilled her more than the idea of education.

She took full advantage of her newfound freedom. She did exactly what she wanted to do. During her college years an interest in writing awakened in her. Her chief association was with a group that wrote for the campus magazine. To gain more time to read and write, she took a room in the home of a poverty-stricken instructor, earning her room and board by doing the family washing on Saturday.

The year is 1916. She began to read about labor unrest and social revolution. It was from such reading that she fell in love with the unnamed and exploited masses. Even though she was doing what she wanted to do, there was still a nagging undercurrent of unrest. She left college after two years, with no idea where she was going or what she would do. She describes her disorientation this way:

"I was seventeen, and I felt completely alone in the world, divorced from my family, from all security, even from God. I felt a sense of reckless arrogance and, with this recklessness, a sense of danger in which I rejoiced. There was a great question in my mind. Why was so much done in remedying social evils instead of avoiding them in the first place?" (Day, op. cit.).

During the next several years, she returned to New York. Even though her family had preceded her there, she made little or no contact with them. Instead, she spent her time job-hunting in the streets of New York. She took jobs with left-wing Marxist publications, such as the socialist *Call and Communist Masses*. It was in New York that she enjoyed the friendship of the so-called radical Bohemians in Greenwich Village. There she would sit over drinks and smoke in the back room of a village bar with the likes of Jack Reed and Eugene O'Neill. It was O'Neill who would occasionally recite for her Francis Thompson's The Hound of Heaven.

When World War I ended, Day was only 20 years old. She was continually troubled by the lack of purpose in her life. A nurse's training course and a year of dedicated hospital work proved unsatisfactory. Travel to England, France, Italy was more a distraction than of help. Upon her return from Europe, she lived a disordered existence, moving from rooming houses, to prison, to nondescript jobs, to meetings with the radicals of the day – all of this was merely frenetic activity by means of which she tried to fill a void in her life.

Her disorientation peaked when she settled down in New York, where she began a relationship with her "common-law husband" Forster Batterham. This relationship was the most fulfilling experience she had ever had in her life. Yet, there was something missing. She herself best describes what was missing:

"Forster, the inarticulate, became garrulous only in wrath. And his wrath, he said, was caused by my absorption in the supernatural rather than the natural, the unseen rather than the seen. He had always rebelled against the institution of the family and the tyranny lf love. It was hard for me to see at such times why we were together, since he lived with me as though he were living alone and he never allowed me to forget that this was a comradeship rather than a marriage." (Day, op. cit.).

It was the birth of her daughter, Tamar Therese, that forced her to ask some critical questions about herself. Lying in a bed in the maternity section of New York's Bellevue Hospital, the poet in her reflected:

"I was so fortunate as to have a bed next to the window looking out over the East River so that I could see the sun rise in the morning and light up the turgid water and make gay the little tugs and the long tankers that went by the window. When there was fog it seemed as though the world ended outside my window, and the sound of fog horns haunted the day and the night. As a matter of fact, my world did end at the window those ten days that I was in the hospital, because I was supremely happy. If I had written the greatest book, composed the greatest symphony, painted the most beautiful painting or carved the most exquisite figure, I could not have felt more the exalted creator than I did when they placed my child in my arms. To think that thing of beauty, sighing gently in my arms reaching her little mouth for my breast, clutching at me with her tiny beautiful hands, had come from my flesh, was my own child! Such a great feeling of happiness and joy filled me that I was hungry for someone to thank, to love, even to worship, for so great a good that had been bestowed upon me. That tiny child was not enough to contain my love, nor could the father, though my heart was warm with love for both."[29]

Reorientation

Day had to make a decision. Whenever she tried to talk about religion or faith to her common-law husband, a wall immediately separated them. His ardent love of creation brought her to the Creator but cut him off from religion. Whenever she asked, "How can there be no God, when there are all these beautiful things?" He would turn from her and complain that she was never satisfied. For her, love between a man and a woman was not incompatible with love of God.

It was shortly after the birth of Tamar Therese that she began to read the *Imitation of Christ*. Cost what it may she was going to have her child baptized. Tamar Therese would have none of the doubting and hesitating, none of the lack of discipline and morality that had been so characteristic of her mother's life.

It was at this time that Day prayed for the gift of faith. She wanted to become a Catholic. She was sure, yet not sure. Becoming a Catholic would mean facing life alone. The great happiness that was hers over the birth of her child was giving way to a feeling of struggle, a long silent battle still to be gone through. The physical struggle of giving birth to a child was a preparation for the spiritual struggle for her own soul. Tamar Therese was baptized. A year later Day entered the Roman Catholic Church.

She began to experience that conversion was indeed a radical transformation on all levels of living. She daily struggled with it, but was determined to fight the good fight. It was at this point in her life she began to write for Catholic publications like *Commonweal, America, Sign. Commonweal* sent her to Washington, D.C. to cover a march by the communist-led unemployed councils. She recalls the bright sunny day as the marchers three thousand strong paraded triumphantly through the streets of Washington.

"I stood on the curb and watched them, joy and pride in the courage of this band of men and women mounting in my heart, and with it a bitterness too that since I was now a Catholic, with fundamental philosophical differences, I could not protest, to arouse the conscience, but where was the Catholic leadership in the gathering of bands of men and women together, for the actual works of mercy that the comrades had always made part of their technique in reaching the workers? ... I kept thinking to myself. They were His friends, His comrades, and who knows how close to His heart in their attempt to work for justice. ... When the demonstration was over and I had finished writing my story, I went to the national shrine at the Catholic University on the Feast of the Immaculate Conception. There and with anguish, that some way would open up for me to use what talents I possessed for my fellow workers, for the poor. As I knelt there, I realized that after three years of Catholicism my only contact with active Catholics had been through articles I had written for one of the Catholic magazines. Those contacts had been brief, casual. I still did not know personally one Catholic layman. And when I returned to New York, I found Peter Maurin – Peter the French peasant, whose spirit and ideas will dominate the rest of this book as they will dominate the rest of my life." (Day, op. cit.).

The reorientation of her life that began with the birth of her daughter took a definite direction after her meeting with Peter Maurin. From the time she started the first *Catholic Worker* "house of hospitality" in 1933 until she died in 1980 at the age of 83, Day's life was filled with the noise, dirt, and strife of the streets. Many only lamented the life of the poor; she lived it.

A "sermon" woman who fed and sheltered thousands but never had a nickel herself, who was jailed eight times for civil disobedience, who swore allegiance to the Church and attended Mass daily. Dorothy always believed that besides talking and theorizing and writing theological tomes about what it means to be a Christian, you have to start living it yourself.

Day, along with the Workers, lacked the comfort most people spend their lives enjoying or seeking, but they cite compensations such as the communal feeling at meetings and meals, the joy of helping someone whose life seems to have been written off, and finally visits to the workers' upstate farm which provide a necessary respite from the heat of the city. There is a freedom in dispelling the fear, a sense of joy in realizing your potential to be drawn outside yourself.

She was a living sermon on Christian discipleship. She willingly denied herself and took up the cross daily. She was childlike in her enthusiasm as she faithfully served the poor. She lacked the comforts that most people spend a lifetime enjoying and seeking. Deep down inside herself there was peace and joy, because she was finally realizing her potential.

Day left us this thought: "It is not love in the abstract that counts. Men have loved a cause as they have loved a woman. Men have loved brotherhood, the workers, the poor, the oppressed – but they have not loved man, they have not loved personally. It is hard to love. It is the hardest thing in the world."[30]

It is difficult to want less, to be convinced that by having less we are not somehow diminished as persons. It is hard because our culture glorifies those who have more – as have most materialistic cultures throughout history. Yet Christ calls us to be more – to be more fully human – calls us to liberate ourselves from selfishness, hatred and greed whether our own or that of others inflicted upon us.

Christ was born, lived and died among the poor to demonstrate the spiritual worthlessness, indeed the immorality, of striving to amass material wealth. His life was a testimony to the higher value of our developing into fully human, fully caring beings.

Her stands against war and in favor of the Church's commitment to the relief of the downtrodden were thorns in the sides of clergy and laity who patriotically supported "just wars" and who enjoyed the fruits of unrestricted, unreflected capitalism. Her fearless and radical views caused uneasiness in the hearts of many "good Catholics."

Many who felt threatened by her brand of Catholicism were quick to disassociate themselves from her. Because she busied herself with the essentials of the Gospel message, one could not dismiss her completely. Due to her lifestyle of voluntary poverty and a life of service to the downtrodden, she was able to address the moral issues of the day without restriction.

As a religious person who prayed daily – Mass and Communion, the Psalms, the rosary – Day used her faith as a buffer against burnout and despair. Fittingly, it will have to be taken on faith that her life of service made a difference. On the subject of results, Day had a philosophy of divine patience: "We continue feeding our neighbors and clothing and sheltering them and the more we do it the more we realize that the most important thing is to love."[31]

There are many who say that Day was theologically simplistic as well as socially naive. She heard these voices raised in criticism of her. Hearing them, she determined to commit herself more and more to a life of voluntary poverty. She had no investments, not even in herself, so there was nothing to lose. She knew she had to please no one except Jesus Christ. Her posture was free from the temptations of power and compromise. Daily she shared whatever she had with the many who came to her. She admitted that it was difficult to rub shoulders or share a bowl of soup with some of the many. Given the choice between writing a check for the poor or eating and living with them, she chose the latter.

Let me close this chapter with a quote from Daniel Berrigan:

"Our best and truest memories are invariably suffused with gratitude. I am grateful beyond words for the grace of this woman=s life, for her sensible, unflinching rightness of mind, her long and lonely truth, her journey to the heart of things. I think of her as one who simply helped us, in a time of self-inflicted blindness, to see. At length, all was said and done; no more needed saying and doing. She stood there, or sat down, like Christ, like Buddha. This is the image of her last years. Her life passed over into passive voice. She was served, reverenced, cherished, protected. Her flame was failing; her memory glimmered and guttered; 'On Pilgrimage' became a barely audible murmur of space and silences as she struggled to say her farewell to the world. ... The best tribute we could offer Dorothy is that we too would stand somewhere, or sit down. ... She urged our consciences off the beaten track; she made the impossible probable, and then actual. She did this, first of all, by living as though the truth were true." (Berrigan, op. cit.).

CHAPTER 21
Have You Had
Your Daily Dose of Divine Love?

"The report about him spread all the more, and great crowds assembled to listen to him and to be cured of their ailments, but he would withdraw to deserted places to pray."

–Luke 5:15-16

Prayer is helping us become more attuned to the personal, passionate, profound love of our Heavenly Father, Jesus, and the Holy Spirit. Why do you pray? You pray to deepen that relationship with the Blessed Trinity and to help you sustain conversion. The word "disciple" means to be a lifelong student. You have to make that kind of commitment, too.

Everyone should expect to experience divine love daily. Everyone. That is the primary way the Blessed Trinity wants to enrich our lives on Earth.

You can discover love with a bird flying by as you're driving, with a child laughing while at play, with nature, with eating your cereal in the morning. There is no limit of opportunities for you to experience divine love every single day. Now, obviously not every experience is going to do that for you. It varies from one moment to the next, from good mood to bad mood, from positive experience to negative experience; but, the ways in which divine love are communicated are absolutely boundless. It is up to you to have, as the Gospel tells you, eyes to see, ears to hear, and a heart to understand. That is what we're all called to do in order to grow in divine love.

Simply put, this lesson in divine love is about being alert to your emotions. Imagine yourself sitting at the table in the morning in the quietness of the sunrise, eating Cheerios … Take away all of the distractions that are to come throughout the day and just sit in silence. It's not as easy as it sounds, is it?

However, if we extend that experience over a period of time, we can condition our minds to love the silence and experience gratitude for the food in front of us, for the light coming through the window; those small, essential moments surrounding us that we often take for granted when we're constantly thinking about what bills we need to pay, who we need to please today, and where we put the car keys! When we silence the mental noise, we have the opportunity to experience divine love. Few people take the opportunity each day to recognize that type of love.

When distractions fill up our minds, an emptiness is created in our souls. What is divine love trying to evoke in you? It's trying to evoke a response of gratefulness and thankfulness. Once that gets rooted, that takes care of worry, self-centeredness, preoccupation ... When you silence your mind, none of those distractions take up residence in your mind, heart, will, soul, and body. You are free. Because people are not attentive to that, what happens? A cumulative effect sets in. That's why the church recommends the practice of welcoming God into your life the moment you wake up each morning.

The opening antiphon of the church is, "God come to my assistance. Lord, make haste to help me." The reason for this is that distraction is inevitably going to set in. Our brains our already in gear! Psalm 1:18 says, "This is the day that the Lord has made." In other words, I don't need to make this day. I don't need to put any pressure on myself. What are we to do with the day that He has given us? It's a free gift. So, rejoice and be glad! The word of God can enable you to set the tone for your disposition toward living this particular day. You trust that He will come to help you, that His grace will be sufficient for you. You trust your Lord and are grateful that He has given you another day to live. In return for these wonderful gifts, you promise to live this day in a joyful manner.

That, unfortunately, gets hijacked for so many people; however, it's not as complicated as we make it out to be.

Without question, life in the 21st century is so much different than life in the 20th century, or centuries before. We live a derivative existence. We're detached from the natural order because we're so obsessed with the technological order. Instead of enjoying the taste of the Cheerios, we're on Facebook. You have to multitask now!

My grandfather would have a real laugh at the robotic way today's people stare at their phones and tablets. He actually enjoyed a meal, because he recognized the importance of being attentive to what you're doing: nourishing your body and sharing a conversation, face to face. You go to houses today and there might be five people at the table – four of them are on their phones! You walk on the boardwalk with a friend; two people walking together, but they're not, because they're both on their phones.

It is a major obstacle to getting to the natural level of our own existence. The technological level pushes its way to "first and foremost." It's another form of addiction. Many people become so tied into that. Even with social media and all of the controversy going on in the world, technology can be dehumanizing, depersonalizing, and a major obstacle to the spiritual life, rather than an aid or a helpful tool to connect us.

Now, they have apps for the Psalms and the New Testament. You can get data and information about the spiritual life, but there's still a certain disconnectedness to it. Instead of it being available, you need it to be a reminder. There's an overdependence on technology to serve reminders to us, rather than us making a conscious effort to remember on our own.

In Christopher O. Blum's and Joshua P. Hochschild's A Mind at Peace, we are reminded of St. Augustine's description of peace as "the tranquility of order."

"We all nod our heads in agreement," the book says. "We know that a tightrope balance is necessary to navigate chaos and cosmos (order) in our everyday lives. It is a constant, daily challenge to achieve and sustain inner harmony of mind, heart, will and soul. If we are full of inner turmoil with ourselves, no amount of external order can bring us the peace we desire."[32]

Oh, how true it is! Blum and Hochschild also reference Sherry Turkle's technological studies. Turkle argued that "our habits of using communications technology are making us 'insecure, isolated, and lonely' and warned of our tendency to seek consolation in machines."[33]

Adam Gazzaley, a neuroscientist, and Larry D. Rosen, a psychologist, call it "ancient brains in a high-tech world." Blum and Hochschild cite these traits as: "anxiety, boredom, weakened memory, poor goal management, general loss of cognitive control."[34]

"It is increasingly clear that our habits of using technology are contributing to interior suffering," Blum and Hochschild conclude. It is yet another paradox. We are so busy now, but we get busier when we are distracted even when we explore our own thoughts, feelings, social interactions … it even leaks into our relationship with Father, Son, and Holy Spirit.

That's why the church in her wisdom won't allow you to go to confession over the phone. It must be a human encounter, because the priest is Christ's natural representation. Implicitly, the priest is the human forgiver. He accepts you in your weakness, in your brokenness, in your darkness, in your sinful patterns of living. So, you receive human acceptance as well as divine. Human touch facilitates divine touch. Is this not another form of divine love?

How Do You Pray?

One of the questions I explored with Fr. Murray was, "How do you pray?" There are three separate methods of prayer: the formal way of praying, using sacred scripture and the Psalms; the ritual way of praying, through the sacraments; and a personal way of praying, through a casual conversation with God. Each of these methods must have a role in your answer to the question, "How do I pray?"

The Ritual Way

We are all creatures of habit, but there is a difference between habit and ritual. Habits can fall into ruts. Ritual frees us from that danger. That whole understanding of what a ritual pattern is gets lost in our culture, today. People want facts and information instantly. People want to be entertained instantly. Because of that, ritual slips through the cracks.

The goal of prayer is to connect to the personal, passionate, and profound love of God. I've come to know that our Heavenly Father calls me by name. When someone calls you by name, there's a personal relationship formed. In confession, God says to us, "I love you, I forgive you, I heal you and uplift you." That is salvation unfolding, which means the healing love of the Lord is trying to heal past and present hurts and anticipate future hurts. We have a choice to make, then. Am I going to be a healing presence in people's lives, or am I going to be a hurtful presence in people's lives? That makes all the difference in the way you live your life and the way you interact with people.

How do I pray? Again, silence is an important part of prayer. That would be captured in the ritual of adoration – when you just sit in front of the Blessed Sacrament, you see the weakness of the host, you experience the silence of the host. This holy moment can fill in the emptiness of your life. Our first duty as Christians is adoration – that we recognize that there is a power greater than our own. Our second duty as Christians is wonder, playfulness, and enjoying our lives. Our third duty as Christians is service

– our willingness to go and be a healing presence for others. Wire that into your mind, your heart, your will, your soul, and your relationships with other people, and you will receive your daily dose of divine love.

The Personal Way

Too often, we fall into just one category of prayer. In the personal, you have a conversation with God. It's most effective through silence, but it's comforting to do throughout the day. The way in which it's conducted can be lost, where it's, "God, give me this, help me do that," or not even asking for things, but simply being grateful without considering the actual meaning of your gratitude. There's a lack of awareness in people who even just believe in a God when conducting personal prayer.

Prayer, in its purest form, is utterly useless. We are all wired to utility. The reason I say that is based on that premise of, "God, help me." When our relationship with God is constantly asking for help, then it is a superficial relationship. It's based on pure unadulterated utility. I'm calling you in when I feel a sense of panic or desperation. "Get me out of this jam."

Believe it or not, our Lord in his goodness does accommodate us on those requests. When do we come to say, "I have to invest more than just a utilitarian relationship"? That does eventually surface at some point. That can be a springboard to going into a deeper, more personal approach to prayer.

I don't like it when people use me for their personal gain. That is a good warning that I should not relate to God in that very way. How do you think God feels as He unconditionally gives His divine love to you, and in return, you ask for more of Him? So, how do you relate to God? Hopefully, you do so in a more humane way, where you can take a walk with the Lord.

I can put in my calendar an appointment to sit with Him after lunch for five minutes. Sit with Him in the morning, or at several points during the day. Make a promise to yourself and to God: I will step aside from my daily responsibilities and spend time with the Lord.

Once you've mastered making time to forming a real relationship with God, you come to a point where you don't just fit God into your calendar anymore. Now, you open yourself up to His unfolding of the day. Then, a major shift has happened.

Mrs. Brown invited Albert Einstein to tea one day and he accepted. She had an agenda. After the tea and biscuits, she says, "Now Albert, I brought you here to explain to me, in terms that I can understand, your theory of relativity." She wasn't ready to allow his theory to expand her horizon! She wanted Einstein to simplify and fit his insight into her narrow, little world. We're constantly doing that with God. We're always trying to fit God in, but He's trying to tell us there's a bigger, greater world out there. You have to be willing to open your eyes and accept this world that is much more expansive than your normal, narrow, constricted version of the world.

I was looking for answers from Fr. Murray, and he was telling me to open my heart and mind to finding the better questions.

The Formal Way

The formal way of prayer can get mechanical and lose meaning, as well. You recite them and don't even know what you're saying. It's drilled into your brain as a kid, but what does it mean? Why is it said when it is said in Mass? Why do you say it when you confess? Why did Jesus share it with us in the first place?

Jesus was extremely reluctant to teach people how to pray. So much so that we only have recorded one prayer: the 55 words, in the English translation of the text, that make up the Our Father. Why was He reluctant? Because He deeply believed that if you lived life the way He wants you to live life, which is abundantly, then you'll pray. You'll become aware of your limitations. You'll also be aware of these remarkable opportunities that are out there.

Prayer – or better put, awareness – in this way avoids the dangerous form of prayer: the mechanical, memorized, meaningless form of prayer. When you pray in the dangerous form, you don't even connect to the words that you are uttering. There can be a collective memory. People don't know the creed, but then once they hear it, they can join in, even though some words have recently changed and it's caused a couple of bumps for people. I think there's something good about changing it, so you couldn't depend on a memorized version.

A seminarian classmate of mine is an example of this dangerous form of prayer, which also was a result of skipping intellectual conversion. He could not have cared less about stimulating and developing his mind intellectually, but he was the first to tell his teachers that he prayed five rosaries, yesterday!

Fr. McNamara used to say that the best way to pray the Lord's Prayer to avoid it becoming mindless is to pray it backward. That's a great task. "Deliver us from evil" is the first statement, instead of "Our Father."

Deliver us from evil – you have to now think, what evil do I have to be delivered from, today? What are the forces of evil that I must be aware of? He said, the Lord's Prayer, as it is taught, is ontologically correct, but if you want it to be existentially effective, pray it backward, so that you end with "Our Father." What you are now saying is, "I'm thankful that I have a Father like you."

CHAPTER 22
Musings on Sacraments in Modern Times

"The self-respecting soul, as soon as he reaches his goal, places it still further away. Not to attain it, but never to halt in the ascent. Only thus does life acquire nobility and oneness."

—Nikos Kazantzakis, Report to Greco (1961)

So many millennials choose hitting the snooze button on the alarm clock over an hour of church every week. What they are missing is the form of prayer of receiving the Risen Lord in the Eucharist: a sacrament we decide to receive or bypass on a weekly basis.

The Lord asks us to give one hour a week. He gives us, freely and generously, 168 hours. He asks for one hour in return. I think when we're unable to fulfill His request, it reflects a certain spiritual poverty. We can't find one hour to give back. Even in giving back, we open ourselves to the Eucharist, where ritual envelops us.

"The grace of our Lord Jesus Christ, the love of our Heavenly Father, and the communion with the Holy Spirit." That language is not the language you're going to hear on the latest hit song on the radio. It's formulaic.

The grace of our Lord – what happens if you're paying attention to that when that initial greeting is presented to you? You're welcomed in to the house of God by grace, love, and communion.

Then, the church says you can be showered with mercy, with a penitential right. "Lord have mercy, Christ have mercy, Lord have mercy." Any hurt can be touched with our Lord's favorite daily miracle: His merciful, forgiving love.

Next, you listen to people you normally don't listen to: Isaiah, St. Paul, Matthew, Mark, Luke and John, and the Psalmists. There's a new language, vocabulary, and hidden meaning in all of that. Its purpose is to enlighten you and expand your horizon.

"We come to give thanks (that's what the word "Eucharist" means), but, we also come to connect with Father, Son, and Holy Spirit, as well as to the mystical body of Christ (that is, the people in the pew beside you)."

Your presence in the pew enriches everybody else who's there. Your absence diminishes. It should be a tripod: I can grow personally in this ritual experience of the unfolding of the Liturgy of the Eucharist; I can be a contributing factor to other people's faith by being there and adding to the mystical body of Christ; and I can be nourished with a gift that we take for granted: a gift of a foretaste of a resurrected order of living.

The Resurrection is the central truth of our Catholic faith, but it means little to most people on a practical level. They haven't sat with it or understood that we can begin a resurrected order of living now and prepare ourselves for the fullness of that unfolding in eternity. You receive the peace of Christ given to you through a gesture – the handshake of someone else. You receive the risen body of Christ – mercy, forgiveness, healing, and enlightenment – through the scriptures that are proclaimed. How do you know someone is important to you? You spend time with them. You waste time with them. That's the importance of the decision you have to make in waking up and going to church on Sunday.

I call this a "grace benefit." It happens when we pray in any form of prayer. It's not the goal, but the indirect result. If you realize that, then you've made a step in spiritual maturity.

"Come Hell or high water, I'm going to be happy today." It doesn't work that way. Happiness is a result, but it's not the end-goal of life. That's the significance of the Beatitudes. That's why the word "content" is a much more adequate word to describe the goal of consistent inner peace. It's a more accurate parallel to the growing discontent in the world. I think happiness is superficial.

We've talked a lot about the three would-be disciples. They are only found in Luke's Gospel. The first disciple shows a lack of awareness, coupled with naivety and innocence. The second disciple says, "I will follow you wherever you go, but let me go home and tell my parents I'm heading off." The third says, "I will follow you, but first let me go and bury my father," which was a very important Jewish ritual, to bury the dead, especially a parent.

Jesus' response to that final would-be disciple is, "Let the dead bury the dead." In other words, you have to accept the opportunity now to live a new understanding of life.

Discipleship is all about accepting the Kingdom of God. Jesus proclaims, even family ties cannot interfere with seeking first the Kingdom of God.

In Matthew's Gospel, it is stated that when the Kingdom of God is presented to people, it will cause division.

'Do not think that I have come to bring peace upon the earth. I have come to bring not peace but the sword. For I have come to set

'a man 'against his father,

'a daughter against her mother,

'and a daughter-in-law against her mother-in-law;

'and one's enemies will be those of his household.'

'Whoever loves father or mother more than me is not worthy of me, and whoever loves son or daughter more than me is not worthy of me; and whoever does not take up his cross and follow after me is not worthy of me. Whoever finds his life will lose it, and whoever loses his life for my sake will find it.'" (Matthew 10:34-39).

What Jesus is teaching is that discipleship has to have a clear commitment to a new understanding of life. The Father's understanding of life is captured in the phrase, "the Kingdom of God." When you pray the Lord's Prayer, you are praying, "thy kingdom come, thy will be done." If you know what you're saying when you're saying that, you wouldn't say those two phrases glibly. No one wants to surrender his or her will to another person's will. We're not wired that way. "Thy kingdom come," or, "I'm going to let go my understanding of life and now adopt this new understanding of life on what Jesus is teaching."

Once you get past the Ego Spirit and listen to the Holy Spirit, you can open your heart to the new understanding of the Kingdom of God. Yet, rest assured, you will still go through the progressions, the trials of the mind, as you go on this journey. Below is an example of the mind's tug-of-war, as written by Nikos Kazantzakis in Report to Greco:

"I am a bow in your hands, Lord. Draw me, lest I rot.

"Do not overdraw me Lord. I shall break.

"Overdraw me, Lord, and who cares if I break!"

He goes on to describe the power we hold once we enter the mindset that it is OK to break: "When the heart believes and loves," he says, "nothing chimerical exists; nothing exists but courage, trust, and fruitful action."[35]

'Lord, let me be chaste, but not yet'

The above subtitle comes from St. Augustine. It presents us the idea of yet another spiritual, inner struggle of our Christian youth in the 21st century. It reminds me still of a time before my full commitment to my vocation, studying at the seminary, struggling with my own questions and doubts.

While in the seminary, I met a man of Italian heritage named Vincenzo, who worked on the grounds. He lived in an Italian neighborhood not far from the seminary. He was a very short fellow and he exuded great joy from many simple things in life, like music and different operas he had memorized. Often, I would be outside on a bench reading a book, and Vincenzo would call me over to inform me that I was wasting my time. Of course, I needed to know why he thought that.

Vincenzo asked me to hand him the book. He would then point to the top line on the page and say, "I start here and read down to the bottom line of the page, and by the time I get to the bottom of the page, I have forgotten what I read at the top!"

Vincenzo had a wonderful philosophy on work: sure and steady. He took great pride in making the seminary grounds eye appealing. As a matter of fact, his philosophy on work was very appealing to me: work, but don't overwork. Don't overwork, but don't cut corners.

After my sixth year, spring 1977, I told Vincenzo that I had to make a decision – whether to live a life of celibacy, or not – and asked if he could offer any advice. With the handle of his rake in both hands, he pondered my request, then looked me in the eye and said, "To see a beautiful woman and not to touch makes the heart grow crabby." It was a hard lesson to learn. He's saying that to live a life of celibacy is almost impossible. He believed that if you really believe in God's grace, you can't do it on your own, but God's grace can help you live this lifestyle in a liberating and healthy way.

In every life, we all depend on God's grace. To think that we can do things on our own is to be spiritually wrongheaded. You trust in His way and His truth and His life. That means a big commitment in allowing the dying to yourself in order to create space for His life and love to guide and direct you in your life. Vincenzo was giving me the advice that it will be an uphill battle, but by depending on God's grace, I could live a life of celibacy in a full and abundant way. That's true of any walk of life.

His advice also echoed in my mother's words: "There is a lucky girl out there that doesn't have to listen to you every day." That helped ease the decision for me, but it didn't make the idea an easier pill to swallow.

When I was first ordained and officiating a lot of weddings, couples were not that much younger than I. Being invited to the receptions – that was a common thing back then – I would enjoy my time celebrating the sacrament of marriage and the great potential of these young couples. However, I would then retreat to the rectory and wonder what it would be like to have a wife. Seeing so many joyful people at these weddings was what triggered these thoughts. I had to learn to deal with the fact that this was not in the future for me. How do you navigate that in a healthy way, not in a self-destructive way?

There's a test among 4-year-olds where they're brought into a room and there's a marshmallow sitting on a little plate. The child's attention goes directly to that marshmallow. The adult says to the child, "You can have the marshmallow now, or if you wait five minutes, you'll be able to have two marshmallows." Studies have indicated that when you can delay gratification, you grow in inner strength. Your life is less driven by needing to gratify. Athletes have to train and delay gratification until they can perform in an event. Musicians have to discipline themselves to practice until they get a chance to perform in an event.

You must also have a mentor and a model to help you remain disciplined. My mother was married for seven years, but she thought she'd have a long, fulfilling marriage that would last many more. She was a model to me that you can still live life in a rich, fully abundant way, even though your husband is physically absent.

The Eucharist says, "Do this in memory of me." Be willing to sacrifice. Be willing to reach for a higher level and goal, even in the gesture of holding up the host and the chalice. St. Paul tells us to set our hearts on the higher realms: faith, hope, and charity. St. Paul tells us to put on the mind of Christ, to find ways in which that becomes real for you, so that you're not caught in web of the cultural trends. It has to be a grounded approach, an acute awareness.

Every time we try to control our destiny, we experience utter and deeper failure. Spirituality and sexuality should go together. Most people find them in complete opposition. The gift of your sexuality is that it's a gift and when that gift matures or develops, people can get frightened of the gift of the power of their sexuality. They run and hide, or they just allow it to control them rather than integrating that gift.

If you don't understand the gift of your sexuality as a gift to be nurtured and expressed in a holy and wholesome way, it will control you in destructive, unhealthy patterns of living. Sexuality cannot be reduced to simply the male and female genitalia. It must be incorporated into a world where there are no modern prophets who can get us to a healthy level of living life. That is why we need to seek role models to understand human sexuality in a spiritual manner.

Fr. McNamara taught many priests that the parish priest should be "the most erotic person in the parish." When he gave this presentation, you could feel the intensity of the tension in a room full of priests! People would get up in arms.

He would say that the true meaning of the word "erotic" is to go out of oneself and to give of oneself. How do you do that in a healthy, wholesome way as a man of God? People can see that it makes sense, they can recognize it in you, but then they wonder what signal is being sent, here. Interpretation is key. It must be free of any hidden agenda.

How do we escape this trap? One method is to recall our prerogatives as Christian men and women: our first duty is adoration, our second duty is wonder, our third duty is service. Adoration and wonder expose hidden agendas, which opens our minds to a new understanding of God's way, allowing us give of ourselves and serve our brothers and sisters.

Even Jesus is caught in an intensely erotic scene in the Gospel when he attends a Pharisee's house for dinner and allows a woman to lavishly pour oil on and wash his feet. The pharisaical approach was, "If this man were a prophet, he would know who and what sort of woman this is who is touching him, that she is a sinner." (Luke 7:39).

But, He didn't. He didn't do that with the Samaritan woman, until He says, "Go call your husband and come back." (John 4:16). Yet, he revealed to her that he knew she had five husbands and would show her how to be free from that chaos when the time neared. Even the woman caught in adultery, He asks, "Has no one condemned you?" (John 8:10).

The Influence of Pope Francis

You have to have absolutes, rules, and laws. The law is there to set and guide, but at the same time, it cannot become so narrow. That was the problem with the Pharisees. Jesus kept calling them hypocrites. To paraphrase the prophet Ezekiel in the 19th verse of his 11th chapter, "I do not write my law on tablets of stone, but on your heart." There is again, a struggle between internalizing the message of the Bible.

Overdependence on the law will not get you to where you want to go. You can use the law as an aid, but eventually, you have to go beyond the law to mercy, forgiveness, healing, and love.

I had a funeral service of a couple whose 52-year-old son committed suicide. The mother came to me and said, "When I was in my late teens, I got married for six months and had this boy, but then I left the father." This first husband has had five wives since. She then met this particular man and has been with him for 48 years. Yet, she feels excommunicated from the church.

I told her, "You're not excommunicated from the church." Relying on the vision of Pope Francis, I could tell she's aching to be active in the church, but she still feels from that mistake that she made 50-some years ago, that she is not free.

I said, "God's mercy is greater than any mistake that any of us make." I strongly encouraged her to come to church and to come to mass. This woman was going through a deep, devastating hurt of the suicide of her son and our Lord wants to be with her at that time. He wants to do anything and everything to heal you and support her. I think that's what Pope Francis is doing with his vision of the Gospel. He prays with us about Jesus the man and Jesus, our God, and what He's all about. Mercy, forgiveness, healing, and love give a newer and richer understanding of holiness and righteousness.

Pope Francis exemplifies that. He listens in prayer more than anything else. His reading of sacred scripture, listening to that and showing up to be influenced by Father, Son, and Holy Spirit, helps him to then go out into the world and recognize that the deepest need out there is for people to experience healing from all of the pains that they have buried alive. The word "savior" means "healing love." Jesus came only as a savior and the church is an extension of His healing, merciful love.

We have to be aware of the hurt that people have in their lives and we have to try to respond in a humane, healing way to them. It's not that the laws are unimportant, but they cannot restrict the mercy of divine love from bringing about healing in people's lives.

Pope Francis is deeply committed to that and it's evident in not only his words, but his actions. He had showers put in for the homeless in Rome. On his 80th birthday, he invited homeless people to a luncheon. That gesture goes beyond the people who were invited and people recognize "healing love" in Pope Francis. Still, there are people who are attached to the law and get very unraveled by his style and his manner of bringing the person of Jesus and His good news to people.

A message sent to St. Matthew's Parish from the Vatican displays his grace:

"Upon all who have remembered him during this holy season, His Holiness invokes the grace and peace of the Risen Lord, and he cordially imparts his Apostolic Blessing."

Free Will vs. God's Plan

When sin is part of our world, which it is, it makes us "less than fully human." Grace tries to restore us and free us from being less than fully human to being fully human. There's a constant tug-of-war between sin and grace. God's life and love flows out of Pope Francis in a rich, recognizable way to other people.

God's plan for everyone has two dimensions: a general and a specific. The general dimension is that He has come for one reason and one reason alone, and that's to save us from sin and death. He wants universal salvation.

Then, He has a specific plan for everyone. That is the more difficult challenge to discern. What specifically does He want you to do with your life? He reverences everybody's free will. He will never compromise that. The task, then, is to recognize the promptings and nudges of the Holy Spirit so that your free will can be blended into God's specific plan for your life. He always gives us clues about what He wants us to do. That's where we have to try to be highly attentive and not miss out on those clues.

It is better to live for someone else than to live for yourself. It's very easy in our world and culture to get caught into trying to establish your own financial security, your own social security, and all of those mundane, daily things that have you worried. The impulse of the Holy Spirit is that your life will be fuller and richer if you let go of that and extend it to helping others.

We live in an age of anxiety. Levels and degrees of anxiety are all around us – economic anxiety, environmental anxiety, political anxiety, international anxiety, personal and interpersonal anxiety. Let's face it: there are some people who see the dark side of every cloud, even one with a silver lining. Some people are always waiting for the other shoe to drop.

Years ago, I officiated the marriage of a young couple in their mid-20s. Fifteen months after their wedding, their first child was born. Unfortunately, he was a fussy baby and cried at night more than he slept. The young mother would wake up her husband and say, "See why the baby is crying."

This pattern happened for several weeks. Her husband would go to work deprived of sleep and it was visible to his coworkers. One day, a colleague gave him a book on infant massage. After reading the book, the fussy baby's father tried it out. Low and behold, it worked! He rubbed the infant's back, arms, and legs, until his son fell into a deep sleep. Now, it was off to bed for a well-deserved, uninterrupted night of sleep.

No such luck.

In the middle of the night, the man's wife would wake up in a panic, jarring her husband from his deep sleep.

"Get up and go see why the baby is not crying!" she exclaimed.

We all know someone like the wife in this story. Even when things are going well, they worry and fret that something bad will happen. They are always stressed out.

When you're struggling with something, there's something of which you must let go. You just have to look and see what it is. The trouble is, it's probably become a pattern. That's where praying and inviting in the Holy Spirit is crucial.

There's a choice between being selfish and generous, honest or dishonest. There are hints and clues that we're all called to recognize. The ability to do so allows us to respond to the Holy Spirit asking us to be joyful, be peaceful, be loving, be kind, be understanding.

The ability to let go of full control is a major skill. In the spiritual life, in prayer and in reading of scripture and coming to understand it all, hopefully, you begin taking little steps so that when you are faced with a dramatic and life-changing experience, you're ready to embrace it. It's like a spiritual muscle. When you can give the Resurrection meaning, it helps facilitate the realization that there is eternal life.

Relative and basic horizons help us navigate life in a way that we don't give every life experience the same value. Certain life experiences give way to a basic horizon in the Pascal Mystery. The gift of life is an understanding of love. Personal suffering is a way to reduce the suffering in the world that is rooted in sin. The gift of letting go is the way to achieving life's meaning and purpose and reaching the goal of living eternally. That enables us to see things, as Einstein said, for their relative value.

You always have to be able to say, "How does this play in the grand scheme of things?" When you recognize things on the relative horizon, you won't allow your consciousness to get tied up in knots. A person who sees all things in the utmost urgency lose credibility and authority over the rest. They cannot distinguish between what is essential and what is relative in life. That's what basic and relative horizon enables us to do. Everything is not a matter of life and death. This too shall pass.

CHAPTER 23
Spiritual Direction

"The saints are the bold ones, daring enough to be different, humble enough to make mistakes, wild enough to be burnt in the fire of divine love, real enough to make the rest of us see how enormously phony we are. They transform passion and raise it to a higher level, where it is freed from the structures of sense. They are passionate pilgrims of the Absolute, restless until they rest in an infinite love that is the intense passion of the Holy Spirit. If they seem to withdraw, it is only for the sake of a fuller life from which the limits of that lower life would have debarred them ... Life is love, passionate and intense. Only in such love is reality touched – the rest is deception, bondage, and spiritual death."

–Fr. William McNamara (1926 – 2015)

This chapter is designed to give guidance, direction, in the spiritual life. Within it, you will find stories, practices, and most importantly, questions, to help you along your personal path. Without asking ourselves the right questions, we may become lost in the daily hustle of the natural life. It is my goal to help you find those questions, just like Fr. Murray helped me.

There is agony and ecstasy in every life. You cannot avoid having valley experiences. The Psalms talk about it. The Gospels personify it. Our Lord takes Peter, James, and John up the mountain and He is transfigured. He doesn't accept Peter's invitation to build three tents there and hang out for a long time. You have to come back down the mountain. As they're coming down, they meet with demons and other obstacles. Any vocation in the Gospel tradition is your ability to overcome obstacles, internal and external. That doesn't change because we're all a part of the human condition.

John the Baptist is the bridge between the Old Order and the New Order, the Old Testament and the New Testament. He is a towering biblical figure. He is the cousin of Jesus, but he has a specific calling in that he is to make straight the way of the Lord. He is to prepare people for the first coming of Christ. All of us have to imitate John in not really preparing for the first coming of Christ, but His second coming.

He was already a towering figure in the community, but he saw who Jesus was right away. He said, "He must increase, I must decrease." (John 3:30).

Contained in the phrase is a conscious deliberate choice to die of your Ego Spirit and recognize the foundational virtue of humility. The more you are connected to the Earth of which you are made, the better connected you are. That's why my grandfather would always say to stay close to the dirt in which you were made. People that have the practice of gardening or landscaping enjoy a spiritual benefit. It keeps us rooted and connected to who we are as human beings.

Jesus doesn't want any of us to dig a ditch and say we're no good, but you should not make your home in your ego, either. One of the most frequent refrains in the New Testament is an offshoot of that idea: those who humble themselves will be glorified and those who glorify themselves will be humbled. That's the tradeoff.

John the Baptist calls people to a new understanding of life; cleansing and purifying of your old way of living so that you can think differently, see differently, hear differently, and behave differently. That's what he calls us to do. You recognize Jesus as your Lord and Savior. Even a brief encounter with Jesus has the potential to change your life. Once you have a personal encounter with Jesus, the opportunity for a new understanding will present itself.

This is true in the 19th chapter of Luke's Gospel, where Zacchaeus, a prominent tax collector, encounters Jesus for the first time. A wealthy man sees Jesus' way, and in turn promises to give half of his riches to the poor and repay his wrongs "four times over." He has found new meaning for his riches, new life in Jesus.

The Greek word *baptizo* means "to plunge." Any person who is baptized is plunged into the Paschal Mystery of our Lord. This sacramental gesture gives the individual a new identity and enables the person to be a contemporary Christ-man or Christ-woman in the world.

Baptism, confirmation, and Eucharist make up the sacraments of initiation. Your baptism forms your identity. The Eucharist engulfs you in intimacy with your Lord. Confirmation builds your integrity – your moral ground on which you stand.

Most, if not all, of life's difficulties can be rooted in our inability to grow in the areas of identity, intimacy, and integrity. These sacraments

---

attempt to offset the obstacles that could result from these vital areas of a person's human and faith development.

What does it mean to be a Christian? It means that Christ is the biggest idea in your mind. He fills your soul like a riot of joy. He sits on the edge of your lips like a shout of praise. He motivates you, haunts you, hounds you, day in and day out. It means that, because of Him, there is nothing more real, more enticing, and more thrilling in significance in your life. You make your decisions, your judgments, your plans in terms of Christ. That's what it means to be a Christian.

G. K. Chesterton said, "There was a man who lived in the East centuries ago and now I cannot look at a raven or a sunset, a lily or a wheat field, a sheep or a sparrow, a vineyard, a mountain, [or a child] without thinking of Him."

Dom Marmion said, "The difference between the saints and the rest of us is that the saints plunge into the consumed fire of God's love."

They come out burned, but magnificently transfigured. The rest of us put our little finger in, get burned, and spend the rest of our lives circling the fire, far enough away never to be burned again and close enough to be warmed by it. That's lukewarmness. That's mediocrity. And that's how we pull it off. Mediocrity is compromise worked out into a system. And the system works, seemingly. In other words, we never lose our reputation. But we don't go storming into heaven and we don't change the world in the meantime.

Reverence is the capacity to be in God's presence full of wonder, gratitude and respect. I love the story of Martin Luther, who, on those dark and discouraging days that we all have, would say to himself over and over, "I am baptized. I am baptized." He affirmed that whatever was happening to him at that moment, he was a child of God.

"The River," a short story by Flannery O'Connor, describes a baptismal scene down by the river. After plunging the little boy into the waters of the river, the preacher raised him over his head and boldly announced, "You won't be the same again … You'll count…"[36]

Sin causes estrangement, brokenness, disconnection with the Blessed Trinity, with our true selves, and with all of creation. That is chaos. Jesus comes into the world to free us from sin and reestablish Holy Communion with the world, with our true selves, and with the divine order. John the Baptist sees this and knows its deep meaning. John the Baptist "saw Jesus coming toward him." (John 1:29).

John the Baptist's purpose, his vocation, is to attract others to Jesus. In the Old Testament, as a lamb sacrificed in the temple atones for people's sins and reunites them to Yahweh. John the Baptist encourages his disciples to "behold" – that is, take a long, loving look, not a quick glance – as a way to overcome alienation and unite all disciples into a deep, profound, holy communion with Father, Son, and Holy Spirit. As you can see, when you keep your hands in the soil of the earth and your heart close to the Blessed Trinity, a purpose, a vocation can be revealed. We are on the horizon of yet another birth.

The 4 H Club

When born into the natural order, we are all called to have a physical experience. As previously discussed, two ways to do so are through humility and hilarity. Jesus wants us to live life abundantly; however, we do not achieve abundance by striving for it. We must accept it in all of its forms, even those unbeknownst to our current situation. Humility and hilarity help us ease that tension in the tug of war between Ego Spirit and Evil Spirit.

When born into the spiritual life, we are all called to develop a new understanding in the ease of that tension through the Holy Spirit, who sits in the middle, guiding us, even if we are blind in the moment. The Holy Spirit asks us to exhibit hospitality and holiness in our quest to live life abundantly. As Zacchaeus encounters Jesus, the Holy Spirit calls him to be hospitable. As St. Paul writes to his pupil, Timothy, we must accept hardship for the sake of the Gospel. In order to do that, we must change. We must exhibit holiness, and part of holiness is accepting hardship. We need to embrace Jesus' way of suffering in love to reduce the suffering in the world, which is rooted in sin. We, too, need to make that change in our lives a conscious one, but that doesn't come naturally. It is the result of being attentive and receptive to God's grace.

Changing appearances is a billion dollar enterprise in our country. Men spend upwards of five billion dollars on products that grow hair and I'm quite sure that women top that figure on oils and creams that guarantee the removal of wrinkles and the restoration of youthful skin. Actually, since the average length of time that a person can stay active is being extended all the time, it is probably true that people don't fear growing old as much as they fear looking old. Since many believe, as Shakespeare said, that clothes make the man, billions more are spent on what we wear, not just to cover up and warm us, but to keep up with the fashions—which is all about appearance.

When we hear this Gospel about the transfiguration of Jesus, we might conclude that Jesus' message is all about appearance too. After all, the incident on the mountaintop is just that—a marvelous transformation in the appearance of Jesus. Never before had Peter, James, and John seen Jesus this way. But if His appearance in such glory were significant, Jesus would not have immediately forbidden these three apostles to talk about it with the others. Also, Jesus would have used this change in His appearance to impress His followers early and often in His ministry. Nowhere in His sermons does Jesus give the impression that that is what He is all about—changing the way we appear to others.

However, the Gospel message is all about change. The season of Lent is all about change. The change that Jesus is constantly advocating is a change in our identity. In a way, we can say that Jesus is guilty of identity theft, since that is what His intention is. Jesus wants to steal our identity. We have allowed our consumer culture and the media to identify us as consumers. We are brainwashed to make us accept as fact that we exist for the sake of our possessions. We live and work for the sake of what we have to such an extent that we identify with the objects that create our life.

Perhaps you have seen the sign: "Ultimate Electronics." This seems an absurd claim until you stop and realize that, in fact, there is something ultimate about the way electronics have taken over our lives: iPhones, tablets, Fitbits, Apple Watches. How much of a family's time and income is spent with and for electronics? Cellphones have become so much a part of our lives that a visitor from outer space might well conclude that they are, in fact, part of the human body. Do we, or do we not, identify with our electronics?

What identity does Jesus want to give us? First of all, we are to identify ourselves as children of Abraham. This means living by faith in God. Abraham had full confidence in the destiny that God determined for him, although, at the time of his call, he was taking a leap into the dark. It was faith in God's promises that unsettled him in his native land. It is faith in God's promises that unsettles us in a world we feel too much a part of. Abraham's faith set him apart from his countrymen. Our faith must set us apart from a secular society whose final destiny is expressed in a slogan such as "Ultimate Electronics." Abraham's faith gave him a different destiny from that of his neighbors. Our faith gives us a different destiny from our neighbors.

Another part of our identity is that we are Gospel people. Saint Paul wrote to his pupil Timothy to accept hardship for the sake of the Gospel. Perhaps you have close friends that belong to an evangelical church. Evangelical churches are attracting thousands of Roman Catholics every day over the entire Western Hemisphere. Obviously, living for the sake of the Gospel has set them on fire. As good Catholics, we do accept the

Gospel, but few of us have the zeal for it to the extent that we spread it the way a fire rages through a forest.

It is clear from the whole message that Jesus preached that we are to change. But the change is from the inside out, not from the outside in. By joining ourselves to Jesus in the Eucharist, we get the strength to bring about that change.

It was Arnold Toynbee who said: "The most dangerous period for a civilization is when it thinks it is safe and no longer needs to face changes."

The scripture tells us that Biblical faith has never been a settler faith. It is a pilgrim faith, a faith that moves out of "what is" in the direction of "what will be."

Genesis' 12th chapter tells the story of how Abraham went out, not knowing where he was going. At 75, he went out of the familiar, out of the secure, out in the direction of the frightening call of God. He became a great patriarch. The church calls him the father of faith. Against all odds, he trusted in God's call.

Matthew 17:1-9 tells us of Peter, James, and John. They, too, answered a call from Jesus. They had their struggles and difficulties in leaving family, friends, and security behind in order to follow Jesus.

Like Abraham they didn't always understand what was going on, or what Jesus' purpose was all about; yet, they faithfully stayed with Him and eventually became His intimate inner circle, preachers of the Gospel, the foundation, with the other Apostles, especially Peter, on whom the church was founded.

We meet them on Mount Tabor where they are given a glimpse of Jesus in His splendor as the Son of God. Seeing this they want to settle there, freeze this moment of glory to make it last forever. "Lord it is good that we are here. If you wish, I will make three tents here," (Matthew 17:4) says Peter.

Peter, James, and John were tempted to think they had arrived and that their life's journey need go no farther.

Jesus knew that this was not the case. He knew He had to climb yet another mountain, Golgotha. His call to follow Him had to include, even for the Apostles, and indeed for us all, a journey up both mountains.

Yes, like Abraham and Jesus we have to undertake a journey up mountains of glory and down into valleys of suffering, persecutions, or crises and experience how God is walking this journey with us. It is never easy to leave what is comfortable and safe to go on such a journey. We often have to leave behind our vision and open ourselves to God's revelation.

But, let's be honest here. Many of us are not risk-takers. We're like Bilbo in J.R.R. Tolkien's story of the Hobbit.

Hobbits are easygoing folk about 3 or 4 feet tall. The average Hobbit lives a well-ordered, sheltered life in a quiet, comfortable hole in the ground.

One day a fellow named Gandalf visits Bilbo, inviting him along on an adventure he is arranging. Bilbo is aghast. "We are plain quiet folk and have no use for adventures," he replies. "Nasty disturbing uncomfortable things! Make you late for dinner! I can't think what anybody sees in them."[37]

That's the way many people feel about life. They like everything to be predictable, orderly. Dull is good.

Thank God for the Abrahams, for the Peters, Jameses, and Johns. Thank God for Jesus. They welcomed the challenge of the pilgrim journey with all its twists and turns, its ups and downs. They were always oriented to the future not like the Hobbits wanting to freeze the present.

Yes, the call to serve God in a life of holiness sometimes forces us to leave our comfort zone; to take stands that are unpopular; to have situations or people who tempt us to compromise what we believe. We cannot be anemic in living the Christian life. Satan loves the anemic Christian. His masterpiece is not the prostitute, the adulterer, the drug addict, the street people.

No, Satan's masterpiece is the self-sufficient person who has made life comfortable, wants to keep it that way no matter how much God calls.

Lent is a season when we journey with Jesus. Read about His journey in Scripture.

Say your morning prayer on your way to work; offer your night prayer when you turn off the TV; pray grace before meals with the entire family; come to Mass each Sunday and recognize the Risen Lord, veiled in our midst, under the appearance of Bread and Wine. Be transformed and don't be afraid to answer Jesus' call to holiness.

At the base of the Matterhorn in Switzerland there is a small cemetery nestled in the shadows near the base.

On one of the stones there is an inscription: "We who lie here scorned the lesser peaks."

There are cemeteries all over the world where you can find the graves of Christians who believed that Christian faith was about more than comfort, who gave of themselves daily that the world might know God's love. They scorned lesser peaks. They walked in the steps of their Master, the greatest Adventurer of all. Yes, they scaled mountains with Christ and got vivid glimpses of Him in the valleys of life in the real world of struggle and frustration.

We are reminded that the season of Lent is a time for all of us to recognize that the world is full of the kindness of the Lord and a time to respond to that loving kindness, a response that will require a letting-go that will result in a transformation in each of us.

The Five Unskippable Steps

After I spoke about this earlier, I hope you had the burning desire to know what these mysterious, five unskippable steps were. It is now time to explore them, define them, understand them, and make changes to live them. These are the steps I have developed to live the spiritual life, which can be reduced simply to Life in the Holy Spirit.

The spiritual life consists of five unskippable steps:

1. Mindfulness
2. Receptivity
3. Conversion
4. Discipleship
5. Apostleship

Step One (Mindfulness): Be awake. Be attentive. Be alert. Be on guard. Be vigilant.

How attentive are we to our experience? Is the thought I am having in the current moment a result of my Ego Spirit, the Evil Spirit, or the Holy Spirit? That's a basic question to which you must be attentive all of the time. The reason is that the Evil Spirit can be very seductive. It's apparently good; that is, we can be easily hoodwinked and seduced into believing that the Evil Spirit is telling us it's good to be dishonest, greedy, etc.

The spiritual life starts by being attentive, or mindful, to the impulse and the movement of the Holy Spirit in your mind, heart, will, soul, and body. The Holy Spirit is influencing each and every one of those levels.

In modern terms, think of it as the devil on one shoulder (The Evil Spirit), the angel on another (The Holy Spirit), and your conscious mind (The Ego Spirit). You cannot become overconfident in your conscious mind. Even if you have responded to the Holy Spirit the last 100 times in the last 100 opportunities you've had, do not think for one second that you've won the tug of war. On the 101st time, for some reason, you could opt to do the wrong thing. That tension exists throughout our lives. It's the age-old battle between grace and sin. God's grace is always sufficient, in most cases in abundance, to help us overcome sinful patterns of living.

Jesus is constantly talking about being alert, on guard, vigilant to what's going on, not only around you, but also within you. You have to be alert and awake to that; be receptive to what the Holy Spirit is trying to offer: peace, joy, kindness, gentleness, generosity, goodness – the fruits and gifts of the Holy Spirit, which we explored in chapter 7. They're given to us in baptism, but we're not at a point to understand them then, so you have to wait until you start to engage that part in your spiritual journey.

Step Two (Receptivity): Be receptive to the spiritual gifts and spiritual fruits of the Holy Spirit and the abundant graces for every situation and circumstance.

Jesus' first invitation is to come and see, come and listen, come and learn, come and gather your strength, come and rest a while, come and be nourished. Why? So you can go in His name. Go and be baptized. Go and heal people, because of your encounter with Jesus. Go preach and teach, and you can bring about a new world order.

What do you seek? What are you looking for? He often answers people's questions with a further question. Jesus' whole ministry is based on parables, telling stories, an indirect way of getting people engaged and aware and then raising questions. That's His method of teaching.

Step Three (Conversion): Pick up your cross daily and follow in His footsteps.

A lot of people say that the first step in the spiritual life is conversion: turn from sin and be faithful to the Gospel. I don't think so. That's where a lot of people go awry. You have to have attentiveness and receptivity in order to make those reasonable judgments and authentic decisions.

St. Paul had a conversion experience. Some people say that there are two types of conversion. The first is initial conversion, the experience when the light bulb goes on in your head. St. Paul was blinded and fell to the ground, and had to be led by the hand. This fiercely independent guy, had to be led by hand. There's always going to be some formative influence in your life, but there's also going to be deformative influences in your life. You have to allow the Holy Spirit to help you come to a deeper, richer understanding of both the formative and deformative experiences of your life. You can't ignore either one of those.

Initial conversion, hopefully, leads to a process of ongoing conversion. You're constantly trying to put on the mind of Christ and set your heart on higher realms. That can then enable you to be a disciple of Jesus, where you become a lifelong student of His way, His truth, and His life. You learn to absorb and assimilate His teachings into your everyday life, and then appropriate his teachings, make them your own so you are deeply rooted in Gospel living.

Step Four (Discipleship): Come be a lifelong student of Jesus. Come and listen. Come and learn. Come and gather your strength. Come and be nourished at the table of the Lord.

You have developed mindfulness of your surroundings and what's going on within you. You have become receptive to Jesus' call, Jesus' way. You have begun following in His footsteps. Not only has the light bulb been turned on, but you are constantly putting on the mind of Christ. Now what?

In the call to discipleship, in the first chapter of St. John's Gospel, Jesus shows us the first way to discipleship. His request to "come and see" is the simple invitation we are called to accept, which brings us closer to Him. All those invitations He extends are unskippable and crucial. We have to hang out with Jesus if we want to grow in the spiritual life. It's not just simply knowing where He lives, or knowing facts about Him, as these would-be disciples desire. It's about developing a deep, personal relationship with Him, because He's going to challenge every disciple after that.

The next step in the call of discipleship is to give of yourself, especially in the world, today, where we're hyperconscious about personal, financial, and national security. Jesus tells us that if someone asks you to walk one mile, then walk two with them; if someone asks for your shirt, give your cloak, as well. He's going to stretch the limits of your generosity.

The third stage is to forgive. People, after hearing this stretching of generosity, will either bail out or just stay on the periphery. To buy into that takes a personal relationship and a belief in His way. Remember, He asks us to forgive 70 times, seven times. It's unlimited, boundless. The only prayer that He teaches us is to forgive those who have injured us and seek forgiveness.

It's a dual role forgiveness plays. We need to be forgiven for our falling short of the demands of the Gospel (missing the mark, or simply, sin) and the challenges that Jesus gives to each one of us, personally.

His first homily was one word: repent. Change your life. Seek forgiveness. At the end of His life, on the cross, He says, "Father, forgive them, they know not what they do." (Luke 23:34). So, forgiveness, is the centerpiece.

Pope Francis would use the word mercy. Forgiveness and mercy go hand in hand, because our Lord's favorite, daily miracle is His merciful, forgiving love. We pray, "Lord have mercy, Christ have mercy, Lord have mercy."

It doesn't end there. There's a stretching of generosity and a real openheartedness of a desire to be healed and to heal anything that has been damaged, injured, or broken in all human relationships. That's a huge hurdle to overcome in people's lives. Some people go to unbelievable extents to hold onto grudges and to remember all the people that have hurt them from early childhood. Remember, forgive 70 times, seven times.

Anyone familiar with the Gospels senses immediately that there is something missing in our approach to conflict resolution. If Jesus were conducting a workshop on conflict resolution, where do you think he would start?

On this matter, He has made Himself perfectly clear. The foundation of peaceful human relationships is forgiveness. No wonder that in the only prayer that Jesus taught us, the Our Father, forgiving each other is at the heart of it. Also, every time Jesus urges us to forgive each other, He connects our forgiving with asking God to forgive us.

Thus, there is a vertical and horizontal dimension to forgiveness. The vertical dimension – God's forgiving us – rests on the horizontal dimension – our forgiving each other.

The vertical axis will topple unless, when we ask God to forgive us, there is also a willingness to forgive each other. What is really needed is not a succession of individual acts of forgiveness, admirable as this is, but a state of forgiveness. We should try to maintain in ourselves a disposition of being ready to forgive each other. In this case, Jesus does, in fact, ask us to be divine.

Medical research has shown that forgiveness can be good for a person's health, while holding a grudge can be harmful. The person who says, "I don't get angry, I get even," might in fact be punishing him or herself as much as the intended victim. Psychologists and sociologists agree that there is not only a religious impetus to forgive, but also therapeutic, social, and practical reasons to do so. There is no question about it – forgiveness has to go beyond the confessional, beyond the church walls.

When we read Luke's idyllic description of life in the early church in the Acts of the Apostles, we find ourselves wishing that such a life were possible now. What makes that life so attractive is its peace and tranquility. These are qualities that are rarely found in today's world of violence and conflict, especially in the Middle East. Peace and tranquility are possible, and Jesus' message of compassion and forgiveness is what will bring them back.

The last step in this stage is to suffer. If you have difficulty in generosity and forgiveness, you're not going to be able to suffer. You're going to avoid suffering at all costs. His suffering is a suffering through love. If you really believe in Jesus and what He is about, your willingness to sacrifice and suffer in love is crucial to trying to reduce the suffering in the world – a suffering that is rooted in sin, evil, violence, hatred, and discrimination. To me, that is the skeleton of the spiritual life.

By becoming a disciple of Jesus, you're growing in spiritual maturity. There's an easy test to determine where you are on the path of the spiritual life. If you can show love to those who have hurt you, you've made a paradigm shift in your spiritual growth. It's not lost on priests who know that the practice of seeking sacramental forgiveness has diminished significantly over the last 20 years or so. People don't even recognize it. The gift that you receive sacramentally in reconciliation is to give that gift generously to people who have hurt you. That is an unskippable step in achieving spiritual maturity.

Step Five (Apostleship): Go in the name of Jesus. Go and teach. Go and heal. Go and proclaim the Word. Go and baptize.

The word apostle means to be sent out, to go out. Every person's life gets interrupted when they sense that they're being called to something. The question becomes, "Are you going to follow that intuition or are you going to cling tenaciously to your own agenda?"

Jesus has come so that you may have life in abundance. Now that you know these unskippable steps, go in His name and proclaim the Word. Thanks Be to God.

Abundance

What is this abundance I've been talking about? It comes in many forms: physical, intellectual, emotional, social, spiritual. In order to experience this, we can follow Lonergan's transcendental steps: be attentive, be intelligent, be reasonable, be responsible, be in love.

To be attentive is to not only have self-awareness, but the ability to ask the right questions. Now, I'd like you to take some time to ponder any of the below. You can come back to these again and again to continue your growth in the spiritual life. The answers can and will change, depending on the stage in which you are in your spiritual development. This is an amazing gift!

The main questions for spiritual direction:

- Who am I as a unique person?

- Who am I?

- Where have I come from?

- Where am I going?

- What does it mean to be a beloved son/daughter of Father, Jesus, and the Holy Spirit?

- What is prayer?

- Who is God for me?

- Where do I belong?

- How can I be of service?

- How can I become aware of God's presence in my life?

- How can I have some assurance that my decisions about work, money, and relationships are made in a spiritual way?

- How do I know that my life is lived in obedience to God and not just in response to my own impulses and desires?

- Should I live a simpler life?

- How do I listen attentively to God? What am I hearing right now?

- How do I find joy? How do I find truth?

- What gifts do I have to share?

- What do I do with my loneliness?

- Why am I so needy for affection and approval?

- How do I overcome my fears, my addictions, and my sense of failure or inadequacy?

- Where is God active in my life right now?

- How do I fit into the web of relationships that is society?

- Can you believe Jesus to be playful with you?

- Can you imagine the Holy Spirit engages you in a lighthearted way?

- Can you celebrate Our Heavenly Father delighting in you?

Identify and name a persistent question at this time in your life. Reflect on a time in your life when a painful or persistent question was dismissed or answered glibly by others.

Spiritual guidance affirms the basic quest for meaning. It calls for the creation of inner space in which the validity of the questions does not depend on the availability of answers, but on the questions' capacity to open us to new perspectives and horizons.

We must allow all the daily experiences of life – joy, laughter, tears, loneliness, fear, anxiety, insecurity, doubt, ignorance, the need for intimacy and affection, support, understanding, and the long cry for love – to be recognized as an essential part of the spiritual quest.

Your Personal Identity

To determine who you are as one of God's unique and wonderful children, you must first identify with your fellow brothers and sisters. We are all these things:

1. I am my authorities
2. I am my needs
3. I am my relationships
4. I am my self
5. I am public, private and secret
6. I am a bundle of irrational thoughts and conflicting emotions
7. I am a touched sinner
8. I am made in the image and likeness of God – Baptismal Identity

Now, as you hang out with Jesus, you can realize His identity. When you are mindful of this, you can grow closer to Him.

The Identity of Jesus

1. Jesus is Lord and Savior
2. Jesus is King
3. Jesus is Suffering Servant
4. Jesus is the Good Shepherd
5. Jesus is the Lamb of God
6. Jesus is fire
7. Jesus is living water
8. Jesus is Rabbi
9. Jesus is the gate, the alpha and omega, the way, the truth, the life
10. Jesus is the bread of life

The truth is much too large to be contained inside of neat, tidy concepts. Doctrine and theology are indispensable, but they are not enough. We have committed the unpardonable sin of transforming an exciting story into a dull system. We must recover the story if we are to recover a faith for our day. We must tell and retell the old story and in the telling of it discover and discern our own story.

Lonergan sums up all of the above in this chapter very nicely:

"Even with talent, knowledge makes a slow, if not a bloody, entrance. To learn thoroughly is a vast undertaking that calls for relentless perseverance. To strike out on a new line and become more than a weekend celebrity calls for years in which one's living is more or less constantly absorbed in the effort to understand, in which one's understanding gradually works round and up a spiral of viewpoints with each complementing its predecessor and only the last embracing the whole field to be mastered.

"Being in Christ Jesus may be the being of substance or of subject. Inasmuch as it is just the being of substance, it is known only through faith, through affirming true proposition, meditating on them, concluding from them, making resolutions on the basis of them, winning over our psyches, our sensitive souls, to carrying out the resolutions through the cultivation of pious imagination and pious affects, and multiplying individual effort and strength through liturgical union. Inasmuch as it is just the being of substance, it is being in love with God without awareness, of being in love. Without any experience of just how and why, one is in the state of grace or one recovers it, one leaves all things to follow Christ, one binds oneself by vows of poverty, chastity and obedience, one gets through one's daily heavy dose of prayer. Quietly, imperceptibly there goes forward the transformation operated by the Kurios, but the delicacy, the gentleness, the deftness of his continual operation in us hides the operation from us.

"But inasmuch as being in Christ Jesus is the being of subject (being in love and knowing it), the hand of the Lord ceased to be hidden. In ways you all have experienced, in ways some have experienced more frequently or more intensely than others, in ways you still have to experience, and in ways none of us in this life will ever experience, the substance in Christ Jesus becomes the subject in Christ Jesus. For the love of God, being in love with God, can be as full and as dominant, as overwhelming and as lasting, an experience as human love.

"Being in Christ Jesus is not tied down to place or time, culture or epoch. It is catholic with the catholicity of the Spirit of the Lord. Neither is it an abstraction that dwells apart from every place and time, every culture and epoch. It is identical with personal living, and personal living is always here and now, in a contemporary world of immediacy, a contemporary world mediated by meaning, a contemporary world not only mediated but also constituted by meaning.

"In personal living the questions abstractly asked about the relations between nature and grace emerge concretely in one's concern, one's interests, one's hopes, one's plans, one's daring and timidity, one's taking risks and playing safe. And as they emerge concretely, so too they are solved concretely." (Lonergan, op. cit.).

Busyness is a Spiritual Illness: It is the Other Side of the Coin of Boredom

There are things to be learned from sin. One is compassion, another is understanding. A third is humility. A fourth is perception. Without the ability to own our own sins, these qualities are all hard to come by indeed. Unless we accept our incompleteness, we can never grow from it. Whatever the heights of our present virtue, the bottomless pit of life stretches always before us, always to be respected, always in the throes of challenging us to look at ourselves again. Humility reminds us that we are all in process always, and to be in process is perfectly all right. As the proverb says, "It is not where we are that counts. It is where we are going that matters."

Busyness is an illness of spirit, a rush from one thing to another because there is no ballast of vocational integrity and no confidence in the primacy of grace. There are heavy demands put upon pastoral work, true; there is difficult work to be engaged in, yes. However, a pastor must not be "busy." A sense of hurry in pastoral work disqualifies one for the work of conversation and prayer that develops relationships that meet pastoral needs. The single most significant phrase that a priest can speak is, "I will pray for you." It means that the conversation in which they have just been engaged will be continued with God as partner to the conversation.

Detachment does not mean that we love nothing but God; it means that we love all in God. It does not mean we learn to love creatures less and less, it means that we learn to love them more and more, but selflessly, as part of our vast undivided love of God. To enjoy any living thing: fire, water, air, animal, vegetable, human, even God Himself, we must let go of it. In detachment is our liberation, and in our liberation the earth is hallowed and God is glorified.

The simple statement, "God is love," has far-reaching implications the minute we begin living our lives based on that statement. When God Who has created me is love and only love, I am loved before any human being loved me.

It requires a lot of inner solitude and silence to become aware of the gentle movements of the Holy Spirit. God does not shout, scream or push. The Spirit of God is soft and gentle like a whispering voice or a light breeze.

Much of Jesus' spousal prayer took place during the night. "Night" means more than the absence of the sun. It also means the absence of satisfying feelings or enlightening insights. That is one reason why it is so difficult to be faithful.

As Henri J.M. Nouwen put it, "Jesus came to announce to us that an identity based on success, popularity and power is a false identity – an illusion! Loudly and clearly He says: 'You are not what the world makes you; but you are children of God.'"[38]

The spiritual life requires a constant claiming of our core identity. Our core identity is that we are God's children, the beloved sons and daughters of our Heavenly Father.

The way of Jesus is the way of downward mobility. It is the way toward the poor, the suffering, the marginal, the prisoners, the refugees, the lonely, the hungry, the dying, the tortured, the homeless – toward all who ask for compassion. What do they have to offer? Not success, popularity or power, but the joy and peace of being children of God.

Too much talk, inane chatter, dissipates our energy. We must know when to speak and when to be silent.

Every person needs silence and solitude in order to exhale the poisons of stress, fatigue, consumerism and sensory overload due to various kinds of pollution.

A particularly dangerous toxin seems to be produced by communication overload. One is left listless and unreflective after being bombarded by news and advertising throughout the day. Every person needs silence and solitude in order to inhale the rejuvenating oxygen of nature, ideas, leisure, the arts: all the essential nutrients which our culture depreciates…

St. Thomas Aquinas makes a distinction between *studiose* and *curiose*.

Studiose involves a chastity of mind whereby a person pursues truth with humility and reverence and has a deep desire to learn because of its great value.

Curiose involves intellectual promiscuity; that is, running around dabbling in various things but never really learning anything in depth.

Busyness is a spiritual illness. It is the other side of the coin of boredom.

Growing Through Stories

It is said that the shortest distance between a human being and truth is a story. Stories connect us to our souls. They are healing to our spirits, enriching to our imaginations. As disciples of the Lord it is vitally important to know the story of Jesus, to know the story of the Church – saints, martyrs and sinners. May God give us the grace throughout our lives to connect our story with the story of Jesus and the communion of saints.

Sarah's Story

There is a story told about a woman named Sarah. One day an angel appeared to this simple woman and told her that God was coming to visit. Sarah became excited because God was coming to visit her house and so in her simplicity she began to try to figure out what she would serve God upon His arrival.

Now, Sarah was materially a very poor woman and so the only thing she could find in her cupboard was a cup of flour with which she baked a loaf of bread, a bottle of wine half-filled and a red apple. "Well," said Sarah, "I wish there were more, but whatever I have I will give to God." Sarah got everything ready and awaited the Lord's arrival. Suddenly a knock came to the door. It was a poor lady with a child. The lady said, "My child has not had anything to eat in two days, do you have any bread?" Sarah said, "I have a loaf for God," but when she saw the hungry child she gave her the bread.

So, Sarah closed the door and sat down again to await the arrival of God. She looked at the table and said, "Well, at least I have some wine and an apple." Then a second knock came to the door. It was a neighbor from down the street who was also poor. He said, "Sarah, tomorrow is my son's wedding day and I don't have a drop of wine to serve as a toast for this occasion. Can you help me out?" Sarah looked at the half-filled bottle of wine that she was saving for God and said, "Here, you can have it."

Once again, Sarah shut the door and awaited the arrival of God. She looked at the apple – now the only thing she had left to give to God. She started to shine up the apple when a third knock came to the door. She figured this had to be God, but when she opened the door she was shocked to see, instead, a man who used to go to school with her and was always unkind to Sarah. The man said to Sarah, "Please forgive me for the past. I need your help – whatever you can give." The man left overjoyed having received Sarah's forgiveness and the apple.

Sarah sat down in the doorway of her home. She was feeling sad, because when God would come she would have nothing to offer. Growing tired from waiting, she eventually fell asleep. The next day the angel woke Sarah. She jumped up and said, "Oh, no! Why didn't you come and wake me up? I was asleep and probably missed God." The angel smiled and said, "You did not miss Him, Sarah. As a matter of fact, God visited you three times yesterday and He was very happy after each visit. He told me how you gave Him bread, wine, an apple and forgiveness.

Bob and Ann's Story

An elderly man, Bob, in his 80s hurried to his doctor appointment at 8 a.m. He wanted to finish quickly because he must be somewhere by nine. The doctor asked Bob what the next appointment was. He proudly said that at 9 a.m. every morning he is at the nursing home to eat breakfast with his wife, Ann. The doctor asked about his wife's condition. Bob said that his wife had Alzheimer's disease, and for the past five years she hasn't known who he is. The doctor was surprised and asked Bob why he continues to go faithfully if she has no idea who he is. Bob replied, "Because I still know who she is!"

Vincent's Story

In 2014, around Thanksgiving, I met a man (Vincent) who was homeless. He had no real address. He did have a sense of community. Vincent was one among the many homeless people who lived on the Philadelphia side of the Ben Franklin Bridge. He lived in a refrigerator box marked with the words "Fragile, Handle with Care."

Vincent claimed those words as his address. He reminded me that those words were everyone's address. He would say, over and over, that when we see all people as fragile, then we will know how to treat people, and when we see ourselves as fragile, we will see ourselves in all people.

Vincent, without a home, really believed that this view of ourselves, and one another, is the way of love.

He had no health care, but he knew how to heal humanity's wounds. He did not have enough good food to eat but he could nourish anyone he met. His sight was limited, but his vision of the world was bright and clear. What a remarkable man living in a refrigerator box – a tabernacle of sorts – a living, visible, real presence of the Word made flesh; broken, shared, and poured out in love and simplicity.

The Parable of the Child

I took a little child's hand in mine. He and I were to walk together for a while. I was to lead him to the Father. It was a task that overcame me, so awful was the responsibility. And so I talked to the child only of the Father. I painted the sternness of His face, were the child to do something to displease the Father. I spoke of the child's goodness as something that would appease the Father's wrath. We walked under the tall trees. I said the Father had the power to send them crashing down, struck by His thunderbolts. We walked in the sunlight. I told him of the greatness of the Father, who made the burning, blazing sun. And one twilight, we met the Father. The child hid behind me. He was afraid. He would not look up at the face so loving; he remembered my picture. He would not take the Father's hand. I was between the child and the Father. I wondered. I had been so conscientious, so serious.

I took a little child's hand in mine. I was to lead him to the Father. I felt burdened with the multiplicity of things I had to teach him. We did not ramble; we hastened from one spot to another. At one moment we compared the leaves of different trees. In the next moment we hurried away to chase a butterfly. Did he chance to fall asleep, I wakened him, lest he should miss something I wished him to see. We spoke of the Father, oh yes, often and rapidly. I poured into his ears all the stories he ought to know, but we were interrupted often by the wind a blowing, of its source. And then, in the twilight, we met the Father. The child merely glanced at Him and his gaze wandered in a dozen directions. The Father stretched out His hand. The child was not interested enough to take it. Feverish spots burned in his cheeks. He dropped exhausted to the ground and fell asleep. Again I was between the child and the Father. I wondered. I had taught him so many things.

I took a little child's hand to lead him to the Father. My heart was full of gratitude for the glad privilege. We walked slowly. I suited my steps to the short ones of the child. We spoke of the things the child noticed.

Sometimes we picked the Father's flowers and stroked their soft petals and loved their bright colors. Sometimes it was one of the Father's birds. We watched it build its nest. We saw the eggs that were laid. Often we told stories of the Father. I told them to the child and the child told them again to me. We told them, the child and I, over and over again. Sometimes we stopped to rest, leaning against one of the Father's trees, and letting His cool air cool our brows, and never speaking. And then, in the twilight, we met the Father. The child's eyes shone. He looked lovingly, trustingly, eagerly up into the Father's face. He put his hand into the Father's hand. I was for a moment forgotten. I was content. I had led the child to the Father.

Conclusion: the Need for Stories

Again, stories relate us to our souls. They are healing to our spirits, enriching to our imaginations. I am reminded of the story of the mother and father taking a trip with their 6-year-old son. It was a hot summer day. The traffic was heavy and there were long periods of waiting. The boy became completely fragmented; a burden to himself and an irritation to his parents. He desperately needed a story. When they reached their destination, the mother, realizing her son's need, told him the story of Hansel and Gretel. The boy listened wide-eyed and silent. Afterwards he went out to play, very calm. He had lost touch with his soul on the tedious ride. The story brought him back together again.

A Lesson in Truth

A mystery, it is worth pointing out, is not something infinitely unknowable or forever incomprehensible – it is quite the contrary, something always to be further grasped, more deeply known.

We do not acquire security by eliminating enemies. Opposition – and sometimes it is intense – is a continuing reality in this world. We get security (Be not afraid … "I lie down and sleep") by putting our trust in God. They are His foes and He will do battle: "Deliverance belongs to the Lord."

The "true" person has roots deep in God's ways: he or she delights in them and meditates on them.

The "chaff" person won't be entangled in such earthy messiness. "Too limiting, too confining, too invisible," this person would probably say.

Today's culture, for all its blather about progress, contains a deep current of ambivalence and pessimism. Many people today fear death and dread life.

People turn to technology to extend life, then quickly consider suicide to end life. Reckless ambivalence has been unleashed and as William Butler Yeats says, "The center cannot hold" any longer because "mere anarchy has been loosed upon the world."

Hostility toward the past, boredom with the present, and fear of the future seem to define the modern malaise. By the way, boredom rarely travels alone. Most times its two cousins, loneliness and restlessness, accompany boredom. If that combination goes unchecked, in most cases, the result will be a compromise of one's baptismal identity.

This reminds me of Thomas Merton's lessons on each of our understandings of our true selves. When we are living life truly, we are not bound by fear. We are living in faith. There is a contrast there. In John's Gospel, we observe, "when the doors were locked, where the disciples were, for fear of the Jews…" (John 20:19). Afraid, cautious, divided, hidden away – what a contrast between how the disciples behave here and what we get from the Acts of the Apostles: a community of believers were of one heart and one mind, with power, the apostles bore witness to the resurrection of the Lord.

The first Christian community was a church that was alive, active, in touch with the needs of its members. They prayed together, ate together, sang together, rejoiced together. They were an active church, a celebrating church, a church that believed greatly in fellowship, service, and outreach. No wonder they experienced such phenomenal growth. The motivating force of the early believers to form a community was their lively faith in the Risen Lord.

However, before the disciples' lives were determined by faith, their fears had to be put to rest. Jesus appears to them and reassures with words of peace and by the warmth of His breath that He is truly alive in body and in spirit. His purpose is not only to reassure them but to send them, encourage them to leave the prison of their fears.

What are you most afraid of? Not being loved? We desire to be loved. What a great opportunity we have in our communities to create an environment of love. Through prayer, through struggling to understand God's Word, through celebrating the sacraments, through our willingness to serve one another – these are examples of living faith in the power of the Risen Lord. We need them to be the foundation stones of our lives so that our lives will be full of life and love, full of faith, and free of fear.

Divine mercy means that we are loved in our weaknesses, our brokenness, our darkness, our sinfulness, and once we become aware of God's mercy, then we can, with grace and the Holy Spirit, overcome all sinful patterns of living.

To Affirm Life in the Face of Diminishment

G. K. Chesterton once said that God hid his mirth from us because we would have been overwhelmed.

Jesus portrays an attitude and style which mixes joy, courage, and freedom. The Middle Ages dubbed this virtue *hilaritas*. It is a joyful confidence, an affirmation of life even in the face of diminishment. It is the celebration of the supper before betrayal and crucifixion, the insistence of the kingdom of another world while in chains before the king of this world, the talk of paradise while nailed to the tree of rejection. *Hilaritas* is a freedom, which does not allow the circumstances of life to totally dictate moods and feelings. The spirit of *hilaritas* runs through Jesus' put-down of worry (Matthew 6: 25-34).

This enduringly beautiful passage does not purport an economic vision or give practical advice on long term planning. It is *hilaritas'* playful reminder not to let worry be the whole story about life.

Hilaritas is not frivolity. It is not flightiness, which is smugly unconcerned with oppression and suffering. *Hilaritas* is passionately involved with the pain of the world but not absorbed by it. *Hilaritas* takes life seriously but not ultimately. It strives for betterment but at the moment of disaster it may wink. *Hilaritas* understands that human growth occurs for the most part by inches (eg. two steps forward, three steps backward, and we still reach our goal).

Hilaritas is permeated with joyous confidence and so possesses the courage and freedom to surprise the world with new acts of love. A Master washes the feet of His disciples; a Samaritan helps a Jew; a Jew shares both faith and a meal with a Gentile. *Hilaritas* is acceptance and transcendence in the same breath.

William James claims that laughter is always a religious experience. Angels move quickly because they take themselves lightly.

The most neglected line in the Gospels is the injunction from Matthew, "do not look gloomy." (Matthew 6:16).

An ancient custom of the Greek Orthodox Church reserves the day after Easter for laughter and hilarity. On this day the sanctuary is filled with festivity and joking to celebrate the cosmic joke God pulled on Satan in the Resurrection. The Resurrection is the source of Christian joy and celebration, the music to which we ceaselessly dance, the Son, which we forever sing.

What does it mean to be a Christian? It means that Christ is the biggest idea in your mind – fills your soul like a riot of joy – sits on the edge of your lips like a shout of praise – motivates you, haunts you, hounds you day in and day out. It means there is nothing more real, more enticing, more thrilling in your life in significance because of Him. You make your decisions, your judgments, your plans in terms of Christ. That's what it means to be a Christian.

Wisdom means a taste for the right things. It comes from the Latin word *sapientia*. To be hungry for God, that's wisdom. Everyone's deepest hunger is a hunger for God. We will never be content until that hunger is satisfied. Wisdom does not make us full. It fills us with hunger. Hunger for stillness, peace, goodness, truth, beauty, union with the Living God. Be a man or woman of wisdom: God-centered, God-filled, God-intoxicated.

Too often, as we grow old, impressive bulk turns into embarrassing bulge.

Distinction Between Mortification and Abnegation

Mortification means putting to death. I put to death a disordered appetite. The virtue that develops through mortification is called temperance. That is, the ability or self-mastery over my senses and intellect as well as my feelings and will.

Abnegation means to deny myself in order to be of service to others. It involves sacrifice. The virtue that abnegation develops within me is humility. Abnegation is aimed at pride. Honest self-appraisal is important. For example, John the Baptist said, "He must increase, I must decrease." I am but a voice, Jesus is the Word echoing through all eternity. Abnegation leads to self-transcendence, that is, focusing on the things that really matter or on the one thing necessary. Abnegation gives one an orientation to life. True abnegation makes one fearless.

Rosemarie Carfagna explains that near the end of Pope John XXIII's life, the pope was entertaining a group of reporters and one of them asked him, "Holy Father, how can you be so serene, knowing that the end is near?" Unruffled by the question, the Holy Father replied with a deep smile, "My friend, today is a good day."[39]

How to Understand God's First Language

Abraham Heschel said, "God is of no importance unless He is of supreme importance." Silence is the pregnant backdrop against which all meaning shines forth. It is His first language.

If we do not have a wellspring of silence within us, we cannot understand our world, philosophy, theology, poetry, literature, music, mysticism, ourselves, others, (community) God.

Three significant demons that we all have to wrestle with are noise, busyness, and crowds.

Any religion that takes seriously God's judgment has the pastoral task of realizing God's mercy, demonstrating in a credible way that judgment and mercy are not opposites but complements.

Character is the psychological muscle that moral conduct requires. A rising tide lifts all boats.

The tragic loss of courtesy and politeness and civility is fast disappearing from our society. Notice the t-shirts and bumper stickers and movies and TV and music. The prevailing attitude seems to be the more vulgar, the more rude, the more offensive, the more shocking, the better.

The task of medicine is to care even when it cannot cure. Suffering – our own or that of a loved one – is perhaps the greatest test of faith we will face, for it seems invariably to raise the basic question: "How can this be happening if there is a God who is both all-powerful and all-loving?" For if God is all-powerful and allows this pain, then God is not all-loving; or if the all-loving God wants to stop this suffering but cannot, then God is not all-powerful. We love earthly life, but we also anticipate eternal life. … Death may also enter into our lives as a liberating friend.

The Line Between Good and Evil

"Morality like art," said G. K. Chesterton, "consists of drawing a line somewhere." We live in an age in which no lines seem to be drawn at all, and it is for this reason that our humanity seems a palsied thing of little reward to us. If we begin to take our sinning seriously, we might at least find that we can be interesting again.

Gradually it was disclosed to me that the line separating good and evil passes not through states, nor between classes, nor between political parties either – but right through every human heart – and through all human hearts. This line shifts. Inside us, it oscillates with the years. And even within hearts overwhelmed by evil, one small bridgehead of good is retained. And even in the best of all hearts, there remains ... an un-uprooted small corner of evil.

Since then I have come to understand the truth of all the religions of the world: They struggle with the evil inside a human being (inside every human being). It is impossible to expel evil from the world in its entirety, but it is possible to constrict it within each person.[40]

Ten Steps to Living Prayerfully

Father Dave Denny, one of the early monks of Fr. McNamara's Spiritual Life Institute, offers these 10 steps to living life prayerfully.

1. Be natural.
2. Live deliberately, ordered.
3. Get up early – begin each day and end each day well.
4. Be faithful rather than flabby – flexible not rigid.
5. Live each moment mindfully – Personal passionate presence. What are you doing now? Just this.
6. Sit quietly every day. Take minute vacations.
7. Have a right attitude about work: not worry, frantic, busyness.
8. Be faithful to prayer, reading, exercise.
9. Be balanced. Was I wild today?
10. Celebrate Sabbath. Do you play enough?

Three Humiliations of Jesus

Dorothy Sayers has said that God underwent three great humiliations in His efforts to rescue the human race. The first was the incarnation, when He took on the confines of a physical body. The second was the cross, when He suffered the ignominy of public execution. The third humiliation, Sayers suggested, is the church. In an awesome act of self-denial, God entrusted His reputation to ordinary people.

Experiencing the Natural Order Through the Holy Spirit

Fasting is never an end itself; that's why it has so many different outcomes, but all the other outcomes are of no real value if compassion is not enlarged and extended through fasting. Besides fasting from candy or cakes and the like, may I suggest that you:

fast from complaining	and	feast on gratitude
fast from worry	and	feast on wonder
fast from bitterness	and	feast on forgiveness
fast from gloom	and	feast on beauty
fast from discouragement	and	feast on hope
fast from gossip	and	feast on silence
fast from fear	and	feast on faith
fast from social media	and	feast on sacred scripture
fast from pettiness	and	feast on patient tolerance
fast from sin	and	feast on virtue

Fasting is good for the soul as well as the body. It serves as a positive penance for spiritual enrichment.

There are three specific reasons why people in biblical times fasted. The first was repentance. They know how deep sin sinks into their lives. The second reason people fasted was to remember. What happened was tragic; for example, Daniel fasted when he remembered the destruction of Jerusalem. The third reason to fast is to rivet our attention on God. Are you ready to worship God right now? Do you have a sense of his presence?

When we fast, we say that there's more to us than just our appetites. Fasting challenges the addictions of the soul that society says are okay, namely, shopping habits, eating habits and sexual habits. Fasting helps us discover the contours of our souls and who we are before God. Jesus expects us to fast. Prayer and fasting are important spiritual practices that help us make important and right decisions in life.

What Does It Mean To Be Physically Fit?

So, what does it mean to be fit? Daniel Kunitz's short list, based on CrossFit guru Greg Glassman's highly influential essay "What Is Fitness?" includes weightlifting (dead lift, snatch and clean-and-jerk), gymnastics (pull-ups, dips, rope climb, push-ups, sit-ups, presses to handstand, pirouettes, flips, splits and holds), and cardiovascular (bike, run, swim, row hard and fast).[41]

You should be aiming for stamina, strength, flexibility, power, speed, coordination, agility, balance, accuracy, and cardiovascular endurance.

Oh, and you should eat meat and vegetables, nuts and seeds, and some fruit. Stay away from starch and avoid sugar altogether. The goal is not to look good naked (although that doesn't hurt), but to be able to hoist a bag of dog food on your shoulder, to carry your child for hours, to move furniture around your home, or to run from a burning building. "You'll never see a person do a bicep curl or a lat raise outside a gym," Kunitz notes, "but you will see them jump, run, and heave loads from the ground over their heads."

If you want to see what fit athletes look like, watch the highlight reels online for the CrossFit championships or the American Ninja Warrior competition. These athletes are inspiring – and fit beyond anyone I saw in the 1980s.

Role Identification

- entire identity is based on performing a role – a role completely dictated by others

- false self; performs to please orders, win acceptance or move up the ladder

- no internalization of values or beliefs

- lost in a persona of performance
- when emptiness sets in, and the expectations of others is not met, or a role cannot be fulfilled, the result is identity-crisis (hollowness)
- resentment for the very people one originally wanted to serve, begins to take over
- the phrase "you become what you hate" hits home
- takes little time off; only feels fulfilled when role-identified and in danger of burn-out
- possible time of enlightenment because one is "forced" by life to reevaluate previous values, beliefs and ideals

Role Orientation

- there is a sense of personal spiritual identity in Christ and the internalization of Christian values and virtues before a particular role is accepted
- a commitment to evangelical virtues of poverty, chastity, obedience
- identity is rooted in Christ and is not dependent upon a need to win approval of others
- interests outside a particular role allow one to find balance, meet new people, and be refreshed
- leisure allows one to pray, play and be re-created
- a soul friend challenges us to drop our masks. A soul friend gives us space to be our true, real self. A soul friend encourages us to relax, supports our efforts and orientation toward poverty, chastity and obedience. A soul friend tells us we are working too hard, taking ourselves too seriously or losing perspective.

Spiritual Direction Conclusion

Transformation is an event that occurs infrequently in one's life, but it leads to a process that continues to reveal more and more of the meaning of the event. We yearn for messages that go beyond information to meaning. For the people of Israel, the fullest communication and the deepest instruction of all was the body of literature we had come to recognize as the Torah, which translates to "instruction."

Who are we? What is life about? What does it mean to do the right thing? The answers to these questions were contained in the Law and the Prophets, and these components were personified, especially in Moses and Elijah.

Each year, on Ash Wednesday, we approach the altar and are challenged by the words, "Turn away form sin, remember you are dust and to dust you will return, be faithful to the Gospel." The ashes are a symbol of our mortality. The cross formed on each of our foreheads is our reminder of the sacrifice Jesus made on our behalf.

I truly hope these truths, stories, and questions stimulated your spiritual muscles. Some of these teachings were long and grueling and others were snippets – bullet points to keep handy – yet, it is now your turn to take what you have read and apply it to your own life. While some of what you read may already be familiar, others may have caused great discomfort.

Dependence on the familiar, however, skews our exploration into God. St. Paul, in his first Letter to the Corinthians, states, "You are not your own. You were purchased at a great price." Illusions, disappointments, and contradictions are part of everyone's lives. They should be expected, overcome, and transformed. The only way this happens is when we make a total commitment to discipleship and surrender to the will of God.

It takes a humorous and stubborn person to overcome the inevitable obstacles from within and from without. What we all need is an irrepressible zest for life. We must take God so seriously that we take ourselves light-heartedly.

We also need a long-range view – the sense of putting things into proper perspective and giving them their proper weight. This is an art and a gift. All of life's experiences need to be filtered through the prism of the resurrection. When we start to get caught up in gossip, pettiness, people's delusions, and manipulation, we need to refocus on the brilliant truth of Jesus conquering sin and death. Convinced that Jesus conquered sin and death, right now for everyone, we realize the central truth of our faith, guided in the resurrection, in both the short term and the long term.

The immediate fruits of the resurrection are: new life, new love, new peace, new joy, and new hope. The long-term benefit of the resurrection is that death is never the final word, life is; abundant life, eternal life, a resurrected order of living.

At the bottom of life's pain is joy. However, too frequently, we get trapped in the pain and are afraid to move through it in order to discover the joy. Jesus reached into the grave and pulled out Lazarus, paraded him around in his death clothes, and had a good laugh.

I remember describing Fr. McNamara, one of my mentors, as "the lone party to a great secret and an even bigger joke." I was deeply struck by his presence, which was simultaneously kind, profoundly still, and unfathomably mischievous. He was clearly a man transformed by the Truth. He often referred to the resurrection as the best "cosmic joke" ever told. Satan and evil thought that they conquered goodness, once and for all, and three days later, Jesus says, "Here I am!" We can all learn a lesson by the way in which Fr. McNamara lived his life and clearly grasped the meaning of the resurrection.

CHAPTER 24
Faith, First and Foremost

"We do not stop playing because we grow old, we grow old because we stop playing!"

—Benjamin Franklin (1706 – 1790), quoted in memory of John Heron (Pop-Pop)

"Many are the women of proven worth, but you have excelled them all. Charm is deceptive and beauty fleeting; the woman who fears the Lord is to be praised. Acclaim her for the work of her hands, and let her deeds praise her at the city gates.

—Proverbs 31:29-31, quoted in memory of Dot Heron (Mom)

As Fr. Murray and Fr. McNamara were spiritual mentors in my life throughout my journey into and through the priesthood, without question, my grandfather and my mother were my spiritual mentors in my early, formative years.

In the ritual of taking my brother and me to visit my dad's grave, my grandfather in those settings taught us to kneel down and pray in three languages. I got a deep sense that he, and we, could communicate with someone who is no longer physically present on the earth. Even though my father was not visible, that did not mean he was not real in that moment. Through my grandfather, I developed a sense of awareness that there is a world beyond the visible that exists.

I believe God gave an incredible gift to those who knew John Heron, sharing His life and love with us. My grandfather's faith was first and foremost, the most precious gift of his life. Faith gave meaning and value to his life – meaning and value that he did not keep to himself, but communicated to others. Many people have their own experience and memories of how he did that for them.

Those who knew him recall how my grandfather was always ready to pray the Our Father in Latin and Gaelic, like he did at my dad's grave. He was proud to tell of the number of times he clerked Mass for the priest – one of many external signs of faith of which he was never ashamed.

My grandfather's sense of humor was an appealing compliment to his lively faith. His sense of humor became visible time and again through his stories, his warm smile, his gentle grin, and above all, his laughing eyes.

My grandfather had an uncanny ability to create an atmosphere of happiness and joy. He did so because he possessed a deep gratitude and reverence for life. He never took life for granted. He derived great pleasure from the simple, ordinary events of life – a hard day's work, a good nourishing meal, a simple conversation or exchange of stories. What gave him the most pleasure was seeing other people content and happy.

The beautiful countryside of Draperstown, with its rolling hills and valleys, nurtured the poet in the man and young boy who grew up there. That was food for his soul. With all its beauty, Draperstown was economically poor and early on he had to use his hands to make the earth produce food for the body. He was a man who communicated truth, life, and beauty through his hands, his words, and his eyes.

My grandfather's life on earth ended on Friday, Sept. 14, 1984. I could not help but reflect on what a fitting conclusion it was, because that's the day the universal church celebrated the Triumph of the Cross. That very event made eternal life a possibility for all of us.

My mother's simple and clear examples instructed me in the many mysteries of life: birth, forgiveness, friendship, suffering, and sacrifice. These simple lessons were the introduction to my spiritual awakening.

Yet, she was so much an Irish mother, so fond of assigning a saying to most every situation in life.

- "That's ridiculous!"

- "For crying out loud!"

- "For heaven's sake!"

- "Phooey!"

- "We're all going to the poor house!"

- And the classic, "What will the neighbors think?"

These were just a few of her sayings to the various situations of raising four children as a young widow. There were others, too.

- "He (or she) is up to his (or her) tricks again!"

- "No cutting the bacon in half," which was homage to my mom's mother, Florence Reilly, who always cut the bacon in half. From that experience she always wanted a whole strip of bacon.

She had to learn to drive after my dad died of the heart attack. She used to say to the four of us in the car (when we had one, of course), "if you don't keep quiet and sit still we are all going to be killed!"

My mom had no business background, other than what her husband had taught her. My dad invested in a wholesale food distributor, Frankford Food Distributor, which delivered the stock over a week. In 1967, Frankford Food Distributor merged with Unity Food Distributors and the money my dad invested was liquidated. Mom had no alternative but to close. She went to work for Acme Supermarkets and for a dentist, but did not enjoy being at work when her four children came home from school.

In August 1968, another food distributor opened in Darby called Montco Cash and Carry. A man for whom I caddied at White Manor Golf Course in Malvern, Pa., gave me $1,500 to open the store again. I was so grateful to that man for his generosity.

As I grew into a priest, my mother's first instruction was to "Be brief in your homilies and the people will love you." She knew I would never master that! She offered one more piece of advice, as well: "Don't be boring."

Father Tom Heron with his mother, Dot.

The most important lesson I learned from her though, was that the Eucharist is what is most real in the world. Even as she lay dying, she, like Mary of Bethany, desired only one thing: a union with God. In a holy and humble way, she died the way she lived, by surrendering all to the will of the Blessed Trinity, who she trusted and who loved her very much.

She encountered God so many times at her parish church, St. Joseph, in Collingdale. It was her place of worship, where she was nourished by the sacraments. It was, in that parish community that she received support, love, encouragement, and strength in her journey of faith. It was there that her children received their sacraments and were formed in the faith. She brought us there to be baptized into the new life of grace. It was there where her eternal life, promised by Jesus, was celebrated.

Jesus understood my family's pain and gave us comfort, hope, and strength in the days that followed her death. My mother was granted the grace of a long and full life. In her last days, she knew she was failing – that the end was near – and she yearned, as St. Paul put it, to have her heavenly home envelop her. Her earthly tent was giving way to a dwelling place God has prepared for her. She died with grace and complete trust in God. Her faith told her that dying was simply a journey from her life on earth to her eternal home in heaven.

Sometimes, we can be easily lulled into believing we would have those we love around forever. Letting go is always painful, because we get used to the fact of their being there. The flood of great memories were what washed away the sorrow we felt so deeply.

Early in her life, my mother made a decision that she would be on God's side in this world. Her faith and her experiences helped me realize that if she was to triumph over any trial that beset her, it would only be with God's help and devotion to the Blessed Mother. She firmly believed that God the Father would grant in the next life the promises made by his Son in the Gospels.

Songwriters have written that the home is a wounded heart – an apt image to describe the Heron home. The heart symbol of much love, affection, and warmth was wounded the day my dad died. Those wound were healed, though, by memory. My mother played the role of doctor, here. Our kitchen table was a very sacred place, a source of physical nourishment and of shared memories. She made sure we would remember our father. Faced with the task of raising four children, all at first seemed dark, but she found salvation in a remembered love. She constantly converted the pain of her husband's absence into a deeper understanding of his presence.

She taught us that love goes beyond the physical presence of the one you love. It finds its deepest meaning in the spiritual being of the person. She knew what the saints knew – that our conversations with those who go before us, marked with the sign of faith, can be as vivid and as satisfying as when they were physically present.

I learned this lesson well, so that through God's gift of memory, I was able to recall, with an uncanny acuteness, her smile, her voice, her look.

To my sister, Suzanne, my mother would often say, "Stop hitting and bossing, Tom, Joe, and Mary around. You are not their mother!"

She would often ask Joe if he could "stop knocking everything over." In humility, my mother never had to correct me growing up! Selective memory is a wonderful and convenient way of remembering the past. Many of my friends and family later refreshed my memory that this was not at all the case!

My mother taught me the importance of the corporal and spiritual works of mercy by example. She taught me when giving alms to not let your left hand know what your right hand is doing. When I was a senior in high school, she stopped me before going to bed one night in the living room, right by the painting of the Sacred Heart, and asked me if I ever thought of becoming a priest. I said yes, but that I didn't think I was capable. Her response was to simply pray to the Sacred Heart and see what happens.

She often played a game of holy solitaire. This was a twice-daily ritual of pulling out a stack of prayer cards and saying a long series of devotions and novenas to various saints as a part of her morning and evening prayer ritual. She confidently told me her prayers are heard and that this practice brought her closer to God each time she prayed. For my mother, prayer was ultimately about love – God's love for us and our return of love to Him.

My mother was a woman of strong convictions. She was Irish to the very core of her being. No one dared enter her corner deli on St. Patrick's day with a red or orange tie. They would immediately be shown to the door and told not to come back without wearing some green. She would often say that anyone who is Irish and Catholic and does not cheer for Notre Dame is mental!

The Eucharist we celebrated for the happy repose of my mother's soul is the source and summit of our Catholic faith and my mother appreciated the Eucharist as the true gift it really is. She knew the Mass was a celebration of Christ's death, resurrection, and ascension, and that through this paschal mystery, we are all redeemed. She made Jesus Christ the invisible companion of her journey. He was never a shadowy figure on the margins of her life.

Her life was inspired by His teaching. Her death was a meeting with a dear, lifelong friend. For my mom, Christ was the King of her life. Christ ruled and governed her thoughts, words, and actions.

Death is for each of us the great certainty, the constant companion on our journey. We are reminded daily, and in so many ways of our fragility, of our mortality. As our lives unfold, we are evermore aware of the precious gift of life and how tenuous it is.

Despite my feelings of sorrow and grief, I am joyful that she is at peace. Her journey on Earth ended, but now she is in the hands of the God she loved so much.

The time of death is a time of faith, when we hold on more tightly than ever to the promise of Jesus that He brings us through this life to a more abundant one. My mother believed this. The gift of love – human and divine – that she received in abundance in this life, she gave as a generous gift to her children and grandchildren.

My mother treasured the gift of life God gave her and she lived it to the fullest – both within her own family and within the larger family of the church. She knew instinctively what many learn only through hard experience – that our characters, our personalities, what we really turn out to be, is now and during every second of our lives on earth, in the process of being formed. We are becoming what we will be forever. Our Risen Lord invites us to practice living a life of love until it becomes ingrained in us and is intimately a part of us.

Dot Heron lived that kind of love, and in the way she lived her life she remains a lasting, memorable model for all of us.

Something happens to the human soul when it is subjected to prolonged illness and suffering. Either it surrenders to despair or it chooses to stand in the fire of pain until purified and transformed into a more compassionate Christ-like person. My mother chose to be purified and transformed.

I will never forget the devotion and heartfelt care with which my mother prayed, "O Lord, I am not worthy to receive You. Only say the word and my soul shall be healed," as she prepared to receive Holy Communion on her sickbed.

All who knew her are more Christian, more human, because of their encounters with her. She is alive in God and by the way we continue to live our lives, she will remain alive and present to us in memory and love. We are grateful for the quality of life she lived and that we were privileged to share it.

My mother blessed us with many family rituals. Before we would go to bed at night, she would hug and kiss us, and say, "Good night and God bless you. I love you very much." I thank her each day for her love and example and am confident that her love will continue to sustain and inspire those who knew her now and forever.

CHAPTER 25
Ordination

"All of us need to be reminded of the nonnegotiable essentials of our spiritual lives from time to time. Otherwise, we tend to forget, and our thinking becomes fuzzy, our actions self-serving."

—Anonymous

Adjusting to seminary life proved to be a challenge for me. Spending many years as the virtual "head of the household," I stumbled upon a mishap or two. Rules, the example of the way my grandfather taught me, were flexible. My grandfather lived the words of Jesus, "The Sabbath was made for man, not man for the Sabbath."

When I skipped Liturgical Music class to play in a basketball game, I was chastised.

"This behavior is unbecoming of a young man studying to be a priest," I was told. Yet, I was undaunted; I would have made the same decision no matter what.

While in second college, I would sneak off the seminary property under the cloak of darkness behind the building. My friends from Collingdale would pick me up at Lancaster Avenue in order to play in a spring basketball league. In one game I severely twisted my ankle and so my friend, Billy McCann, had to drive onto the seminary property with his lights off. Pat Tursi and Vince Conway, neighborhood buddies, assisted me onto the elevator by the refectory. Bob Kulp, a seminarian and classmate, secured a pair of crutches. The next morning I was asked what happened and I replied truthfully, "I sprained my ankle playing ball last night," conveniently leaving out the detail that it was in Collingdale, off the seminary property.

In September 1971, while moving into the seminary to begin his second year of formation, I was summoned into Father Frank Loughran's office.

Fr. Loughran was the Dean of Men in the college division. It had been reported to him that I had been arrested in the summer in a Wildwood bar with a young woman.

The truth: I was arrested for swimming out to a sandbar, spent five-and-a-half hours in a jail cell in a wet bathing suit, was escorted, handcuffed, into an air-conditioned courtroom where the judge decided because I had disregarded the lifeguard's whistle, that I was guilty of endangering the lives of one million people. The judge sentenced me to three days in jail or paying a fine of $75. Several seminarians who were down the shore that weekend chipped in to pay the fine. I reimbursed them promptly.

In July of 1976, I worked at the Ventnor Vacation Home for Priests. One evening I dined alone with Cardinal John Krol. Two other priests who were there decided to go out for dinner upon hearing that the cardinal was coming. After some pleasant exchanges, the cardinal asked what work my father did. I replied that my father died when I was 4-and-a-half years old.

"How old was your dad at his death?" asked Cardinal Krol.

"Thirty-three, Your Eminence," I said.

"How old will you be if I ordain you?" he followed up.

"Twenty-five, Your Eminence," I replied

Musing aloud, the cardinal said, "If you only live as long as your father, you will only give me eight years of service. I don't know if I should ordain you."

"Your Eminence, kindly pass the salt and pepper," I said, with no hesitation. End of conversation.

That September, I embarked on my third year in the theology division and after a silent retreat at Mt. Savior, a Benedictine monastery in Elmira, N.Y., I made the decision to be a deacon. During my four years in the college division, I received a J. Wood Platt Caddy Scholarship. I received a letter from the scholarship committee that I was entitled to a fifth year of scholarship money because I would not turn 22 until November. The Rector, Monsignor Vincent Burns, was thrilled to receive the additional income.

On Fridays during 1973-74, I would accompany three other seminarians to the children's hospital to give platelets for children battling leukemia. The brother of a classmate of mine at Monsignor Bonner High School was one of the patients. He died in April 1976.

Among my field education assignments was one to Mercy Vocational Tech School in North Philadelphia, an assignment that would prove a blessing in my early priesthood. The Mercy tradition lives the Gospel in word and action and promotes service to others. This mission aligned very closely to my passion.

From seventh grade through high school and including my seminary years, I was in direct contact with 30 priests who left the active ministry. These were difficult times, but in spite of that reality, I was ordained May 20, 1978.

CHAPTER 26
The Call

"The most valuable gift that the church can offer to the bewildered and restless world of our time is to form within it Christians who are confirmed in what is essential and who are humbly joyful in their faith. The more this happens, the more it helps us create climate of 'mutual esteem, reverence, and harmony' in the church and learn to 'acknowledge all legitimate diversity ... For the ties which unite the faithful together are stronger than those which separate them; let there be unity in what is necessary, freedom in what is doubtful, and charity in everything."

—Our Hearts Were Burning Within Us: A Pastoral Plan for Adult Faith Formation
in the United States, Statement of the U.S. Catholic Bishops (1999)

You just got hit with a significant amount of spiritual teachings. I am proud to say these are the lessons I've learned through my birth into the natural order, followed by my birth into the spiritual life. What I hope to have imparted upon you is the genius of the Resurrection. Jesus was the only one who rose from the dead. He unlocked for us the experience we are all meant to experienced: courageous trust, radical risk, and ultimate surrender. This is all meant to diminish the emphasis we have on fear.

The apostles went out and shared the Good News with everyone that they could. Experiencing these births makes us at peace with our bodies (natural) and our souls (spiritual); however, it doesn't stop there! When we experience the births in the second half of this book, we become at peace with our minds (vocational) and our salvation (birth into eternal life).

To tie the spiritual all together, I'd like to tell the story of a young man pondering life's questions. In doing so, he approached a wise elder to ask why some people remain faithful and others do not. The wise man responded with a story of his own.

One day, a dog spied a rabbit and began to chase it. The barking dog attracted other dogs who joined in on the chase. The rabbit was out of sight. Soon, the other dogs tired and dropped out of the chase. The only dog left was the first one to pursue the rabbit. The chase continued until the rabbit vanished. Once the dog realized the rabbit was not to be caught, he returned home to await the next chase.

The young man frowned and said, "I don't get it!"

The wise man replied, "The first dog was the only one that actually saw the rabbit. To remain faithful, one must see the vision."

The young man went on his way to consider his new lesson.

The Easter season comes but once a year, yet it remains with us throughout the year, throughout our lives. What is next on the spiritual journey for you and me? What new vision of Jesus as Lord and Savior do we have? Ask yourself during the Easter season, "Have I become a different person since Ash Wednesday? How have I changed?" Then, ask yourself next Easter if you are a different person than the year prior.

No matter how profoundly life-changing the Lenten season was, the year was, we have work to do as individuals and as a community of believers. That work is the task of conversion, of changing our lives to mirror more faithfully the life of followers of Jesus Christ.

St. Francis of Assisi said at the end of his life, "Let us begin again for up to now we have done nothing."

We begin again on the road to conversion, which is the journey of faith. It commences with a starting point and moves through life's vision to reach a destiny.

While fear may open us to change and conversion, as Christians we are not to remain in our places of fear. Into our tense places of fear, Jesus offers His comforting, "Peace be with you." He promises his peace to us in our illnesses, in our poverty, in our loneliness, in our tragedies, in our doubts. His peace can transform fear into rejoicing in the knowledge that God is near.

Jesus' greeting of peace is accompanied by an incredibly wonderful gift: the gift of the Holy Spirit. The Holy Spirit is the Lord's gift that gives us power; we depend on God, not ourselves. The Holy Spirit is the gift that offers us new life to pass along the Good news and continue Jesus' work in the world. The Holy Spirit gives the Christian community the vision of God's grace in the world.

You and I may not have witnessed Jesus in the flesh in the upper room, but we do experience Him in the Eucharist. To that experience of the Lord Jesus Christ, we exclaim, like Thomas, "My Lord and my God!"

We are invited not to put our finger and hand into His wounds, but to take Jesus into our hearts. Then, we can profess our faith in Him more powerfully and announce the Good News of His resurrection to the world.

What Leads You to Christ?
What Leads You to Your Calling?

The story of the Magi is one of the best known in all of Christian literature. It is filled with mystery and intrigue. These "kings" from the East see a strange star in the sky and decide to follow it. They sought out on a journey, not sure of where exactly they were going. But they had this innate curiosity, this inner drive, this desire to find out what the star meant and where it would come to rest.

In many ways, this story of the Magi's journey represents our own journeys to discover the truth. Evelyn Waugh describes the Magi as patrons of all late comers; of all who have a tedious journey to make to the truth; of all who are confused by knowledge and speculation; of all, who through politeness, make themselves partners in guilt; of all who stand in danger because of their talents.

We, like the Magi, make complicated journeys to God. Some begin close to God in families of faith and then drift away through distractions and complexities of life. We lose the light as the magi did for a while and we get ourselves into dreadful, muddled situations, which involve others as well as ourselves. The Magi lost their guiding light and politely, but unwittingly, betrayed Jesus and the Holy Innocents when they went to Herod.

Others are not so fortunate to begin their journey to God within a family of faith. They start out in darkness and stagger about like blind men and women. They have no star to guide them, no one that is, to show them the way. But sometimes, by God's grace, a stranger might come into their lives and help them recognize something important about themselves – what is best in their lives, self-discovery, a hidden talent. We all must be prepared for such manifestations in our lives – surprise epiphanies that shine light on our darkened lives; where we had been following the false light of our pride and self-righteousness, now we can follow, with confidence and a sure step, the true light that lightens the path to God.

Whenever we set out on a journey of discovery, we run the risk of failure. This risk seems to be a constant companion. It keeps many people at home, afraid to venture forth on what could be a most exciting journey of the soul. Many are afraid about what they might discover. They may discover what they do not want to know. We want clear and easy signs, fixed stars, a good, reliable map. Sadly, there are many Herods out there who would deceive us, lead us astray, involve us in their wicked, evil schemes.

Yes, the story of the Magi is our story. They are our patrons. We can learn a lot from them about the courage and inner drive necessary to go on a journey of discovery. We will find, as they did, Jesus on the way. This story reveals that all men and women who honestly seek God are acceptable to Him.

What life experiences do you have that lead you to Christ? Once you discover Him, do you recognize the priceless value of that discovery and that encounter? Jesus didn't just come to save the chosen people; he came to save everyone. He reached across certain lines to touch all of humanity.

There's a universal call that everyone receives. Everyone is called to the invitation and to make a response by the ways in which they order their lives. Even the idea that the Magi returned home in a different way is really a hint to say that they are radically changed by their encounter with this infant, who they recognized as The Messiah. Once you have that encounter, you can't go back to your old way of living. You embark in new pathways. You hitch yourself to a star. You try to elevate yourself to become fully human. That is the key – not to be anything else, but to live life in a fully human way: on the physical, emotional, intellectual, social, and spiritual levels.

PART III: VOCATIONAL BIRTH

"Our vocation is to restore divine order and proclaim the Good News."

–Thomas Merton

CHAPTER 27
To Be a Priest

"We are not perfect. That should not be a goal. It is unrealistic and unhealthy. Just be kind and generous to others and yourself. That's enough for now."

—John Wooden

There is an Irish proverb that says, "A good beginning is half the work." This is sage advice, when one considers all the false starts, hesitations, and uncertainties that can easily claim our minds for such a long time before the actual act of beginning. Too often, we postpone when we should take the plunge and begin.

When the mind is ready for a fresh beginning, unforeseen insights and connections can emerge. By default, that is how beginnings often occur.

There is probably no active churchgoer, who at one time or another in his or her life, hasn't wanted to impress someone – somewhere along the line. When we have succeeded, we feel a bit uneasy about someone who comes along who is smarter, more talented, more attractive, more athletic (e.g. a singer in choir, a player on a sports team, a computer expert). What do we do in such a situation? Pray for them? Encourage them? Or do we allow fear and envy to get in the way?

John the Baptist was a fierce and fiery man with some rough edges in his personality. Yet, he was a great prophetic voice. Crowds of people came to hear him. He didn't mince words. He had a significant impact on people's lives. Then, one day while John the Baptist was preaching, baptizing, and having all kinds of success, out of the crowd steps Jesus.

John the Baptist admittedly didn't recognize Jesus at first. Through the power of the Holy Spirit, John was able to see that this is the one whose way he was preparing.

John the Baptist knows Jesus is gifted in the ways of God far beyond his own gifts. John the Baptist was proud of the work he was doing. Now comes someone who can do it much better. Imagine his feelings. He was to step aside now. He was to fade into the background and let Jesus take center stage. John had accomplished his task, which was to reveal Jesus to the world when He came. John the Baptist remains a role model for us. Like John the Baptist, we too need to learn how to discern divine love in our everyday life experiences.

Vocational birth is the belief that **we are all called** to play a role in the plan of salvation history. If you don't have that belief, you're never going to work with the Blessed Trinity – Father, Son, and Holy Spirit – and discern their love for you in your everyday life experiences. That's the key to vocational birth. It's not about you and me. You are the conduit. My goal as a priest is to help people believe they have a role in salvation history and to discern divine love to support that plan. Every person plays a part in the Kingdom of God. Every person has to figure out where his or her life fits into God's great plan. It's not our job to determine how that plan is carried out. It is our job to find our place in it.

Each of us has the task of revealing Jesus to our world, the world of our families, our workplaces, our homes, our parishes. This task doesn't need any spectacular display. If God is in our hearts, He goes wherever we go. How do we reveal Jesus to the world? In the way we speak to each other. In the value we place on other people and possessions. In the right care we take of ourselves. In the courtesy and compassion we show to the needy. In the way we care for the elderly. In the way we assist the young and in the way we value all of creation, especially the unborn.

Sometimes we might be confused or uncertain about our mission in life or just how to go about it. The same Holy Spirit who revealed Jesus to John the Baptist, Jesus' cousin, will come to our aid. Christ asks us to bring healing to our world; bring forgiveness, comfort, encouragement and hope.

"Here I am Lord, I come to do Your Will."

Can you say you woke up this morning with this refrain on your mind? Did you go to church on Sunday to renew your commitment to discerning the specific role you are to play in the plan of Salvation History? The general Will of God is that we all will be saved. It is up to us to figure out how we can reflect His life and love in our daily lives.

Another question to reflect on: "How would you describe your core identity?" The answer is that you are a beloved son or daughter of the Blessed Trinity.

Children experience God's merciful, forgiving love for the first time in the Sacrament of Reconciliation. After each child confesses their sins, I respond by telling them, "No strings attached, you are completely forgiven."

I also tell them that the reason God forgives is because He is wildly in love with us and when we are convinced that we are loved, we live life differently – more fully and freely. For a child's penance, I ask them to repeat the following: "Lord, help me to be a peacemaker rather than a no-good, rotten troublemaker."

Every time we sin, we are troublemakers. Does God want any of us to be a troublemaker? Do you want to be a troublemaker? What does God want you to be? He wants you to be a peacemaker. The baptismal font is where you became a child of God.

Once in the check-out line at a local supermarket, the gentleman in front of me was wearing a t-shirt that had this saying on the back: "Life is uncertain, order dessert first." That expression was a moment of grace for me.

It certainly puts life and the future in perspective. How do we bring God's peace to the world each and every day? How do we do that concretely and consistently, and what difference would it make in our lives and our relationships with one another? Being a peacemaker is a universal call to every person who claims to be a disciple of Jesus. In a similar vein, the prophet Isaiah, in his 49th chapter, acknowledged that Yahweh called him to be a light to all nations. We, like Isaiah, are also called to bring the light of Christ to a world of darkness.

Not long ago, I had a face-to-face, unpleasant conversation with someone who told me that I belong to a false religion and Jesus is not in any tabernacle throughout the world. This person continued to attack the Catholic faith, the priesthood, and the Eucharist. Remarkably, this conversation was also a moment of grace for me in this way:

I learned to absorb these attacks in silence, because I was able to discern that any attempt I made to refute these remarks would fall on deaf ears. To compound the sadness of this experience, the person has battled multiple forms of addiction for a good portion of his life. I ask that you remember this man in your prayers.

Think of God's plan as a series of voices. The first voice, thunderously loud, had certain advantages. When the Voice spoke from the trembling mountain at Sinai, or when fire licked up the altar on Mount Carmel, no one could deny it. Yet, amazingly, even those who heard the voice and feared it – the Israelites at Sinai and at Carmel, for example –

soon learned to ignore it. Its very volume got in the way. Few of them sought out that Voice; fewer still persevered when the Voice fell silent.

The voice modulated with Jesus, the Word made flesh. For a few decades, the voice of God took on the timbre and volume and rural accent of a country Jew in Palestine. It was a normal human voice, and though it spoke with authority, it did not cause people to flee. Jesus' voice was soft enough to debate, raise questions, or cause a listener to walk away, a would-be disciple to leave.

After Jesus departed, the voice took on new forms. On the day of Pentecost, tongues of fire fell on the faithful, and the church, God's body, began to take shape. That last voice is as close as breath, as gentle as a whisper. It is the most vulnerable voice of all, and the easiest to ignore.

The Bible says the spirit can be "quenched" or "grieved" – try quenching Moses' burning bush or the molten rocks of Sinai! Yet, the Holy Spirit is also the most intimate voice. In our moments of weakness, when we do not know what to pray, the Holy Spirit within intercedes for us with groans that words cannot express. Those groans are the early pangs of birth, the labor pains of the new creation.

Let us all pray that we can make a conscious effort to present ourselves to God – Father, Son, and Holy Spirit – each day with the words from Psalm 40: "Here I am Lord, I come to do your Will."

'The Blissful Life That God Himself Lives'

Erasmo Leiva-Merikakis, in his book, Fire of Mercy, Heart of the Word, says "In the Sermon on the Mount and elsewhere in the Gospel, Jesus constantly returns to the fundamental requirement for discipleship: poverty of spirit, an interior state and virtue that could not be defined better than Pascal did when he listed the nothingness and other things that we begin to feel within ourselves precisely when we come to total rest. And so we have to face squarely the paradox with which the Gospel presents us: that what we most need in order to become a disciple of Jesus are precisely those things against which our fallen, ego-centered nature most revolts. If we are ever truly going to become anything worthwhile, we must first recognize and embrace the truth that, of ourselves, we are nothing."[42]

Letting go of our Ego Spirit, fighting off the Evil Spirit, we come to a full, richer understanding of the guidance of the Holy Spirit. We cannot do this alone. We must rely on God – Father, Son, and Holy Spirit to help us with our worldly concerns.

"Paradoxically, insisting on our own self-sufficiency, worthwhileness, and competence can only have the effect of freezing us into stagnant inertia, whereas the humble admission of our radical neediness opens wide the doors of our being to all manner of transformation and movement," Leiva-Merikakis continues. "At length we, too, recognizing ourselves as new beings, can exclaim with the Psalmist: 'I praise you, for I am fearfully and wonderfully made' (Ps 139[138]:14, NRS)."

Think of this like Lonergan's philosophy on conversion. Skipping any of the steps will only hinder us as we try to grow, spiritually. We've been born into the world and our faith, but are blinded by what's directly in front of us. This blocks us from finding our true purpose – our vocation in God's plan.

Leiva-Merikakis goes on to strategically quote the Bible: "'He who finds his life will lose it, and he who loses his life for my sake will find it' (10:39). 'Unless you turn and become like children, you will never enter the kingdom of heaven' (18:3). 'Blessed are the poor in spirit, for theirs is the kingdom of heaven' (5:3). 'Whoever would be great among you must be your servant, and whoever would be first among you must be your slave.' (20:26-27).

Leiva-Merikakis and I share an admiration for the above biblical entries. These are the core musings we both follow to fulfill our four births.

He finishes, "These are the dynamic principles by which that person must think, live, and act who has '[fallen] into the hands of the living God' (Heb 10:31). Experience bears out that these pronouncements from the Lord's own mouth are the laws of the highest life possible to the human spirit, because they are, in fact, the laws of God's own Being. Although at first they must be terrifying to the self-indulgent ego and pose the greatest threat to my existence as I have lived it until encountering Christ, in time these 'laws' are seen to communicate nothing less than the blissful life that God Himself lives."

Leiva-Merikakis leaves us with such a powerful message: God's blissful life is within our reach. We must pray hard and discern every day in order to live that universal truth.

This overall concept captures language that is inviting and challenging. It invites you to "come and see," but then it challenges you to live life not according to the ways of the world, but the ways of our Lord.

Most people recognize poverty as a very negative force to avoid at all costs, but Jesus says when you embrace your own poverty, then that becomes the setting for you to grow in healthy and greater dependence on grace.

I often think of the story about the fellow who wants to change the world and he realizes that is just a little bit too ambitious. Then, he wants to change his community. After a while, he realizes that's still too much to bite off and accomplish. Then, he wants to change his family and soon realizes that's not as easy a task. He finally comes to the conclusion that he needs to change himself and have a relationship with the Lord in order to bring about the change. He then sets out to sustain that singular change in himself with an *ongoing* relationship with the Lord.

Sometimes in our youthfulness, we have big ambitions. If we're attentive, we soon learn that they get pared down to a point where if we can bring about personal conversion – our own change – then we've done a lot for the world, for the community, for our families, and ultimately, for ourselves.

Jesus, in the eyes of the world, is a failure. But, in the eyes of faith, He continues to call us to a new understanding of life. His word endures even in death and suffering, because no human being escapes suffering or death, and suffering and death is not the end.

Lazurus, a good friend of Jesus, dies. His two sisters, Martha and Mary, also good friends of Jesus, are angry with Him for not coming in a timely way. He came to raise Lazurus from the grave. That was a foreshadowing of something even greater: His own death and resurrection.

There's a common joke … How do you make God laugh? Tell Him your plan. We all have our own game plan, but must be humble enough to revise it and accept the game plan that's rooted in the Gospel and in our personal encounter with our Lord.

The Modern Disciple

"How long does it take to become a priest after you graduate high school, Father?"

"Eight years," I said. "Four years in the college division and then four years in the theology division."

"Wow! That's a long time."

Well, that's just about the usual answer I receive when I tell someone eight years – "that's a long time." I suppose it does seem like a long time to spend in a seminary; a long time to prepare, a long time to get ready for ordination to the priesthood.

We know the commission that Jesus gave to his first disciples: Go teach all nations. But before He said, "Go," Jesus said "Come." Come follow me, come close to me, come listen to me, come gather your strength from me.

As a modern disciple, the priest must also come to Jesus. A priesthood that is not based on closeness to Him is not a priesthood. The task of every priest – to make Jesus present in our world – is an impossible task to accomplish, or even to begin, without the strength of Christ.

So, if we look to the task involved with this preparation for the priesthood rather than the time involved, eight years is not a long time – neither is 20 years, nor even a lifetime.

My curiosity turned into my vocation because of my observations of the type of relationship my mother had with our Lord in receiving Holy Communion. That's what triggered it in me. It was that experience of seeing something change in her after receiving Holy Communion, even if it was just for the remainder of the mass. It intrigued me and caused me to wonder: What is happening? Why is it happening? How can I have that same experience?

We can be awakened spiritually, but that's not enough. It ended up being a vocation for me. Everyone is called, but not everyone hears or follows the call.

In vocation, you can be called to a single life. People can wonder, "why are you still single?" Is it by default or is it by an undercurrent that is saying you are called to remain single or called to the married state? There is a call involved in the priesthood. It took six-and-a-half years in the seminary before I made the decision that I was called to be a priest. That came through many meetings with Fr. Murray, because there's a natural desire to be married and to have a family. How do you recognize that and not feel that your life would be incomplete without having a spouse and having your own children? With good guidance and prayer, a peace comes into the person searching to know his call. You can get severely twisted in an unhealthy way unless a man discerning priesthood can clearly believe that this life, with all of its peril, can be lived in a healthy, wholesome way, and not in a compensatory way.

The First Love I Experienced

The first love I experienced was that of my mom and dad. Their natural love, sanctified by faith in the Risen Lord, saw to it that before I was born, they prepared a healthy family atmosphere in which I was able to open my eyes to light, my soul to life, and my heart to love, as I grew in age.

My mom and dad enriched my life in ways I know and appreciate and also in ways too profound for me or anyone to fathom in this world. Human love and divine love were wrapped in mystery in their marriage, and generously shared with me and my three siblings. Even after my dad died, I firmly believe that faith and love united my parents. That enrichment continues to shape my understanding of life.

A child's innocence is so easily exposed to danger. A child's heart is like wax to be molded. Wax, however, is not molded by merely protecting it from melting. It needs to be worked upon with a conscious design. So, in molding my heart, my mom and dad had to know themselves and know what they were training me to become.

I entered St. Charles Seminary on Sept. 10, 1970. I was young and innocent, with a heart already molded by my parents, yet still in need of more molding. I met Fr. Murray.

I am sure Fr. Murray did not know initially what was to transpire between us. I remember early on in our relationship he told me that prayer taught him that teaching is something that flows from the very core of his being. That made a deep impression on my mind. My mind was seeking and searching for the purpose and meaning of life. Dan Murray took it as his personal responsibility to challenge me to ask questions rather than seek answers.

Our friendship spanned 44 years, from 1970 to June 26, 2014. We walked a lot of roads in all kinds of weather and it was a great deal easier because we walked them together. I recall the lyrics to Elton John's "Your Song," which said, " I hope you don't mind that I put down in words, How wonderful life is while you're in the world." (John, op. cit.).

The love of my parents, the love of my spiritual director, Fr. Murray, prepared me to be open, attentive and receptive to the love of the Heavenly Father, the Son, and the Holy Spirit. When this threesome loves me it means they take delight in me. The love of the Blessed Trinity is personal, passionate and profound. Their love is a powerful expression of living life abundantly. When we live life abundantly on all levels: physical, intellectual, emotional, social and spiritual we show the world our delight in Father, Son and Holy Spirit.

Often, though, they suffer under our lovelessness and in the face of our sinful patterns of behavior they are overcome by a kind of helplessness- "Ephraim, what shall I do to you?" says Yahweh. "Judah, what shall I do to you?" Human words fail to describe this love. St. Paul helps us: "Through the Holy Spirit given to us, the Father's love has flooded our hearts." (Rom.5:5) And again a passage from St. Paul I never tire reading or hearing: "I am convinced that there is nothing in death or life, in the realm of spirits or superhuman powers, in the world as it is, or the world as it shall be, in the forces of the universe, in heights or depths – nothing in all creation can separate us from the love of the Father in Christ Jesus Our Lord." (Romans 8).

The Cyclical Nature of Our Births

One time, down the shore, I had a long conversation with Fr. Murray. We were sitting at the bottom of the steps of a duplex.

He said to me, "If you would leave the seminary and get married in a year, you'd be a disaster as a husband and a father."

I remember reacting very angrily to that. Who did he think he was to be able to predict something like that? Years later, I realized he was right. I was emotionally underdeveloped and too needy. I hadn't achieved a maturity that would have been necessary in marriage.

They were very long and deep conversations that I needed to have in order to grow. He was extremely patient in waiting for that maturation to happen. He possessed a humble authority about life. He was a very gifted man, intellectually. Now, it's one thing to have a great intellect, but it's another thing to have a rich understanding of the Gospel.

A classmate of mine referred to Fr. Murray as "Desert Dan the Gospel Man." I always enjoyed that. In St. Mark's Gospel, there's a Greek word, *proboling*, which basically means to throw it out there, or to have distance and see how to come to a good resolution to it (it is closely related to the English, "problem"). It was the Holy Spirit that kept *proboling* Jesus further and further into the desert. That should be in your life, too. Some people found Dan too much to take, because of his intensity in explaining biblical words and sacred scripture. He was a very demanding teacher, but his lessons were what threw me out into the desert to find myself: from natural desire to spiritual curiosity, and eventually to vocational fulfillment.

In the document "Vatican II Council," vocation is known as a universal call to holiness, not just priesthood and religious or monastic life.

Danish philosopher Soren Kierkegaard realized that we cannot be truly ourselves by ourselves.

Another philosopher recognized that if a disciple of Jesus is not living some process of ego-dying in order to serve the other, then his or her faith is not authentic.

Each person has a specific role to play in the plan of salvation history. Each person needs to learn to discern what that call is. For example, in 1961 Dag Hammarskjold, a single man, and Secretary General of the United Nations, wrote in his diary, "at some moment I did answer Yes to Someone – or Something – and from that hour I was certain that existence is meaningful and that, therefore, my life, in self-surrender, had a goal."

CHAPTER 28
The Steep Learning Curve

"It's not what we don't know that gets us in trouble. It's what we know for sure that just ain't so."

—Commonly attributed to Mark Twain (1835 – 1910)

My vocational birth occurred May 20, 1978, the day I was ordained to the priesthood. The next day, my spiritual director, Fr. Murray, delivered the homily at the first Mass I celebrated on Sunday, May 21, 1978, at St. Joseph Church in Collingdale, Pa.

The First Assignment

In January 1978, an assistant priest was transferred from Immaculate Heart of Mary Parish in Andorra, and was not replaced. Later, I discovered that pastor informed the Chancery Office that he would wait until June with the hope of getting a newly ordained priest assigned to the parish, which turned out to be me.

At my first meal in the rectory, the pastor informed me that when I celebrated my fifth anniversary as a priest he would be celebrating his 35th. He strongly suggested that we combine our celebrations. I did not even think that any priest celebrated his fifth anniversary. After dinner, the pastor wanted me to come with him to the church hall, because the eighth graders were having their graduation dance. I agreed. He introduced me to the eighth graders, the faculty and chaperones, and asked me to offer a prayer. So, I obliged. The pastor came up to me and said it was the "most magnificent prayer he'd ever heard."

The next day in the rectory, the other assistant priest told me that after communion at every Mass, two weeks before my arrival, the pastor told parishioners, "St. John Neumann has been appointed to this parish."

With a chuckle, the assistant said, "You have big, big shoes to fill." This brief conversation stirred in my mind the words many told me as a 4-and-a-half-year-old boy that after my father died I was to be the man of the Heron household. Now, on my second day as a parish priest I was expected to be as holy as St.John Neumann. I quickly had to learn to deal with unreal expectations.

A number of unsettling incidents had caused me to request a transfer from this parish. In August, I consulted my spiritual director, Msgr. Murray, who encouraged me to persevere until June 1979. This seemed untenable to me, and so he encouraged me to speak to another priest.

On Aug. 6, Pope Paul VI died. As I watched his funeral on television, the thought crossed my mind that I was dying in this assignment.

I set up an appointment with Father Jim Meehan, a well-respected priest in the diocese. After filling him in for five minutes, Fr. Meehan interrupted and said, "get the hell out of there."

I informed the pastor that I was calling the Chancery to request a transfer. He wasn't happy about the news, but I felt as though I was being smothered. I'd already made my decision.

Money Matters ... or does it?

The first year I was ordained, Margaret Coakely from Collingdale bequeathed me a gift of $10,000. I was taken aback by her generosity and did not know what to do. I knew I did not deserve it. I knew I had not earned it. Therefore, I thought I needed to be rid of it as quickly as possible. My Uncle Jack had been laid off from work and he and his family was struggling financially. So, I went to the local bank, deposited the $10,000 check and asked the teller to make out two checks in the amount of $5,000. The next day I drove to my aunt and uncle's house and handed them a check for $5,000. They were deeply grateful and greatly relieved.

The other check was sent to Dorothy Day and the *Catholic Worker* in New York, where I had just went on retreat for three days with my friend Bill Mattia. I knew that money would help the homeless people on the Lower East Side, immediately.

As a priest, my salary each month was $200. I felt so relieved that I didn't have to be weighed down by this great sum of money.

Later that week, I proudly informed Fr. Murray what I had done. His initial response was stunned silence. Then, he told me I was foolish, because I could have invested it and distributed it to many people over a long period of time. This was during the Carter presidency, when Certificate's of Deposits were giving a 17 percent rate of return. The lesson I had learned was that money doesn't have to be a burden. If used wisely, money can become a long-term source of good.

The Second Assignment

I was transferred to Saint Michael the Archangel in November 1978. My first weekend at St. Michael's, I was confronted with a pastoral dilemma. I was meeting with a young couple that just recently had given birth to their first child and had come to the rectory office after Mass to make an appointment for their daughter's baptism. In the basement of the rectory, the ushers were counting the Sunday collection. After they finished counting the collection, they would play cards and drink beer. Their conversations were loud and salty. Their earthy language rattled the young couple.

The same incident occurred after another morning Mass. A couple came to the rectory to register as new members of the parish. The tenor and tone of the ushers heard by that couple left them with an unfavorable first impression.

On Monday morning, I reported these two incidents to the pastor. Not knowing what to do or say, he mumbled, "I'll get back to you." He called the head usher to discuss the matter. On the following Tuesday morning, four ushers arrived at the rectory at mid-morning to install soundproof ceiling tiles in the basement of the rectory. Dilemma resolved.

The leadership styles of my first two pastors were so very different. Grace and sin exist. In the parable of the weeds and wheat, the Master of the household (Jesus) instructs his slaves, "Let them grow together until the harvest, then at harvest time I will say to the harvesters, 'First collect the weeds and tie them in bundles for burning; but gather the wheat into my barn'" (Matthew 13: 30).

Throughout the rest of my time at Saint Michael the Archangel, I would open up a sort of "thrift store" in the rectory basement getting shoes and clothing donated – some brand new.

As the youngest priest in a rectory of four priests, I was asked to visit the classrooms in the school, help with the PREP program, i.e. children receiving instruction in the Catholic faith one hour a week as they attend public school. I was also asked to be a chaplain at Bishop Conwell High School, an all-girls school on the campus of St. Michael the Archangel

Parish. I would visit Bishop Conwell High School one day a week, to teach class and counsel the students and faculty.

I was moderator of the CYO and also coordinator for the World Peace March in 1982.

Love is Blind
and Marriage is a Real Eye Opener

In my first 13 months of priesthood, I celebrated 88 weddings! Most unusual were the four weddings celebrated on Saturday, Aug. 19, 1979! This was an active parish, to be met by an active young priest.

The sacrament of marriage has become an important piece of my vocation. At weddings, I always make an agreement with the bride. The agreement is this – for every minute she is late arriving at the altar I add two minutes to my 15-minute, standard-length homily.

Then, I present my favorite quote by e.e. cummings, "we cannot be born enough, we are human beings for whom birth is a supremely welcome mystery."

The sacrament of marriage is another form of birth. The couple courageously, boldly, and passionately proclaims to one another that they will love and honor each other for the rest of their days. This proclamation erupts from deep within their souls. And it will echo forever.

The altar at which they recite their vows is a symbol of the covenant between God and us. It is a sacred meeting place. It is where Jesus himself teaches us more than we ever need to know about self-giving love.

Marriage is a spiritual reality. The couple is called together to fulfill the mission that God has given them. They are united together for life, not just because they experience deep love for each other, but because they believe that God loves each of them with an infinite love and has called them to each other to be living witnesses of that love. To love is to embody God's infinite love in a faithful communion with another human being.

Our Lord asks the couple to become a flesh and blood witness of His love. Through the Eucharist that we celebrate, Our Lord gives them the grace to love one another, to forgive one another, and to heal one another as personally and as passionately as he loves, forgives, and heals us all. It is an adventure of human and divine love wrapped in mystery.

We do not know what the future holds, but we do know who holds the future: Almighty God. That truth is more than sufficient for us to face the future with confidence and hope. More than anything else God – Father, Son, and Holy Spirit – desires to gift those celebrating the sacrament of Holy Matrimony with their abiding, faithful and enduring love.

It takes four words to adequately translate the one English word – love. Those four words, it seems to me, describe the full and complete meaning of marital love.

First, there is the word for romantic love. God's will for the couple is that they always be lovers. May you never fall into the trap of losing the freshness, newness, and wonder of being in love. There is an old rabbinical proverb that says: "God will hold us accountable for every joy that we did not experience."

The second concept of love, as contained in the language of the New Testament, is affection. And we need to understand that romance and affection are not the same thing. Romance floats on cloud nine. Affection has both feet on the ground. Romance is Saturday night. Affection is Monday morning. Romance celebrates the festive moments of life—the soft music, the glass of wine, the candlelight dinner. Affection celebrates the importance of the routine. It is the call in the middle of the day. It is the gift that is given for no reason at all, other than "I love you." A wise counselor once said, "If married couples will look after the little things, the big things will take care of themselves.

The third concept of love, in the language of the New Testament, is friendship. Friendship is the things done together and the thoughts and feelings shared with one another. Perhaps the highest compliment that a husband can pay to his wife and a wife to her husband is for either of them to say, "I am married to my best friend."

The fourth concept of love, in the language of the New Testament, is a word that describes an indestructible good will. This is the word that is used to speak of God's love for us; it is also the word that is most often used to tell us how we are to love one another. In his first letter to the Corinthians, Paul wrote a very beautiful poem about this kind of love.

Part of that poem goes like this: "Love is patient and kind. Love is not jealous, it is not snobbish. Love is never rude, it is not self-seeking, it is not prone to anger: neither does it brood over injuries. Love never fails. There are in the end three things that last: faith, hope and love; and the greatest of these is love."

As God loves us, not always because of ourselves, but sometimes in spite of ourselves, so we are to love one another.

These are the four dimensions of love that I would, if I could, include in my gift to those I help celebrate the sacrament of Holy Matrimony. God's children need them all – romance, affection, friendship, and indestructible good will. But no one can give us that kind of love; it must be built within ourselves and between ourselves. That is the message I give through the celebration of the sacrament of marriage.

Jesus doesn't want us to live a survival existence by just getting by. He wants us to live life every day abundantly. That's the reason He came. What's your game plan to live life abundantly on all levels? How do you engage in spiritual intimacy? When I ask that to couples who are getting married, they usually look at me like I have three heads!

How do you engage in healthy social intimacy without having all the social media being the great disruptor? How do you engage in intellectual intimacy?

I joke with them. "Some Friday night you two should just work out calculus problems together." If you're just engaging in physical intimacy, it's going to be a dissatisfying experience. The more you can engage a person in all levels, the more fulfilled you will be. Play and pray is a great balancer. It's a good question for an examination. How often was I playful today? How often did I pray today? If those two things dry up, you're in for a dark existence. Play and pray and you stay.

I ask, why do you want to be married in Christ? That really is a question that most people never really think about. They think, "Well, I was raised a Catholic." However, that isn't my question. My question is, you're coming to this parish, in this church, you might be practicing or not practicing. You want to be married. Why here? Some of them honestly say that the reason is because of their parents or grandparents. That's fine. I try to lead them to connect being married in a church and at an altar to its being a symbol of a covenantal bond of love.

This couple picked this day, at this church, at this altar, because they want divine assistance and help so that their love can be a faithful love, a growing love, a prosperous love, a permanent bond of love. In a world of relativism, that is a monumental shift, because for you, for me, your truth and my truth might not be the same thing. That is my primary concern. I ask, "What does Jesus want for you?" If you want to be married in Christ, what do you think Jesus wants for you? He wants you to have a life and love that is abundant. What does it mean to live life abundantly? It means being able to live life on all five levels: physical, intellectual, emotional, social, and spiritual. It is to learn to engage in intimacy and intercourse on all of those levels.

Why do you want to marry this person? Her great attention to detail? His ability to give you another perspective on life? But, do these things carry on through, say six months into the marriage? You can go from great attention to detail to being a nag! That's surely two sides of one coin. These are broad strokes. Men and women are wired differently. I would say to the man, "If you're getting married June 5, 2018, after that date, you won't have to remember any of your mistakes." Why is that? There's no sense in two people remembering the same thing. A woman remembers all the details! Her expectations are always high.

Lou Holtz was interviewed one time with his wife sitting beside him. They're talking football, and finally the interviewer asks Lou if he loves his wife more than football. He responds, "I love her more than I love basketball." So, there's a necessary lightheartedness in marriage. Men can stonewall. You have to be able to know how each one is differently wired and learn how to love the thinking patterns of the other person.

In intimacy, you must make yourself vulnerable. That means the one that you believe you love the most in life is the one that you have the potential to hurt the deepest. When contempt for the other person sets in, that should be a clear signal that you have to resolve this sooner rather than later. You can't keep pushing it aside or pushing it away because contempt has a way of festering and when that starts to grow in a person's mind, heart, will, or soul, it unfortunately becomes, for so many couples, an insurmountable obstacle.

"Play and pray," is based on my observation of my own mom and dad in the four years of my life. There was a playfulness and a prayerfulness to the two of them. How do you engage in spiritual intercourse? What are the burning big questions in your life? How do you navigate them? I tell the couple that they both have to have a game plan. Just like a coach wouldn't go into a game without a game plan. You both have to have the flexibility to adjust the game plan. You have to know your own game plan. Couples must find their own patterns and rhythms, too. There's no set rule that says we have to do everything together. That can get suffocating. They have to have healthy attachment and healthy detachment. They have to have independence, healthy dependence, and healthy interdependence. All of those different fibers have to be woven into the tapestry of their relationship.

I recall one couple that was married for 72 years. They were 93 and 92 at the time. I asked if they'd be willing to come to church to celebrate with the whole parish. Their 71-year-old son sat beside them. Five generations of family filled 15 pews that day, Oct. 28, 1979. There were more than 1,500 people in church. After communion, I announced, "we have a joyous occasion." I prayed nuptial blessings. "A few moments ago, I extended my hands over the bread and wine. In the same way, I'm going to extend my hands over Margaret and Charlie so that they may uplift one another and make each other an acceptable gift back to the Holy Trinity." I lay my hands over them. "Be a holy woman, faithful wife, loving mother; be a holy man, faithful husband, loving father." This was followed by a thunderous applause. As the crowd settled down, I asked this couple what advice they could give to me, a newly ordained priest to assist couples to enjoy such longevity in marriage. The husband, Charlie, said in a rough voice, "Father, tell them this: love is blind, and marriage is a real eye opener." You could see all the couples in the pews playfully nudging each other. It was a wonderful response with laughter and joy.

Yet, despite the joyous nature of celebrating the sacrament of holy matrimony, there are challenges the church must face in all of her wisdom. In this day and age of political correctness, the intention is not to offend; yet it is so important to be vigilant to the language you say or write. We are experiencing a cultural trend that ignores 5,000 years of traditional valued norms. Consider same-sex marriage, transgender rights, friends with benefits, couples living together before marriage, divorce and re-marriage, the definition of the family has radically shifted. It is a remarkable pastoral challenge. I don't have easy answers. I do know that a priest must accept each person with respect and dignity, recognizing the face of Christ in them.

Most of my pastoral experience concerns co-habitation and the indissolubility of marriage. Ross Douthat writes in his book, *To Change the Church*, "The Catholic Church's teaching on marriage begins with the Gospel of Mark. Jesus is teaching a crowd in Judea, and the Pharisees appear with a testing question: 'Is it lawful for a man to divorce his wife?' Jesus answers by asking the about the law of Moses, and they remind him that 'Moses allowed a man to write a certificate of divorce and to send her away.' At which point Jesus, as elsewhere in the Gospels, makes the law more demanding, more radical, more transcendent:

- "And Jesus said to them, 'Because of your hardness of heart he wrote you this commandment. But from the beginning of creation, God made them male and female. Therefore a man shall leave his father and mother and hold fast to his wife, and the two shall become one flesh. So they are no longer two but one flesh. What therefore God has joined together, let not man separate.'

- "And in the house the disciples asked him again about this matter. And he said to them, 'Whoever divorces his wife and marries another commits adultery against her, and if she divorces her husband and marries another, she commits adultery.'

"From the first, this vision of marriage's indissolubility, its one-flesh metaphysical reality, was crucial to Christianity's development and spread. It taught the fundamental equality of the sexes in a world defined by patriarchal power, and it promised permanence and protection to the women and children. But more than that it was theologically important, because St. Paul's vision of human marriage as a 'mystery' connected to Christ's relationship to his church was embedded deep into its self-understanding as the 'bride of Christ.'"[43]

The church affirms four conditions for a valid sacramental marriage: permanent commitment, a faithful commitment, openness to children (new life) and freedom to fulfill those responsibilities. These must be present at the exchange of vows. The couple confers the sacrament together professing to "love you and only you until death." Freedom has become an elusive criterion today. What actually determines being free to accept those responsibilities? Age, maturity, psychological stability, cultural influence, all of which are complicated by a society fraught with addiction, depression, war, violence.

Co-habitation, divorce, and re-marriage ... the pastoral challenge is always to figure out all the different dimensions and then make an authentic decision that reflects the Lord's mercy and maintains divine order.

A father in his early 50's whose daughter was getting married outside of a church building asked me to come and officiate the wedding. I asked if they were both Catholic. They were. The mandate is that they must be married inside a church unless there's an extraordinary circumstance. For example, I've celebrated a wedding in a hospital. Part of the form of the sacrament is that you are married in the church to witness to people the significant role of divine love. This father could not understand why I could not perform his daughter's wedding at a venue like the beach.

The couple is publicly proclaiming a covenant bond of love. That is why they stand at the altar. This exchange of vows at the altar roots their covenantal bond of love in sacrifice and willingness to suffer for the sake of the other.

Every time you enter a Catholic Church three key symbols are prominent: the altar, symbol of a covenant bond of love, a tabernacle, a symbol of real presence, a cross, a symbol of sacrificial love. These three symbols draw you into the mystery of divine love.

These three symbols make up a silent homily present at every celebration in church. It brings Trinitarian love into each ceremony.

The Importance of Leisure

"Play and pray," even applies to your personal life, because without it, the stress and monotony of daily living can bleed into your spirituality. In any field, whether it's medicine, law, music, business, law enforcement, everybody has in himself or herself a unique DNA. The first step in the spiritual life is be attentive to it.

Some people say they don't mind working overtime, but if that becomes the pattern, then they have to have the ability to discern why they're consistently putting in 16-hour days when they're only required to work eight-hour days. The reverse can happen.

A young man took on a job and thoroughly immersed himself in it. He learned all he could, extending that learning into special training. After 10 years of outstanding performance, with the workplace requiring of him 70 hours a week, he felt as if his workplace was taking advantage of him. He had to make a choice to continue or look for work that would allow him more time with his wife and daughter. He decided to leave that job. That was a great risk, but he's come to realize he did not have enough quality time with the most important people in his life: he did not have enough leisure.

Can you learn to work leisurely rather than compulsively? Compulsive work blurs healthy boundaries. If you think about it, "all work and no play" (or very little) is an affront to the Creator who, Himself, rested!

Friday is my Sabbath. I take off on Fridays. I do that because Jesus, Himself, did and I understand the implicit value in affording myself time away, time alone. The Masses, meetings, and ministerings of priesthood are very like the demands in the workplace. Our bodies and minds need some time to recover in order to bring our best selves back to the task at hand.

Thomas Carlisle credited the Industrial Revolution and Thomas Edison's invention of the light bulb with seriously disrupting the natural order of light and darkness. Slowing down seems impossible to most parents trying to raise children. Their weekend activities or the pressure of our culture to get things done has nearly obliterated the idea of leisure and co-opted the very idea of "Sabbath rest."

All of us are significantly over-scheduled with no built-in checks and balances. Far from being interrupted, the cycle intensifies producing frustration and fatigue.

Parents can live vicariously through their children, putting enormous pressure on the child to succeed. "I want my son/daughter to score the highest in the SAT's, to be the best musician in the band, the best athlete, etc." This derivative existence of parents does no justice to a child in formation! When a parent says, "I am proud you graduated from high school or college," what is really being said? The pronoun, "I" is a give-away! Is the child's achievement really the parent's victory? Perhaps a truer phrasing might be: "You should be proud of yourself, I am!" This is not silly semantics. Language shapes reality and reality shapes language. That reciprocity, especially when dealing with children, cannot be overstated.

When you read the Acts of the Apostles, you wonder, "What happened?" What enabled fearful, cowering men locked inside a room to suddenly begin boldly proclaiming the word? They had to have receptivity with the Holy Spirit that transformed fear into fearless, bold proclamation. They had to have a personal encounter with the Risen Lord.

Jesus says to lower your net deeper. What He's saying is that we must dig deeper into our minds, hearts, wills, and souls to discover a new catch. That image of lowering your net is to not allow yourself to skim along the surface of life. Superficial living is not compatible with Gospel living. Everybody needs to be guided to ask the further question so that they can come to a newer, deeper understanding of his or her vocation. Everybody needs a Moses figure to lead him or her in life. Everybody needs a Jesus figure to lead him or her up the mountain of transfiguration.

My method of approaching people is always based on coming to an awareness of their life experience. This is what Jesus did in the Gospel. He met people where they were. Whether it was Mathew as a tax collector, Zacchaeus as a chief tax collector in a tree, Nicodemus coming at night; Jesus always would deal with people exactly where they were.

CHAPTER 29
The Teacher and the Coach

"Be more concerned with your character than your reputation, because your character is what you really are, while your reputation is merely what others think you are."

—John Wooden

In June 1982, I was assigned to teach high school at Archbishop Kennedy in Conshohocken and took residence at St. James in Elkins Park. I quickly learned that many of my students weren't very interested in theology class. Some even slept right through it. My enthusiasm and zeal was often met with the "sophomore stare."

That summer, before the school year began, I studied the four textbooks I would use for the four different courses I was assigned to teach.

On a Friday afternoon in a fifth period , the topic was the Gospel of Matthew's Sermon on the Mount. The lesson I was trying to convey to these students was to protest the nuclear arms crisis, and to have outreach to the poor.

One student said to me, "Father give us a break, we're only 14 years old." Joe Casciato was a bit more coy in his attempts. He pulled me aside after class and said, "Father, you're a nice guy, but I think you have to lighten up a bit." I responded, "What do you mean lighten up?!"

I reflected on the conversation while driving home from the football game that night and realized he was right. My intensity was more of an obstacle than a bridge to connect my students to the Gospel. I heard that many of times from Fr. Murray.

"You have to check your spiritual, emotional, and intellectual intensity," he told me. "You like to turn the volume up to 10. People might be able to handle a 5, but they can't handle 6 to 10 unless they've known you for a long time. You have to learn how to temper your intensity, and at the same time not lose your zeal, passion, and enthusiasm. In trying to be persuasive to any group, the substance of what you're saying is crucial, but the tone and the manner in which you deliver it can be either a hindrance or a help."

I frequently had to teach and remind myself to have substance, proper tone, and a manner that is not off-putting or distracting to the message that I'm giving.

Not being satisfied with the sophomore stare, I learned to switch my teaching methodology and engaged the class by having them act out Gospel scenes. I deeply believed the proverb, "I hear and I forget, I see and I remember, I do and I understand."

My strong desire to have students absorb, assimilate, and appropriate Gospel truth, enabled me to move the classroom acting to a broader arena. I hoped to have the students write and perform skits on relevant topics occurring in their lives. It was to be a peer-to-peer form of evangelization, but it was not to be – not at Archbishop Kennedy High School. That would come later.

I coached basketball for four years – two years coaching girls and two years coaching boys. I taught Joe Dempsey in his senior year and played basketball with him. He ended his 14-year tenure as head coach of LaSalle High School in Wyndmoor, Pa., in April 2018. He had served the program for a total of 27 years. As head coach, he won 208 games, and in 2014, he led his team to a 23-7 record and the PIAA Class 4A championship game.

He was well known amongst the faculty at Kennedy for his famous impersonations of me. Mockery truly is the best form of flattery! He would imitate the way I would write on the chalkboard with my left hand and the manner in which I asked questions and engaged the class. He was so good that other teachers in the school would have him get up and do the Fr. Heron imitation.

At the end of Joe's senior year, I was asked to participate on a panel program on Channel 6. I didn't know it, but the principal had the whole school watch that half-hour program. When I returned to school, the students considered me a local celebrity. Joe had his impersonation already cued up and ready to perform.

Joe was a very talented basketball player. He was Bicentennial All-League and went on to play Division II basketball in college. He had a great interest in the Catholic League. His goal in life was to teach and coach basketball.

I told him the story of going to Monsignor Bonner with 965 freshman boys and 550 of them trying out for the freshman basketball team. Only 10 of them made the team. He enjoyed anything laced in the history of the Catholic League. He always wanted to practice and ask questions. I was able to connect with an entire group of high school students at Archbishop Kennedy High School, because I was able to play basketball. Being involved in basketball had a mentoring influence on Joe. He was a good student and is a good man.

Joe received his degree in English literature and taught high school for many years. Now, he owns a coffee business. He has been someone that I continue to see periodically. I always enjoy his company. He invited me many times, once or twice a year, to say Mass for his team. He was always grateful for that. I've attended a number of games that he's coached.

My coaching style resonated with Joe. I emphasized to my players to enjoy the game, to internalize the game to learn something deeper about themselves; to discover and use the talents with which God had blessed them. My coaching style once led an official to comment, "This team is one of the most disciplined I've ever seen."

After dialing back, as Fr. Murray had instructed, and finding a way to connect with my students through athletics, I began to get more adjusted to teaching and mentoring. I found new ways to deepen my relationship with my students.

When I met Brian Bransfield, he was a sophomore. His mother died when he was in eighth grade. He was very shy. He frequently came up to me after class. His demeanor reminded me of the stories of Nicodemus. He never asked questions in class, but after class, it was always, "Father, can I see you?" Of course, I obliged every time.

I tried to get him to ask his questions in class so his classmates would benefit. By his senior year, he came out of his shell and was asking questions in class regularly. I helped Brian navigate high school, which was difficult. He was the fourth of five children, but his mother's death made for a very difficult life situation. The simple act of telling the story of my dad's death was an inspiration to him. He was profiled in the *Catholic Standard and Times*. He mentioned me as the one who had the most influence on his decision to become a priest. Even while in the seminary he would come to visit me and I often visited him when he was in his first assignment as a priest. Our conversations proved fruitful in helping him negotiate different challenges that present themselves in the early days of priesthood.

Today, Brian serves the secretary for the U.S. Catholic Bishop's Conference. It's an important position for the church in the United States. At the time of this writing, he has written seven books. That's unbelievable! His books are all spiritually driven. He wrote one on the addiction to pornography, which is very timely. He has attended bishops' conferences in Poland and Rome. He gives presentations on relevant church topics and spiritual retreats to priests throughout the United States.

A Wave of Exciting Projects

While I was at Archbishop Kennedy, almost simultaneously, another young teacher was having a similar effect on the student body at Bishop McDevitt High School in Wyncote, Pa.

In 1982, Mrs. McKenna had begun her second year teaching in the secondary school system of the Archdiocese of Philadelphia. She, too, was young and energetic. In the middle of her first year, she was moved to teaching seniors, with a minor revolt by the junior class she had to leave behind.

In June 1986, I was appointed School Minister for Bishop McDevitt High School, which was technically a part of the school's administration. Since my residence was at St. James, a feeder parish, I already had a familiarity and reputation with many students and parents.

All of the administrators had to give a presentation for the new school year in September 1986. I talked about cognitive structure, without using that phrase. As an educator, the word means to lead out of the darkness of ignorance into the light of knowledge, wisdom, truth, and understanding; and in my position, into the truth of the Gospel. I explained that everybody has his or her life experiences and to the degree that we are attentive to our life experiences, we will be able to acquire intelligent understanding and make reasonable judgments and good decisions. We are aided tremendously as educators by understanding ourselves.

Mrs. McKenna and I taught Junior Morality. The year moved along with hardly a nod between us until I volunteered a guest speaker for the junior classes. He was a young man from St. Joseph's University with a message and a request for Aid for Children, a Campaign Against Hunger. I introduced the young man, who gave a wonderful presentation. Mrs. McKenna promised to get involved in the project with her class.

A Balloon Launch for Hunger Awareness on the front lawn of Bishop McDevitt made headlines and memories, plus it raised thousands of dollars for food for hungry children in underdeveloped nations. It was our first collaboration.

Easter 1986 class retreats were scheduled for Holy Week. No regularly scheduled classes would be held. It eased us all into a needed spring break.

My homily began with a humorous story about being small as a child and growing into the big guy I am now at 5-foot-8. Mrs. McKenna sensed a setup with the story. She was right, but not prepared to be radically affected by what was to come. Included in this homily was a metaphor to understand the Eucharist. It was the story of my dad and his death, but more importantly to Mrs. McKenna, a story of my mother, left with four young children to raise. Mrs. McKenna left after the homily in tears. I never knew until much later that the story had provided strength for her to raise her two children, also fatherless.

After the successful balloon launch, our next collaboration was a retreat in September 1987. We took a group of students on a retreat to Camp Neumann, in Bucks County, Pa., with a team from the diocese, which conducted the retreat. It was a mini-kairos experience, which eventually developed into a successful retreat program for high school students, nationwide. At the retreat, a mime was performed as a part of a prayer service.

Mrs. McKenna had a degree in theatre arts. After the retreat, she came to me and said, "You want that to happen at McDevitt? It can happen."

We created a mime and enlisted students to perform. The mime symbolically offered Jesus as a way through the obstacles and traps, which high school students experience, such as underage drinking, drug abuse, and engaging in sex before marriage. The mime became the centerpiece for the senior retreat and was well received by the senior class. Next, it was performed for the faculty, freshmen, sophomore and junior classes.

In 1988, I presented Mrs. McKenna with the idea of creating skits about chastity. By now, she had learned that if I had an idea and she could flesh it out, it would be not only worthwhile, but also full of grace.

We set to recruiting students, eventually receiving 12 commitments to the project. They began writing skits, a few written by Mrs. McKenna, a few from her homework assignments, and a few from students. "Inasense" was born. It was staged, choreographed, rehearsed, and videotaped.

A morality play of scenes was developed with the virtue of chastity shown to be a valued life choice. The scenes were about struggles with conscience, drinking and partying, a game show on the purpose of sexuality, falling into "too much too soon," the tragic response of an unwanted pregnancy ending in abortion. Twelve scenes were presented with the prevailing message on the benefits of "waiting until marriage" to experience the intimacy of the sexual expression.

I set out to promote and publicize "Inasense" and it went "viral" (before that was even a commonly used term)! The "Inasense" troop was covered in the Philadelphia Inquirer, The Catholic Standard and Times, Channel 6 AM Philadelphia, and Reel to Real Channel 17. Requests for performances flooded the ministry office. The student and parent response was immensely positive. The audience was filled with spirit.

It was fast moving and extremely entertaining, yet a remarkable teaching tool. After the program was over, we would hold a question and answer period at the assemblies. Some high school students could really be rough and ask extremely personal and direct questions. I felt that we couldn't expose the high school students to that, yet they rose to the occasion. Perhaps a peer response like this carried more weight than words I might have spoken as "the priest." One student stunned a group of high school students by saying that the performers truly believed in the message. "We're like you, we struggle with this, but in the long run, it's more freeing and liberating," he said. This really impressed me.

This collaboration was one part of my mission for the Bishop McDevitt community, but it didn't stop there. Our formation of the urban-suburban partnership really took off, as well, which was similar to Habitat for Humanity. We took 16- and 17-year-old students to what was the toughest neighborhood in North Philadelphia, at 23rd and Burks, in order to help repair impoverished homes.

We also introduced students to another section of Philadelphia on Saturday evenings to feed the homeless. The students were trained on how to handle various situations before embarking on their mission. Participants left with us from the McDevitt parking lot at 5:30 p.m. to go down to Center City and hand out bagged lunches to the homeless.

This all took place over the course of two to three years. These were very productive enterprises. Almost everything we attempted to present to the students of McDevitt was extremely well received.

As the moderator of the football team, I attended many school events. I was not just going about the school day and then disappearing. Because the principal recognized that our adult involvement elicited great response from students, we received the help we needed.

During my three-year tenure at Bishop McDevitt, the community suffered three tragic deaths. A freshman on a skateboard was killed in a collision with a car; a junior succumbed to cancer in a matter of months from the time it was diagnosed; and a drunk driver killed a senior – slated to begin studying at Notre Dame University – walking across the street during senior week.

At all three untimely deaths I tried to be an ever-present source of prayer and strength to the struggling students, the suffering parents, and the school community that was mourning.

Despite these tragic times, it really was an extremely fruitful three years. I could not have done that on my own. I just didn't have the time, energy, or skill to organize all facets of our projects. The talent Mrs. McKenna brought to many of these activities was the driving force. It was so much more important to us both to be able to teach the Gospel through living action than to have the students take notes and pass tests.

The McDevitt community would say that in every case, every situation, every relationship, every circumstance, with great intensity I could be found laughing, joking, crying, high-fiving, cheering, encouraging, uplifting, rejoicing, reflecting, watching, and praying. This allowed the human experience to set the stage for the divine to breakthrough. Mrs. McKenna put it best: "He is school minister, retreat master, teacher, coach; but most of all, he is a priest."

CHAPTER 30
New Challenges Arise

"You cannot escape the responsibility of tomorrow by evading it today."

—Abraham Lincoln (1809 – 1865)

My time at St. Charles of Borromeo Seminary spanned seven years, beginning in September 1989 as a member of the newly formed Formation Faculty. By January 1990, I was appointed as acting dean of the theology division and continued in that role until June 1991. I was reluctant to be dean.

The Formation Faculty was to assist the seminarians grow in human formation, intellectual formation, pastoral formation, and spiritual formation. This would be outlined and enforced in Pope John Paul II's *Pastores dabo vobis*. In time other seminaries adopted this Formation Faculty structure.

I didn't know what my role was supposed to entail at first, but meeting Fr. William McNamara at Seton Hall in a summer 1989 workshop on priestly formation offset much of that unease and uncertainty. When a soul is open, it is given to know what is needed.

Fr. McNamara's workshop was full of spirit, an enlightening experience. It was an opportunity to get out of the small parochial world of just Philadelphia. I found it very refreshing and an expansion of my personal horizons.

I returned to my work excited. I was able to bring Fr. McNamara to St. Charles Seminary. He brought Mother Tessa Belecki and Fr. Dave Denney. Together they provided conferences and a retreat to the seminarians that were very well received.

I met with fourth college and second theology on a weekly basis, discussing my pastoral experiences in rectory/parish life and teaching high school, helping seminarians to anticipate what they may experience as priests.

Seminarians needed a place to "come away and pray." Surely the beautiful chapels at St. Charles are that. Within the magnificent building where classes were held, the Formation Faculty, with the help of Sara and Claude Lessard, re-imagined two large and beautiful rooms. No longer mere classrooms, they became meditative spaces for student to come for a few moments, a bit of an escape from the strictly shaped academic structure of studies, field assignments, and other tasks. The one room admitted of a flowing fountain surrounded by living plants. The other suggested the calm and quiet of a desert. The flowing waters and peaceful environment promoted a feeling of restfulness. These formation rooms enabled the seminarians a place to reflect on their vocation to the priesthood. To me, creating an "environment" of tranquility and silence that is visible and audible goes a long way in helping one develop a proper internal disposition to life and to prayer.

Our faith has to embrace fresh language and fresh ways of presenting the Gospel. It will not be handed on without making the necessary adjustments and adaptations to the particular young man who's presenting himself to be a priest. Faith is a dynamic gift that needs constant refreshing. Instead of a deductive method from high to low, you have to learn how to work from the ground up and move people up the mountain of faith.

My most treasured memory of my time on the faculty at St. Charles was being able to work with other priests. That was very enriching. We shared a common vision and a common desire to help these new guys, many of whom would eventually be ordained priests, reflect Gospel values and Gospel truth, and live them in a holy and wholesome way.

After 24 years of service at the seminary, Dan Murray, a monsignor at this point, was assigned to be a pastor. He was replaced in 1994. I knew my time there was also running out.

In May 1996, I was assigned to St. Albert the Great in Huntington Valley, Pa. I had requested to be assigned to a parish in order to be closer to my mother, whose health was failing. This was not close to her.

In September 1996, I was assigned to St Cyril in East Lansdowne. By June 1997, my mother's health had declined significantly, and I was granted a leave of absence to be her primary caretaker, that lasted one year.

CHAPTER 31
The Dark Days

"Experience is a hard teacher, because she gives the test first, the lesson afterward."

—Vernon Sanders Law

I arrived at Good Shepherd in Southwest Philadelphia on Monday, June 15, 1998 at high noon. The first phone call I received was from Tim Votta informing me that his brother, Bob, ordained in May 1979, had died of brain cancer the day before. Bob was the deacon for my first Mass. We were good friends throughout our seminary years. We were assigned together on field education placements – North Light Boys Club in Manayunk. We played basketball and shared a common understanding of priesthood. Bob was 44 years old when he died, giving 19 years of priestly service to the Church.

Two weeks later, I was installed as pastor of Good Shepherd parish, which was the home parish of Bob Votta.

One hour after my arrival, the parish secretary informed me that $1,500 of tuition money (cash) was missing. I asked her if she had any clue how this cash had disappeared. She did not know. This is all she knew: she had put it in a locked metal box in her desk at 10 a.m. and had discovered it missing at 12:45 p.m.

My first night, I reviewed bank statements, bank accounts, and check books, only to discover glaring mistakes, miscalculations, and misspellings. It is unusual for a pastor to call the Archdiocese Office of Audits and request an audit, even more so only after two days into a new assignment.

In my first two years, I was more a detective than a pastor. I uncovered three major embezzlements: one by the principal of the elementary school in the amount of $134,000 with indisputable hard evidence, one by the aforementioned secretary in the amount of $40,000, and one by a seminarian in the amount of $10,000. The seminarian admitted stealing parish money when confronted, paid restitution, and resigned from the seminary, and returned to live at home.

I met with the secretary privately to address my findings. She acknowledged her struggles with alcohol abuse and drug addiction to me in this meeting. I informed her that if she cooperates and gets immediate help, she could keep her job.

With crocodile tears and two rivers of black mascara streaming down her cheeks, she thanked me, told me she would call the emergency contact number that I gave to her.

The next day, she returned to the rectory and handed me a six-page letter accusing me of harassing her. This served as supporting documentation for her eventual termination, due to the many grammatical and syntactical errors and misspellings contained in the letter.

She called me on two occasions after her last day, Aug. 7, threatening to kill me.

The last embezzlement I uncovered, regarding the elementary school and the principal, took a full year-and-a-half before it was finally resolved.

A lifetime parishioner of Good Shepherd and the volunteer "business manager" hinted that there were irregularities regarding the last two years in school. For example, the principal held a sleepover for 20 students in the gym and charged $40 a student. She claimed she spent $500 of the $800 budget on popcorn to feed the 20 students.

I responded that the Phillies do not spend that much money on popcorn at Veteran's Stadium to feed 40,000 fans.

The principal was away for most of July and August. When she returned, I informed her that the secretary had been fired for financial mismanagement. I also informed her that a seminarian is no longer studying to be a priest and is no longer living in the rectory, and furthermore a diocesan auditor would be reviewing the school, the convent, church and rectory.

To all of this, she replied, "Is something wrong?"

I replied, "Yes, there are serious misappropriations of parish and school funds."

I was forced to close the elementary school, which incited a great deal of anger. I tried to salvage this financial burden first by attempting to sell the building to the Philadelphia School District, an attempt that did not materialize. My leasing the building to charter schools only resulted in more vandalism and damage.

There was an incident where an 18-year-old stole a very expensive statue of St. Martin de Porres – the only saint of African origin in the Western Hemisphere, known for freeing African slave women[44] – from the rectory. I ran him down, tackled him to the ground, and had him arrested.

An action like this is something for which you cannot always prepare, but for which you have to be willing to risk. It would be an easier path to just close your eyes and hope that other community leaders would take a role.

The responsibility I received from my father as "business partner" when I was 4 years old led to my eventual willingness to take an active role in correcting wrongdoing. I felt that as a church leader, it was necessary to have a presence in the neighborhood. Today, Pope Francis strongly encourages priests leave the "stuffy sacristies" and "go out to the peripheries."

I visited every registered member of that parish. That hadn't been done in years, having once been a practice in all of the churches of the Archdiocese of Philadelphia. I felt it was necessary and good. As pastor, you go and bless a family's home, but you also listen to their concerns. You learn a great deal and then you try to come up with a way to heal the wounds of an individual family or of an entire community.

Meanwhile there was the ever-present mentally challenged man, who would come to daily Mass with a portable phone (not a cellphone) in his hand and carry on an imaginary conversation. In the middle of celebrating Mass, he would approach me on the altar, hand me the phone, saying, "It's for you Father." On another occasion, he moved up and down the center aisle of church as though he was landing an airplane, and would loudly recite the Lord's Prayer with "It's MY FATHER!" He was often found ranting up and down the street in front of Church. The parishioners angrily asked for his removal, but I insisted on letting him be there.

In St. Mark's Gospel, Jesus attended to the blind Bartimeus when he cried out as He passed by. Peter and James healed a beggar at the gate in the Acts of the Apostle's, which got them thrown into to jail in the name of Jesus. I hoped I was doing the right thing.

My time at Good Shepherd posed a pastoral challenge of trying to minister to three distinct groups, which for the most part, kept an arms-length distance from one another. The old guard was a group of white community members. The Vietnamese were a newer group of residents who kept mostly to themselves. The African-American population, mostly from Liberia, was also growing in the parish.

What might bring those three communities together? It was a great challenge. It was something to which I gave much prayer.

When you would come into Good Shepherd church you'd instantly notice that it was a magnificent church. The dwindling white community sat to the far left on the Blessed Mother's side. The Vietnamese sat on the far right. The Liberians took their seats in the middle.

I watched this pattern occur over and over again, week after week. The parish council and I tried coffee and donuts to get them to socialize with one another. That didn't work out, initially. Until finally, it dawned on me: I'm going to have to get everybody to come into the middle to receive Holy Communion. So, I changed the pattern for distribution of Holy Communion.

To receive the Sacred Host, everybody had to come to the two ministers distributing the Eucharist in the center aisle and receive the Precious Blood from the cup on the two side aisles. After doing that for several weeks, believe it or not, the three communities began to come together as a parish. Can you believe it? It was all made possible by a simple change in the way people approached the altar to receive the Eucharist. Theologically, the source of unity, my changing the schematics symbolically brought together these three disparate groups.

They began to engage one another. In such a simple gesture were the beginnings of a turnaround in the isolation of the three communities into one. Then we had coffee and donuts and there was a marked difference in the behavior of all three groups. "Coffee and donuts" slowly became a meeting ground as parishioners began to engage each other. Quietly the parish became "community." It was not this way in the neighborhood.

There were many Catholics, not practicing their faith. They weren't seeing the unity occurring in the church, so they stayed in their biased positions. The neighborhood was not only in transition, it was in decline, decay, and depression. I took photos of burned down and neglected house. I understood that constantly having that environment "screaming" at you negatively affected any vision and hope.

I saw the detriment of the neighborhood leak into the parish. Good Shepherd was also the parish to a tall, single, white woman, who seemingly didn't want the 1950s to end. She was a very pious woman. She would come in and pray, but then make demands on everybody. She didn't like the fact that I was trying to welcome the Liberian community to the parish. "Maybe they should have their own church," she'd say. She reminded me of a female Archie Bunker.

On Monday, May 15, 2000, she expressed her prejudice and racism toward African Americans acting as a spokeswoman for several other parishioners who were displeased with my attempt to reach out to that community and welcome them into the parish, giving as an example, my baptizing black children during Mass.

She always wanted to be the last to receive Holy Communion. If we would be running out of hosts, we would have to break the host into smaller fragments. She would say, "Don't ever give me a fragment of the host." She thought if she only got a fragment, she wasn't getting the Risen Body of Christ. It was bad theology. Despite her nastiness, I visited her in the hospital and brought communion to her in her home while she was sick. I did some of the things that would've been done in the 1950s that she appreciated.

In trying to bring the community together and bring it up to date, some still voiced displeasure and resentment.

As a pastor, you deal with people who have physical, mental, emotional, social, and spiritual issues. You can't predict a person's receptivity to personal growth. Yet, you're called upon to be patient, listen, understand, and then come up with a creative strategy that will help them grow to a point in which they can take care of themselves and eventually answer the calling to mentor others.

This takes a priest being available, being approachable, being friendly, being willing to listen, going back and trying to understand, and praying, trying to come up with a way that can break through personal dysfunction and spiritual paralysis.

Jesus would heal people who were physically paralyzed. There's a spiritual and emotional paralysis, too. Jesus would heal people who were blind or deaf, but there's also spiritual blindness and deafness. Some only hear what they want to hear and dismiss everything else.

Parishes are complex organisms, and sometimes they fall into an evil pattern: people know how to scapegoat and rid themselves of a pastor, mostly by making so much noise and trouble that the situation becomes unbearable to everyone concerned. Because they know how to do this, it becomes what they do, again and again. Over the years if a parish is not healthy, this pattern of behavior takes a toll.

St. Paul would liken the effort to bring the Gospel to others as planting seeds. You triumph if you plant the seeds. Jesus and St. Paul would caution not to think that you have to see the planted seeds break ground, blossom, and bloom. Someone else might have to come along and water, nourish, and refresh the seed that you planted. Someone else might come along and see the fruits of those labors. I've had experiences where people have made what I would call a true, breakthrough conversion, by the diligent work of those who have sown seed.

I'm reminded of the words of Fr. Murray at my ordination, as he described the role of a priest. "The priest becomes the living reminder of God to his community as Peter, Paul, John were to theirs," he said. "The Priest hears, sees, touches, and tastes so intimately the Word, Who is Life. How can he be other than a living reminder that all we hear, see, touch, and taste reminds us of God, of the origin and purpose of our lives? Tom, as priest, you are to reveal the connection between our sufferings, and the story of God's suffering in Jesus. You are to reveal the connection between our life, and the life of God within us.

"As priest you are the living reminder that our faith is the achievement of ages, an effort accumulated over the centuries; you are the living reminder that if we cut off our rich past, we paralyze our future. You are the living reminder that the true test of character is not whether we follow the daily fashion, but whether the past is alive in our present."

The Hard Times Continue

By June 1999, the school and the convent were empty and I was left to figure out what to do with these two unoccupied buildings. I spoke to a representative of the Bartram Cluster of the Philadelphia School District that summer. He informed me that due to the lack of funds from Harrisburg, the decision of Superintendent Hornbeck to step down, and the change in membership with the school board, the Philadelphia School District would not purchase the convent in the near future. He informed me that aside from the cost of purchasing the convent for $600,000, the school board would need $750,000 for renovations.

I projected an August 2000 date, which was dismissed immediately. Pressed further, he responded by saying that the cost to purchase and renovate the building would prohibit the school district from purchasing the convent in the near future, but that he was attending a meeting on July 24 to which he would bring my concerns.

The parish needed to find a prospective buyer. It was suggested to me that it be used as a halfway house. I decided we should pursue that. I was informed that St. Bonaventure's rectory in North Philadelphia is used as a halfway house.

The next three months were filled with vandalism, robbery, and even murder, within the boundaries of the Good Shepherd community. The straw that broke the camel's back for me occurred on Sunday, Oct. 15, 2000, 10 minutes before the 11 a.m. liturgy.

I approached a parishioner who was talking to a woman in her 20s in front of the Blessed Mother statue in the church. The parishioner informed me that this woman wanted to drop off food and volunteered to take the young woman into the rectory. The young woman claimed she had made arrangements to do so with "one of the Fathers," yet she could not give me a name.

I then asked the woman if she was alone. She told me that there was another woman with her. I told her to wait and I went in to the sacristy.

"Make sure that she has the food with her when you take her into the rectory," I said to the male sacristan. "I will take care of setting up for Mass."

I gave the sacristan strict instructions to stay with the two women until they left. The sacristan accompanied the two women into the rectory to deliver the food; however, he left them alone and returned to church. I told an altar server to tell him to go back to the rectory. When he returned, the women were no longer there.

He went upstairs to discover that they were in my suite. He asked them what they were doing. They told him that they were "jumping on the bed." He proceeded to escort them out of the rectory.

He then called the police and they told him to ask me if anything was missing from my room. After Mass, I went to my room and discovered $25 in change, $300 of All Souls money plus the All Souls envelopes, $360 of block collection cash, $150 of Mass Intention money, and approximately $200 of personal money all missing from securely locked drawers and closets within my quarters. They must have found the keys I hid in a coffee cup being used as a bookend.

I discovered later on Monday, Oct. 16, that these women attempted to rob Saint James Episcopal Church shortly after 8 a.m. on Sunday, Oct. 15, and also attempted to rob St. Clements Church shortly after 9 a.m. on the same day. They were unsuccessful in those two locations. The women were later identified from their attempted robbery of St. James Episcopal.

The Good Shepherd community endured more vandalism, robberies, and murder over the course of the next three years of my service, which concluded in June 2003.

I felt as if a millstone were hanging from my neck until somehow each one of those cases was finally resolved. I talked long and hard with my spiritual director, Msgr. Murray, who gave great guidance and said, "Even though they're telling you to just forget about it and let go, you have to be true to your own conscience and address it, but you also have to learn how to recoup your own life without that becoming a consuming preoccupation."

A Sense of Loneliness

When I arrived at Good Shepherd in June 1998, there was a feeling amongst the parishioners that the archdiocese was abandoning this parish. By June 1999 the three priests living in the rectory reduced to one – only me. In its heyday, the rectory was home to six priests. The needs of the parish did not warrant three priests.

I think when a priest lives alone without having another priest with whom he can confide; this isolation may allow unhealthy patterns of living to go unchecked. I don't know if that issue has been addressed fully, to this day.

The interesting thing is, the only way I survived the craziness of being the pastor at Good Shepherd was by being a good, faithful, disciple of the Lord. I celebrated the Eucharist, sought out the Lord through the sacrament of reconciliation, prayed, had my friendships outside of the parish, and made sure I exercised. Most importantly, I took time for leisure.

In order to understand myself, I had to remember the words of Msgr. Murray's homily at my ordination: you have to search your memories.

"In the Old Testament, remembering is never simply looking back nostalgically at past events," he explained. "To remember is to bring those events into the present and celebrate them here and now. To remember is to participate in and have an intimate encounter with the real acts of God's love. Through memory, a gulf is spanned. That's why they remembered Abraham, Isaac, Jacob; that's why they remembered the Exodus every year. To remember is to recapture the original vision. The first words of Genesis indicate this: "In the beginning... The entire Bible can be summed up in one word: 'Remember!'"

Further, Msgr. Murray wove this idea into the life and suffering of Jesus. "And so when Jesus says, 'Do this in memory of Me,' He wants His friends to make all they have experienced, and will experience with Him a present reality; He wants them to remember so as to participate in and celebrate His life, death and resurrection; He wants them to remember so as to capture the original vision. Jesus' friends did not forget.

"In fact they state that their first obligation to the people is to make them remember what they have received and already know. Peter says: 'I consider it my duty to keep refreshing your memory as long as I live, even though you already know and are firmly rooted in the truth you possess.' Paul tells the Romans that he has no doubt of their goodness; nevertheless he writes to refresh their memory, and writes somewhat boldly at times, because he considers it his priestly duty to do so. John tells us that Jesus promised the Spirit who will remind us of all He taught and more besides."

If you don't have flexibility in a parish setting, you'll never survive. School has a fixed pattern and structure to it. A parish doesn't. Although at times I felt that loneliness as a pastor at Good Shepherd, I am still grateful for the experience and the lessons I learned, which I took with me over the next 15 years of my vocation in order to better serve new neighborhoods and other parish communities.

CHAPTER 32
Physical Illness and Spiritual Wounds

The millstone in front of the church reminds all of us to take Jesus's words seriously. "Whoever causes one of these little ones who believe in me to sin, it would be better for him to have a great millstone hung around his neck and to be drowned in the depths of the sea." (Matthew 18:6). The millstone is a visible reminder of the serious consequences that are involved in ignoring Gospel mandates. To those who have had their bodies violated, their trust betrayed and their faith shattered, we pray for healing.

—Millstone Installation outside St. Matthew Church, Conshohocken, Pa.

I was appointed as pastor of St. Gabriel in Norwood, Pa., in June 2003 and spent five years there. The parish house and church at Saint Gabriel's when I arrived was in disrepair. The pastor, whom I replaced, invited me to visit before I was to take over. He walked me up to his room, he pointed to a chair, and told me to sit down. He sat down in a chair close by and the chair broke. I sat down in the chair he told me to occupy, and it, too broke.

He laughed heartily and said, "This is what you are inheriting." He asked if I wanted the room painted before I arrived. I looked at the bare walls and noticed it hadn't been painted in many years.

Shortly after my arrival, I began to experience significant adverse health issues – rashes on my skin, distended stomach, profuse perspiring, raspy voice – all while saying Mass in the Parish House Chapel.

One night at dinner, I detected an unpleasant odor, but initially could not figure out from where it was coming. With careful attentiveness, I realized it was coming from the bookcase.

I asked Father John Large, "Who owns these books?"

He replied, "They were left behind from when the St. Joe nuns occupied the building as a convent in the early 90's."

The carpet throughout the building was never stretched or shampooed. It looked like somebody worked on a car engine on it in many parts of the building. There was very little artwork on the walls. Under microscopic observation, I was made aware of two different types of mold festering in the chapel's paneled walls.

The convent building, now the parish house, sat on a high-water table and a sewer system. My personal physician and an environmental doctor wrote a letter to the Archdiocese in April 2004, declaring to them that the rectory "is a sick building and should be demolished." No action was taken.

Shortly thereafter, I was diagnosed with Celiac Disease, which doctors said was triggered by two types of mold. I remained at St. Gabriel's from June 2003 until December 2003. Health issues forced me to accept a temporary assignment at Our Lady of Charity in Brookhaven.

Upon my return to St. Gabriel's, I initiated a Capital Campaign to clean up the church and the parish house. Before this project started, I remember a conversation I had with one of the parish secretaries. I entered her office, which was in terrible disarray. Her desk, tilted, only had three legs. Since there was zero cabinet space in the office, there were stacks of papers in every inch of available space. Yet, somehow, this secretary managed to have the personal organization to know where everything was!

After absorbing the visual disarray, I couldn't help but notice a very unpleasant odor. I asked her if she also detected the smell.

She said, "You mean like the odor of a subway station in Philadelphia?"

"Yes," I responded.

"Oh you'll get used to that," she said. "We all have."

I visited the classrooms in the school every day and also visited and taught in the PREP program. I was involved in visiting the sick, homebound, nursing home, and hospital. The parish averaged three funerals per week. In one four-month period, I sadly buried six suicides – a young, 10-year-old who'd hung himself in a bathroom, an 80-year-old man weary of caring for his sickly wife, a 43-year-old father who, with his two teenaged children at home, shot himself on their front porch, and a 30-year-old man and two teenage girls who, on separate occasions had jumped in front of oncoming trains.

Saint Gabriel in Norwood was four miles from Good Shepherd Parish. The people of the parish had their roots in the city of Philadelphia, but due to working at Scott Paper and General Electric, were able to purchase a single home in the suburbs. However, in 2003, the economy declined and these two places of employment shut down. Significant unemployment and alcohol and drug abuse played major destructive roles in the lives of many parishioners.

I remember finishing baptisms one Sunday afternoon in June and walking back to the rectory. An elderly gentleman on a motorcycle approached me and asked if he could speak to me. I agreed. He parked his bike outside the parish house and we entered the office. He began by saying that he was going to kill his grandson who was addicted to drugs and was stealing from him and his wife. I tried to have a reasonable conversation with the distraught man. He was not receptive. To show me how serious he was about his decision, he pulled out a loaded gun and placed it on the desk that separated us.

When I asked him why he'd come to me, he said, "My brother told me to speak to a priest before you kill your grandson."

Following this 10-minute exchange, I went to the Norwood Police Department to report the man about whom, the police officer told me, they were already aware.

A Much Needed Break

Because there had been no rectifying the physical plant at St. Gabriel's my health again deteriorated. In October 2007, for the second time, I had to leave the parish house and find refuge in another rectory. While residing at Sacred Heart rectory in Manoa, I divided my eight months between hospital visits for my personal health conditions and assisting at the parish whenever needed.

In June 2008, Monsignor Tim Senior asked me to assist Father Jim Hutchins at Saint Pius X in Broomall while keeping my residence at Sacred Heart. St. Pius was an uplifting experience.

Prior to my appointment at St. Pius, I was suffering from serious self-doubt. It almost immediately left me, and for the first time in a very long while, I felt that everything had fallen into place, that I was operating "on all cylinders."

I visited classrooms at the school and found the students engaging. One day, as I walked across the schoolyard, an enthusiastic young girl shouted in a deep, raspy voice, "Hey Fr. Heron! How's it going?!" I was amazed that a youngster could have such a booming voice! It was music to my ears, a balm for my soul.

During my assignment at St. Pius, I would come to enjoy very positive feedback from the community. It was truly an affirming experience, a healing remedy for all I'd been through with personal illness as well as the weight of having known so much despair and death over the course of the previous 10 years.

Soon enough a priest learns to deal with being demonized or deified for certain actions. Neither reaction, we come to realize is necessarily true and both, dwelt upon for too long, can cause a priest to lose perspective.

In your vocation, in order to find your place in salvation history – your purpose in the world – you must be aware of grace in the present moment and in retrospect. You can find new meaning in the resurrected order of living your faith, your memory, and your love.

In retrospect, grace was flowing in my life through my life when six suicides occurred in the St. Gabriel community. Grace was pouring out and over a brief personal encounter I had with a dying parishioner at St. Pius Parish about whom I'll speak in a later chapter. It is only after Karen Purcell was born into eternal life that I was given a new understanding of the Resurrection.

There are some moments in life that fade away in a manner of minutes, hours, days, or weeks. The lights go out, darkness envelopes a person, and you forget. There are other moments that can inspire you for 20 years. The difference between the novice student and the wise disciple of Jesus is that the wise disciple of Jesus knows to remain attentive to the disconnectedness in times of darkness. Those moments return and one's understanding evolves.

At St. Pius, I was able to do communion calls, which I enjoyed. It was kind of like my backyard. I had the great opportunity to be connected to Sacred Heart, St. Pius, and St. Anastasia's, which were all in close proximity on West Chester Pike. I was able to cast a wide net.

Those experiences both inside and outside of every assignment I had as a priest were linked to the celebration of the Eucharist in the church. From my work in schools, the PREP program, communion calls, hospital visits, my goal was to connect people's humanity to divine love. Grace was alive and flowing, and the current of energy traveling up and down this metaphorical cable connection between this community and God was strong – so much so that I experienced it with all of my senses and felt it in my very soul.

I didn't have to work to find grace hidden within chaos. I wasn't the pastor. I didn't have administrative responsibilities. This gave me the opportunity to simply interact with people. Since I was struggling with Celiac Disease, it was a good time to serve in this type of role. In terms of just enjoying being a priest, it was a good experience. It was relaxing and a lot of fun, but as is the nature of this vocation – and anybody's life – I would once again have to move on.

Pastor Again

I received a call from Msgr. Tim Senior, who asked if I was interested in becoming a pastor again. I accepted the opportunity to return to St. James in Elkins Park, Pa., in June 2009, – this time as pastor – returning to a familiar place, where I was an active resident priest from 1982 to 1989. Soon, I would realize how much its landscape had changed.

One of the first things I asked the pastor I was replacing was what he recommended I do that he wished he had done. "That's easy," he replied. "Move First Holy Communion from Saturday morning to what the church has recommended since 1965: Sunday Liturgy."

I approached the principal of the school with the idea; she thought it a good one, as did the head of the PREP program, garnering the support of the teachers.

In September 2009, I met with parents to put forward the plan. Although only two out of 40 parents objected, the disdain of those two parents began the swelling of an insurmountable tide of opposition against me.

Around the same time, the school was in jeopardy of closing. The parish was in financial distress. I was faced with raising $300,000 in order to keep the doors open at the school.

Many different circumstances ignited a host of accusations on the part of parishioners to discredit me.

Within the boundaries of the parish lived a Jewish family whose son was kidnapped during a trip to the Middle East. I read about it in the *Philadelphia Inquirer* at the end of August 2009. I immediately went to their home to tell his parents that the parishioners of St. James would be praying for their son's safe return. They were very happy and asked if they could come sometime to thank the parishioners. They came at Christmastime. The parishioners, instead, became very upset.

There are seven synagogues in the boundaries of St. James parish. As a part of my community outreach, I wrote to each of the rabbi's. Two of them invited me to give talks in their synagogues. The congregation picked the topic of Catholic spirituality. I spoke to 250 people at each of the sessions.

A parishioner publicly attacked me in back of the church, in an unsettling, verbal uproar toward the end of my tenure.

"You ruined the school, you ruined the parish, now you're trying to ruin the neighborhood!" The final point predicted on my being too friendly with the Jewish community, which accounted for 65 percent of the neighborhood's population at the time.

People would scream during mass, shouting out horrific things about me, like "He's an evil man!"

The parish financial records were nowhere to be found in the rectory. It took me a long time to put together the pieces, but when I did, I discovered a donation of $1.5 million given more than 20 years prior to my investigation. That money dried up by the time the school's necessity for funds were at the forefront of this parish's list of concerns. We never raised the $300,000 and I had to announce the closing of the school. Unsurprisingly, that caused an uproar.

With the inevitable closing of the school, I decided to lease the school building to those who oversaw the care of special needs Jewish children. Parishioners were appalled and in retaliation, community members painted swastikas on the building. It was abominable, a climate that sickened me.

Surrounding all of this was a drawn-out campaign against me. A small group of individuals first went to the Vicar, then wrote letters to every parent who had a child in second grade, and finally proceeded to meet every week, discussing ways in which to get me removed from St. James and expelled from the priesthood. However, after having to talk to multiple lawyers, it was determined that all of these accusations and others were unfounded.

The attacks were vicious. I was spiritually paralyzed. I would say mass, come back to the rectory, and just sit in a chair. It affected my spiritual and physical health terribly. It was the deepest, darkest valley that I had ever experienced.

"What a scumbag," one unhappy parishioner said of me. "Closes two schools, comes to St. James, destroys the parish, closes our school, and leaves a few months later. I think there is a show about him called *The Closer.*"

The swastikas appeared on the school a second time in August 2010. I called Msgr. Dan Sullivan and said, "This is enough. There's no way I can be in any way effective in St. James parish."

Msgr. Fran Meehan wrote a letter to Msgr. Sullivan as a result of his counsel over my concerns. In it, he said, "I wish to communicate to you my own conviction (added to yours), that Tom has truly suffered huge injustices, unconscionable hostility, shocking defamation, false accusation – all of which seem to have risen to a level of real evil. Sometimes when a good priest is defamed in such a dramatic way, I begin to wonder about demonic forces. By this you understand, I am sure, that I do not accuse Tom's accusers of being demonic people, but simply that a spirit can set in that is an instrument of the demonic – no matter how unconscious and unknowing such a dynamic might be within the individual people involved."

Msgr. Sullivan granted my request, and in September 2010, my 15-month stint at St. James was finally over, as I was appointed as Parochial Vicar at St. Coleman in Ardmore.

CHAPTER 33
Finding Peace

"The abundant love of Father, Son and Holy Spirit does not compel but penetrates our souls by sharpening our ability to cooperate with grace in order to make authentic decisions."

—Anonymous

Father Jim Sherlock, pastor graciously welcomed me to St. Coleman. The parishioners of St. Coleman's were also kind and supportive to me.

I lived and served at St. Coleman for nine months, leaving in June 2011. I was appointed as administrator at St. Matthew's Roman Catholic Church in Conshohocken, Pa.

Upon my arrival, the person who spearheaded the campaign against me at St. James called the principal of St. Matthew's school and told her that every child in the school was vulnerable because of my presence in the parish. I had no choice but to threaten to sue him for defamation of character if he did not discontinue raising these false allegations. Finally, the nightmare was over; the torment ended.

Being at St. Matthew's reinvigorated me. People were hungering for the Bread of Life and hungering for the Living Word of God.

I was familiar with Conshohocken from my four years teaching at Archbishop Kennedy High School. Conshohocken reminded me a lot of my own hometown of Collingdale. They both have a square mile of land. They both had about 8,000 – 10,000 people. They're a hardworking people. There are people who have become successful or famous, but they don't build mansions. They live modestly. They have a genuine concern for the community.

Conshohocken brought back warm memories of my youth, St. Joseph in Collingdale; more particularly, recollections of Fr. Andy Lavin, the parish's pastor, and one of the few priests whose appointment came from

Cardinal Dennis Joseph Dougherty. I have many vivid memories of Fr. Lavin: serving his Masses, ringing the parish bell to announce the death of his brother, Fr. Tim Lavin. Our lives were closely intertwined for the better part of 25 years. His life as a priest inspired me.

In my early days of Conshohocken, I prayed for people, proclaimed the gospel, and served the community. Those are three key responsibilities to being a priest. Your first duty is to pray for people, your second duty is to proclaim the good news, and your third duty is to be of service in the community. Overall, it continues to be an enjoyable pastoral experience.

However, the culture was changing. There are plenty of studies out there – one most recently –reporting that Catholics in the 1980s were between 35 and 40 percent actively practicing their faith. Present day statistics are much more grim. Depending on the research, 20 percent or less are practicing today.

While I was the parochial administrator at St. Matthew's, the parish school closed. That decision was 85 percent made before my arrival. Many parents had already taken their children out of the school. The enrollment went down to 95 students across eight grades. When St. Matthew's merged as Conshohocken Catholic in 1997, their hope was to have a school enrollment of 250. They started with 237 students and each year the enrollment declined until in 2012 enrollment fell under 100 students. It was clear the Conshohocken Catholic could not sustain itself.

There was a major study of the educational system, and archdiocesan officials decided to make the elementary schools regional. So, Conshohocken Catholic School closed, and parents were encouraged to send their children to newly formed regional schools.

In my second week as parochial administrator I was informed that Conshohocken was being considered for a pilot study for the merging of parishes. Eventually, Coatesville was selected. I determined not to initiate any major changes in my first year, but listened attentively to understand the workings of the parish.

Knowing that my colleague, Mary Kay McKenna, was ready for a career change – having taught high school students for 30 years – and aware of an opening at St. Matthew's for a parish director of religious education, I invited her to consider taking the position. I thought it would be a new and invigorating challenge for her. After introducing her to St. Matthew's, she accepted that role and began her new duties on July 9, 2012.

Still, it was a difficult transition. She went from teaching high school students – a position she not only knew well but excelled in – to working with young children, their parents, and parishioners, very unfamiliar territory! By God's grace, under Mary Kay's supervision and my support and encouragement, the PREP Program grew into a visible and active part of parish life.

At Thanksgiving, the children recited grace before meals in the various languages of the families' ethnic heritages: Italian, Spanish, Polish, Gaelic, and Swahili. We celebrated a tree lighting ceremony on the fourth Sunday of Advent in which the children presented, on the altar, the Birth of Jesus according to the Gospel of Luke and closed with the congregation moving to the front lawn to light up the Christmas tree and Nativity for all of Fayette Street. Confirmation and First Communion ceremonies involved much of the parish community again, spotlighting the children receiving the sacrament.

At former parishes I introduced what became an annual tradition. On Pentecost Sunday, following the celebration of Mass, the congregation left the church and assembled outside. With prayer and pomp I released a beautiful, pure white dove from its cage. I enlisted Mary Kay's help to institute that event into parish life at St. Matthew's.

Mary Kay organized a procession of banners of the gifts and fruits of the Holy Spirit to lead the dove to the altar where it was displayed during Mass. At the closing of Mass the entire congregation moved to the front lawn of the church and the dove was released amid the cheers of the people. We continue the tradition yearly. One year, the procession was composed of several sets of twins in the parish of every age, another, families with four generations of parishioners led the dove.

In 2013, Father Gasper Genaurdi stepped down as pastor of Saint's Cosmas and Damian due to health issues. I was appointed administrator of SS Cosmas and Damian and continued as pastor of St. Matthews.

The Mass on the Street, the Merging of Parishes

Every parish experiences tragedy as well as triumph. While at Good Shepherd, St. Gabriel's, and St. James furnished the extremes of sadness and despair a priest may come to experience in a parish community, St. Matthew's has known sorrow. In my tenure here, three suicides and a murder have taken place.

Each parish I have served is touched by divine grace. It is alive and at work. Through it people become instruments of forgiveness, examples of genuine peace and witnesses of love – human and divine. Such human triumph offsets human tragedy.

The Archdiocese of Philadelphia's announcement of closures and mergers wreaked havoc on many church communities. Conshohocken was no different. A study was conducted beginning in September 2013. The result of this study was to merge St. Gertrude's, St. Mary, SS Cosmas and Damian and St. Matthew into one faith community, July 1, 2014.

In May 2013, I called for a parish synod at St. Matthews – a gathering together of all parishioners. Its purpose was to gather together all the various organizations of the parish to reflect on the past and create a plan for the future.

The synod opened with an outdoor Mass on Fayette Street, the feast of St. Matthew, Sunday, Sept. 21, 2013. This was Mary Kay's first big challenge in her new role.

"I watched not only the parish come together in those summer months preceding the Mass, but the entire town come together to support the mass on the street," she recalls, "the mayor, chief of police, fire police, borough council members, and parishioners of every age and group."

Five hundred people attended the mass, and because of its popularity, it was repeated on Divine Mercy Sunday in Spring 2014.

Both masses were spiritually uplifting and well attended. We were fortunate that the weather was glorious on both occasions.

The painful process of merging four parishes into one commenced in October 2013, one month after the synod. Eight meetings followed the initial October 2013 meeting to assess all four parishes' potential to accommodate the parishioners of all four communities.

St. Matthew's was the oldest and most visible parish of the four. It had the most parishioners and was the most sacramentally active parish.

Only two pastors were serving over four parishes at this time. That was an indication of a shortage of priests, which was a key factor in the merging process. One presided over St. Mary's and St. Gertrude's, the other over St. Matthew's and Ss. Cosmas and Damian.

Ultimately, St. Matthew's was selected as the parish for this community and I was appointed pastor of the newly formed, merged parish.

The statues at Ss. Cosmas and Damian and St. Gertrude were brought to St. Matthew's and placed in the Parish Center. Now, they are displayed in the actual church. The former parishioners were very happy about that. We made every attempt to try to be sensitive to the emotional attachment of our new parishioners to their former parishes. We made changes to the bulletin, kept the pastor names, and in a spirit of inclusivity adjusted the sign outside the church to read, "A Newly Formed Parish," listing all four parishes, in alphabetical order, to show the origins of the new St. Matthew's parish formed on July 1, 2014.

In September 2017, an archdiocesan group was to meet to recommend the relegation of St. Mary's. It had yet to be relegated. The other two church properties had been relegated and sold. A day before the meeting, I received a call from Msgr. Sullivan with a proposal from the archbishop. Instead of relegating St. Mary's church, the proposal requested bringing in the Fraternity of St. Peter's Society, a group that only celebrates mass in Latin. The fraternity already has 36 parishes under its care, nationwide. The fraternity is planning to come September 2018.

Hard Work and Goodness Prevails in Conshohocken

Our research and the of the number of baptisms at St. Matthew's each year helped determine a local need for a daycare to be incorporated into the parish. The borough supported this decision, granting us all of the necessary permits. Additionally, we needed a place for PREP, a parish hall, a kitchen, and office space.

The renovations done at St. Matthew's enable the parish to serve the community with daycare service, early childhood service, the PREP program, and parish socials. The offices in the rectory were relocated to the parish center, making for more efficient service to our community.

At the time of this writing, we have more than 300 children in daycare and early childhood programs. There's a waiting list for both programs, which have fulfilled a serious community need.

The construction of the school building, underutilized since June 2012, began in 2015. An area of open concrete walls set beneath the first floor of the school was transformed into a modern, top-notch daycare facility boasting an open playground. The front entry, an open porch, was unable to be used due to major water damage. This was re-fashioned, becoming a portico, enclosed with stained glass windows and a stone sculpture of the Last Supper. It provided a sense of the sacred upon entering the building. As it faced the church, I thought it would be a reverent transition from the church to the newly renovated Parish Center.

Two dedications were held to bless the Parish Center the first in September 2016 with Bishop Michael Fitzgerald presiding, and the second on Sunday, May 20, 2018, with the installation of another stain glass window.

Momentous changes have taken place in the seven years I have served the people of St. Matthew's. My relationship with the Risen Lord enables me not only to be willing to accept the burdens of the parishioners, but to learn how to do so and still deal with my own struggles and challenges.

The action of grace, God's gift of life and love, has strengthened me as pastor to liberate some whose anguish is deep and to lift some of the weight of other's suffering. Grace acts like a "spiritual transfusion." Daily prayer and the reading of Sacred Scripture enables me to go out into the community, as Pope Francis advises, so that "the scent of the sheep" becomes part of my life.

The duty of this assignment has been to unite four distinct parishes – with long histories and traditions – and welcome everyone, comforting the aching hearts of the parishioners. While each of my previous assignments have come with high and lows, I have accepted these challenges each and every day by faithfully attending to my relationship with Father, Son, and Holy Spirit in prayer.

CHAPTER 34
The Work of Salvation

"There is still work to be done, the work of salvation."

—Richard Stern (1928 – 2013)

The vocation of the priesthood is a perilous journey. The vocation of the priest is a call to so immerse himself into the life, suffering, death, and resurrection of Jesus Christ – that His words and His actions penetrate every part of his life so that he can be prepared for his own death.

It is unavoidable: a priest faces death head – on. Often I celebrate three funerals in one week! I try to connect my personal belief in the central mystery of our faith, namely the resurrection; to that of those present at the Mass of Christian burial. I always attempt to unite the mourners by affirming our purpose in having gathered: to pray for the happy repose of the soul of the deceased and to re-examine the reality of death as a crucial component of the Paschal Mystery.

Confronting death is a life-changing event, particularly when the departed is someone you have loved or someone who has loved you.

In that confrontation lies an invitation for us to call upon the Holy Spirit, to ask the Holy Spirit to help us come to a newer, deeper, fuller and richer understanding of life, because life doesn't end with death. Death is not the final word. It is the doorway to eternal life.

In her wisdom the church teaches this: life is changed, not ended. Intrinsic to every funeral mass is the grief of those in attendance. Sometimes the anguish can be so deep as to defy consolation by mere human words.

This is a considerable challenge for a priest. It is precisely why and when we depend of the living word of God to come to our assistance. How to acknowledge anguish that is real and palpable?

It is essential for every priest to unite grief with hope. To do so is to unite earth to heaven. Perhaps even more demanding is to bring sensitivity and love to such articulation, to affirm that the spiritual relationship that the living person has with the deceased is not terminated by physical absence.

This was the most important lesson I was taught by my widowed mother who never imagined her marriage would last a mere seven years. She never stopped speaking about him to the whole family.

At Sunday afternoon dinners, she recounted stories about their first date, their hopes and dreams, and the significance of the bond of faith which united them.

In her simple way, she made it very clear to me – even as a child – that she was deeply in love with my dad even though he had died. Until her death 46 years later, the depth of that yearning and love for him was evident.

The pastor and parish priest tried to be "matchmakers" as did neighbors and siblings. She was widowed at 34 and when she was coaxed into going on a date by their suggesting, "Your four children need a father," her razor sharp response was, "I'd have to love the guy that I'm marrying."

The implication was clear although many couldn't grasp the fact that she was still in love with her husband. This truth was palpable to me until the day she died.

I have no doubt that the deceased communicate with the living through dreams, memory, faith, and love. It is healthy and good to be attentive to those experiences and unafraid to share them. Oftentimes, they are catalyst to comfort and healing.

The life of Jesus cannot be grasped without embracing suffering, death, and resurrection. It is the meaning and model of the Paschal Mystery. As human beings, we're inclined to skip past the suffering and death and bask in the resurrected order of living. However, suffering and death, as the Master showed us, are the way to arrive at resurrection. Without Jesus' dying and rising, death would be the final word. It takes a mature desire to be a disciple of Jesus, to cling to His being the way, the truth, and the life.

Life is as fragile as our breath. Built into that reality is the inescapable fact that we all shall die. "For the wages of sin is death, but the gift of God is eternal life in Christ Jesus our Lord." (Romans 6:23) The Gospels offer us countless ways of grasping the mystery of life and death: Jesus' words, his action in images and stories, and finally and definitively by His own willingness to suffer, die, and ultimately be raised from the dead and so rob death of its sting. Death is swallowed up in victory. "Where, O death, is your victory? Where, O death, is your sting?" (1 Corinthians 15:55).

There's a tale told about two people in their late 20's who grew up as friends. They had graduated from college and entered the work force but still labored under a great deal of stress. They had burning questions and considerable uncertainty about their future. They felt they needed some guidance.

They learned that a holy man was living in a desolate area near a body of water. One day they decided to make the 50-mile journey to visit him. The warmth of his greeting impressed them. They blurted out, "Our lives are directionless, filled with doubt and confusion." The old monk smiled when they asked to be his disciples.

He said, "Come with me." And so, the two friends followed the monk to the nearby lake. He motioned them forward, and soon enough, they were standing in the lake with the monk!

All at once he clasped their heads and thrust them under water for what seemed to the young men to be an eternity. Releasing his grip the friends, reeling from lack of oxygen, began gasping and coughing and struggling for breath.

The monk calmly inquired of them, "What did you need more than anything in the world when your heads were under the water?"

They responded in unison, "Air!"

Then, the learned monk said, "When your desire for God is as strong as was your desire for air, come back and see me. Only then can we talk about discipleship."

This parable poignantly emphasizes the simple fact that if God is not of supreme importance, He really is of no importance.

We can relativize our "relationship" with God and call on Him in times of crisis or celebration.

It is a living, daily commitment to bring ourselves to Him, to allow His Spirit to know us and to allow ourselves to be known that constitutes real relationship with Father, Son, and Holy Spirit. Such commitment will impact our thought and speech and actions. Through it we will come to know unbridled love, peace and joy.

Léon Bloy, a French novelist, once wrote, "The only real tragedy in life is not to become a saint." This remarkable insight is echoed in *Lumen gentium, the Second Vatican Council's Dogmatic Constitution on the Church*: "all the faithful, whatever their condition or state, are called by the Lord—each in his or her own way to a holiness of life."

Pope Francis repeats this universal call to holiness in his latest apostolic exhortation *Gaudete et exsultate*. If everyone is called to be a saint, no two are called to be saints in the same way. Pope Francis believes personal holiness is achieved through "small gestures." He gives an example:

A woman goes shopping, she meets a neighbor and they begin to speak, and the gossip starts. But she says in her heart, "No, I will not speak badly of anyone." This is a step forward in holiness. Later, at home, one of her children wants to talk to her about his hopes and dreams, and even though she is tired, she sits down and listens with patience and love. That is another sacrifice that brings holiness. Later, she experiences some anxiety, but recalling the love of the Virgin Mary, she takes her rosary and prays with faith – yet another path of holiness. Later still, she goes out onto the street, encounters a poor person, stops to look him in the eyes and say a kind word to him and offers him something to eat; three small steps that make a difference in another person's life.

God has given us freedom to choose the foundation upon which we build our lives. There are many foundations from which to choose.

If our desire is to spend our lives chasing the almighty dollar, we are free to do so. If our goal is perpetual pleasure, we have that right. We can, if we're so inclined, spend our lives rebelling against everything we have been taught!

However, wise people understand that some foundations cannot endure. All foundations are not created equal. Jesus said in Matthew 7: "Therefore everyone who hears these words of Mine and puts them into practice is like a wise man who built his house on the rock. The rain came down, the streams rose, and the winds blew and beat against that house; yet it did not fall, because it had its foundation on the rock. But everyone who hears these words of mine and does not put them into practice is like a foolish man who built his house on sand. The rain came down, the streams rose, and the winds blew and beat against that house and it fell with a great crash." (Matthew 7:24-27).

On Sept. 10, 2001, Howard Lutnick's greatest motivation for going to work was to make money. Lutnick, CEO of the investment firm Cantor Fitzgerald, was at the top of his game. But on Sept. 11, a terrorist attack destroyed the World Trade Center and killed 657 employees at Cantor Fitzgerald. That moment changed many people's lives, including Lutnick's. He made a public commitment to the families of his deceased employees that Cantor Fitzgerald would provide healthcare coverage for the families for the next 10 years. In addition, 25 percent of Cantor's profits for the next five years would be given to the families of those killed in the attack.

As Lutnick said, "I didn't want to wake up in the morning and go to work to make money. It wasn't worth it. It had to be for a different reason. And that reason is that I loved so many of the people I lost ... THAT became my motivation. THAT became my driving force."

Lutnick needed a better cornerstone than greed. He found one. There are as many foundations as our imaginations will allow: the pursuit of power, prestige and possessions, the esteem of family and friends ... some will prove to be more worthy than others.

There is, however, but one cornerstone that will not fail. That cornerstone is Jesus. Grounding our life and work, our effort and desire in Jesus will never mislead us.

Some might recall this lyric of an old Gospel song: "On Christ, the solid rock, I stand. All other ground is sifting sand, all other ground is sifting sand."

Any good architect, ancient or modern, knows the cornerstone to be the quintessential piece of a building's foundation; it provide the security, the strength upon which every stone rests.

Jesus Christ is the only enduring foundation for a satisfying life, "built upon the foundation of the apostles and prophets, with Christ Jesus himself as the capstone." (Ephesians 2:20)

Eventually all other foundations crumble, they dry up, they perish.

Only one foundation is eternal.

"You, also, like living stones, are being built as a spiritual house into a holy priesthood," says Peter, (1Peter 2:5), "to offer up spiritual sacrifices acceptable to God through Jesus Christ.

"For this is contained in Scripture: 'Behold I lay in Zion a choice' stone, a precious corner stone, and he who believes in Him shall not be disappointed.'" (1Peter 2:6).

The only cornerstone that will not ultimately disappoint you is the person of Jesus Christ.

The Rewards of Priesthood

The real rewards of priesthood are neither measurable nor tangible, but only observable. Perhaps they are not calculated by the number of people in the pew or the influence we exercise by virtue of the office, but by the signs of service to which dedication to our vocation calls us.

My energy and enthusiasm to say Mass, preach a homily or give a talk is not predicated on numbers, but is directly informed by the grace that is offered in daily prayer born of a desire to do God's will, a desire that has not waned in all my years of priesthood.

I love to baptize. In the case of infant baptisms it gives me unadulterated joy to lift up the newly baptized child and present him to the congregation full, as he is, of the new life he's received from Father, Son, and Holy Spirit. To hear the thunderous applause with which he is received is an emotional experience for me.

"You are made in my image and after my likeness." You are wonderfully made and precious to me." No matter the wording this is the first and most important truth of Scripture. Without doubt, it is children who continually energize my desire to share it. For I have come to know that if you believe yourself to be profoundly and passionately loved, you live life differently, abundantly.

In September 2005, I volunteered to bless the newly decorated pre-kindergarten room at Saint Gabriel's, as well as all of the children. I wanted this service to be "High Church," so I arrived at the classroom with alb and stole, holy water bucket, and aspergillum.

I welcomed all the children and asked each of them to tell me his or her name. I introduced myself to this group of wide-eyed 3- and 4-year-olds who sat in undivided attention and rapt curiosity. I told them that the most important lesson anyone in this world can learn is that God loves them dearly. I also informed them that I would bless them so that they could grow in the love of Father, Jesus and the Holy Spirit. They were eager and ready.

One month later, as the parishioners exited church after Mass, one family stopped to introduce themselves to me. The mother, with her husband and three children, told me of her youngest daughter's response when I came into her classroom that day for the blessing.

When she picked up her daughter at school, she asked her how her day was, to which the child responded, "It was great! Big daddy came into the classroom today."

The mother chuckled and asked, "Well, what did Big Daddy do?" With child-like innocence and sincerity, her daughter responded: "Mommy, Big Daddy put Jesus in my heart."

I could not wait to share this wonderful story with the principal of the school. However, she responded by saying, "Father, I don't want to burst your bubble, but we almost lost a child when you went into the classroom that day".

She went on to explain that a 3-year-old, went home and told her mother hat she was never going back again.

"Why", asked the young girl's mother.

"Because Father came into the room today," she responded.

"What did Father do?"

"He wet me and my Oreo cookie."

Fortunately, the mother was able to explain what it means to be sprinkled with holy water, and the young girl returned to school the next day.

I receive joys like this almost daily. Anointing, blessing, consecrating, forgiving, and reconciling others … these are the rewards of sharing in the one priesthood of Jesus Christ.

What Fine Work
Will You Do in His Name?

I am looking to turn the oddities of my life and vocation as a priest into words – words that are lean, muscular and vibrant. I need to discover an "inner voice" in which language is spare and lush all at once.

This inner reflection is what I use to continue to guide my vocational experience. There is still work to be done.

Do you have a special place to go to "get away from it all"? Be it a cabin in the woods or near a river? Maybe it's a favorite, comfortable chair in which to relax and read or even fall asleep. It could simply be the memory of such a place.

It might be that listening to a particular piece of music transports you to a calmer, more peaceful space that restores you. It is even possible that the mere use of your imagination provides a very real escape from the stress and demands of life.

Some find making retreats the perfect way to reflect and reorient their lives, to discover what in their life is truly important. Being in surroundings that invite deep, conscious breathing, one may be blessed with a key insight or direction for the course of his life.

While our times and culture may seem especially stressful and complicated, even bewildering, we are not the first ones who have sought to get away, desiring to renew our lives by re-calibrating our priorities and responsibilities. The mountains have been a place where, in many cultures and throughout history, people have gone to find God, to be with God, to have one of those life-changing experiences of the divine that puts everything in its proper place. Both Old and New Testaments are full of such efforts: God appeared to Moses in the burning bush on Mount Horeb, Moses encountered God again on the mountain to receive the Ten Commandments, and the Jesus encounters Moses, Elijah and His Heavenly Father in the Transfiguration story in the New Testament.

Away from it all, up on a mountain, glorious experiences occur. Throughout the Bible, the "mountain" is a metaphor for a sacred encounter with divinity. It truly is God's sacred meeting place.

The problem for us is that we have to come down from the mountain. The exhilaration of new insight and rest comes to an end. The retreat is over, the telephone rings, the music stops, the alarm clock beeps and we are back to "business – as- usual". All the gratifying feelings of tranquility and peace are all too soon eroded by the reality and demands of the day.

When Jesus goes up to the mountain, in the Transfiguration story, (Mathew 17: 1-6) to confer with Elijah and Moses, representatives of the Prophets and the Law, the three disciples who had trekked up there with Jesus were amazed and utterly wowed by what they saw. They wanted to build booths or tents to try to prolong this epiphany, this grand revelation of Jesus's identity as the Son of God.

"This is My beloved Son with whom I am well pleased," God thundered from the clouds. The wonder of it all brought them to their knees.

Then, the epiphany was over; it was time to go back. So, down the mountain they went, ordered by Jesus to say nothing of this to anyone, "until the Son of Man has been raised from the dead," an order that surely would have bewildered the disciples on many levels.

We can almost hear the questions forming in their minds: "Why do we have to go down the mountain? Why keep this beautiful experience quiet? What does "until the Son of Mas has been raised" mean?

The apostles were not given much of an answer, really. All of that would come clear in time. For now it was time to return to the business of salvation: healing, preaching the Kingdom of God and teaching about Jesus' dying on the cross.

The same is true for us as present-day disciples. The altar becomes the new 'mountain' and we are awed and amazed at what happens in this holy space. Bread becomes the Risen Body of the Lord, wine becomes the Precious Blood of the Lord in the celebration of the Eucharist: the source and summit of the church's life.[45]

"I believe I shall see the good things of the Lord in the land of the living." (Psalm 27).

Perhaps Jesus' ultimate act of faith was not so much in coming to earth as in leaving it. After a lifetime of preparation and only three years of implementation and training, He had to look at His mission and then let it go. "It is finished," He said in His dying breath.

In His final recorded prayer on earth, Jesus said to the Father, "These people were Your gifts to Me." (John 17:6). They were not projects to be completed, sinners to be changed, fools to be corrected, worms to be transformed, corporate pawns to be maneuvered until the plan was in place ... They were gifts to Him.

What fine work He did, this carpenter of human souls.

Jesus saw people as His greatest accomplishment and in so doing He built them a table to last.

"There is still work to be done", says Richard Stern. "The work of salvation."

What fine work will you do in His name? Each of us is called. To discover that call, we must look to Jesus. To carry out that call, we must trust in the guidance of the Blessed Trinity – Father, Son and Holy Spirit.

Russell Shaw, in his book *American Church,* recalls a conversation he had with a friend on the topic of new evangelization in the Catholic Church. Shaw's friend offered this keen insight: "the biggest problem of all – and the cause of all the rest – is that we have not preached holiness."[46]

We readily proclaim justice, peace, generosity, giving to the latest disaster relief campaign. We encourage parishioners to become active in one or more of the ministries in the parish,.

Are we forgetting to remind everyone of the unique role each of us plays in the plan of salvation? St. Paul urges us to "live in a manner worthy of the call you have received, with all humility and gentleness, with patience, bearing with one another through love." (Ephesians.4:1-2).

As my friend and mentor Msgr. Murray preached at my ordination, we cannot grasp the totality of God's gift of love.

"Every liturgy is celebration, because of its constant reminders of the meaning of all things: spring, summer, death, life, suffering, joy, words, music, woven together into a meaningful pattern."

"Celebration is a receptive attitude of mind which opens us to mystery, to a time of peace in the depths of the heart, to the realization that there is within each of us a place where beauty and the holy dwell."

PART IV: BIRTH INTO ETERNAL LIFE

"The fear of death follows from the fear of life. A man who lives fully is prepared to die at any time."

–Mark Twain

CHAPTER 35
At the Hour of Our Death

"Our task in discerning what is good and holy in the world of the arts, is to ask the question: 'Does this book, song, film, or poem lead me into the light? Or does it leave me in a fog, or worse still, a darkness?'"

—Bill Donaghy, Archdiocese of Philadelphia

From the moment of our birth, we are moving inexorably toward the most important event in our lives: our death. It is not how healthy and strong we are that is most important. What is of greatest importance is how we prepare for the hour of our death.

Why the "hour of our death?" The church uses the great prayer to our Blessed Mother, the Hail Mary, to emphasize its importance. Repeated over and over in our rosary, the Hail Mary turns into a plea to our Heavenly Mother for our salvation: "Pray for us now and at the hour of our death!"

We may well ask, "Why at that particular moment?" From the lives of the saints, we learn that the battle for our soul is most intense just before we die.

It serves as a clear reminder of my mother's dying days. Alternating from rest to consciousness throughout that time, there was a moment where she woke up and called for help.

"I don't know what to do, Tom," she said. "Help me."

I consoled her in that moment, telling her to do what she always did, "Trust in God's providential love." She nodded and her countenance changed from fear to peacefulness. Mom was a good Irishwoman to the core. She prayed the rosary every day and was a good friend of the Blessed Mother.

A nurse brought in a cup of orange water ice, and I found this to be the greatest irony of my life. In this very moment, in my mother's final hours, I was able to feed her this orange water ice; for 51 years, my mother fed me with rich fare, physically and spiritually, and all I could find was a wooden spoon! It was a great honor, despite the sadness of the situation.

Our lives follow rhythmic patterns. We are born into the world physically, explore our faith and grow in God's way, truth, and love, serve Him through our passion, finding our place in salvation history, and hopefully come in contact with Him for all eternity. In our dying days, we all experience the cyclical nature of our four births. Despite my mother's impending journey to heaven, she still got to enjoy the natural experience, tasting the sweet, cool refreshment of an orange water ice. In spite of her pain, she still thirsted.

When Jesus exclaims his final words, he experienced genuine anguish. Why? It was because he took on humanity. He experienced hunger, thirst, anguish, and suffering in a real way. That quote, ""My God, my God, why have you forsaken me?" (Matthew 27:46), is really a quote from Psalm 22: "My God, my God, why have you abandoned me?" (Psalm 22:2). It starts out in deep distress and near despair, but as you go through, the prayer, you work through that anguish.

We come to encouragement and hope. If you live life long enough, no one does escape suffering. You might not be privy to an individual's pain, but part of humanity is going to involve doubt (like Thomas), pain and suffering (like Job), setback (as in the early days of the church), and hardship (like the many sinners with whom Jesus encountered). But, how do you integrate that into forgiveness, mercy, generosity, and kindness? It's blending all of that together that enables anyone to live life abundantly.

Jesus was a person of prayer. Time and again, the Gospels report that Jesus went into a deserted place to pray, sometimes spending a whole night in prayer. A major mission of His was to teach His disciples, first of all, how not to pray (don't make a public display of your praying on street corners and don't multiply words) and then positively how to pray using His familiar sample prayer, the "Our Father."

In the closing days of His life, we hear Jesus Himself pray. The night before He died He prayed, "Father, if you are willing, take this cup away from me; still, not my will but yours be done." (Luke 22:42). Just before He died on the cross Jesus prayed a series of short, poignant prayers: his reference to Psalm 22, continuing with "Father, forgive them, they know not what they do," (Luke 23:34), and concluding with His final prayer, "It is finished." (John 19:30).

We are also privileged to hear Jesus pray not in short spurts of words, but in 26 verses of chapter seventeen of St. John's Gospel. Situated during the Last Supper on the night before He died, the prayer was prayed by Jesus in the presence of His disciples and addressed to His Heavenly Father.

As lengthy as this prayer is, there is one word that captures and holds our attention. It is the word glory. No less than six times, this word, glory, appears in noun and verb form. Jesus asks His Father to give Him glory so that He in turn may glorify His Father. Jesus sums up His earthly mission as one of having glorified the Father on Earth by doing the work the Father gave Him to do. Now, in turn, Jesus asks the Father, "Glorify me, Father, with you, with the glory that I had with you before the world began." (John 17:5). Finally, Jesus prays for His disciples, those in whom He has been glorified.

The glory of Jesus is too powerful to be contained in a singular Gospel passage. So, six more times, glory spills over into the prayers and the readings of this Easter season mass. The Opening Prayer reminds us that Christ lives with the Father in glory. The Prayer over the Gifts asks the Lord that "this Eucharist brings us to Your glory." The Prayer after Communion petitions that God "give us hope that the glory given the Risen Lord will be given to the Church, His body."

Jesus' prayer to God is a call to give the glory to His Son, so that He may give eternal life to all. "Now this is eternal life, that they should know you, the only true God, and the one whom you sent, Jesus Christ." (John 17:3).

Peter's First Epistle remarkably associates glory, not with the resurrection and ascension of Jesus, so obviously at the center of our Christian Glory Story, but with the sufferings of Jesus. The author, Saint Peter, encourages us to rejoice that we share in the sufferings of Christ because those sufferings are the link to His glory. So, if and when we are insulted for the name of Christ, then the Spirit of glory rests upon us. Our sufferings as Christians are not the source of shame but the cause of glory for God.

What, then, is this glory that saturates every celebration of the Eucharist? We all have some idea of what glory is, what it means. We associate glory with such words as beauty, splendor, magnificence, exaltation, power, majesty, honor, radiance, brilliance, wonder, and dazzle. Glory takes our breath away but leaves enough wind in our lungs so we can shout or whisper, "Wow!"

It is important to remember that this Glory Prayer of Jesus came before His suffering, death, and resurrection, not afterward. Rather than complain, worry, or be anxious about the formidable future of pain and anguish He was about to face, Jesus concentrated His prayer on the glory that He hoped would be His when His burial stone had been rolled away. Then He would emerge as He had been previewed at His transfiguration when His face shone like the sun and His clothes became white as light. Now that's glory!

This glorious celebration is our challenge to become more aware of the glory that suffuses our lives if we have eyes of faith, hands of hope, and hearts of love. In a war-weary world where the only news worth televising, broadcasting, and printing is bad, sad, and mad news, we need to keep on looking for the glory of the risen and ascended Jesus who still "remains with us until the end of time."

Every random and deliberate act of kindness, every kind word we speak, every bit of help we give those in need, every prayer we pray, every smile we give to loved ones and strangers, every effort we make to be patient, forgiving, helpful, and loving will erase the grime from our world and bring out the glory. The glory is here, for we believe God made our world and saw that it was not just good, but very good.

Yes, Jesus is a person of prayer. He just told us in John's Gospel, "I pray for them." The "them" is we who come together like this week after week to pray, "GLORY to God in the highest, and peace to His people on earth."

What better preparation for death than a lifelong practice of prayer? From this grows an ever-increasing love of God, devotion to the Mother of God, and attachment to our guardian angels, those pure spirits whose purpose for being is to aid and guide us to eternal salvation!

Is all this prayer and preparation exaggerated? Excessive? Well, let's examine it, as in any battle, a battle to save our souls against "the wiles and wickedness and the snares of Satan." He who is prepared by training, knowledge of the enemy, conviction, and devotion to the prize, is more likely to succeed than he who leaves to the moment of conflict – or temptation – his preparation for survival.

To draw an analogy to the world we live in … Take the serious young people who aspire to achieve academic excellence in any or all of the subjects, languages, sciences, law, and medicine. Do they just decide that language, or science, or math, is going to be their cup of tea and that the necessary skill will come without practice? Of course not. First comes an understanding of the challenge and what it takes to succeed – to star on the athletic field, or behind the footlights, or in the laboratory or courtroom. Then comes practice, practice, practice.

Now, if this is so on the worldly level, why would we expect to attain the far more treasured spiritual and heavenly prize with far less commitment than that required for the worldly prize? The level of commitment required is determined by the value of the prize we seek and, for eternity in glory with Father, Son, and Holy Spirit, it requires a lifetime of dedication.

This is what St. Paul tells us: "For I am already being poured out like a libation, and the time of my departure is at hand. I have competed well; I have finished the race; I have kept the faith. From now on the crown of righteousness awaits me, which the Lord, the just judge, will award to me on that day, and not only to me, but to all who have longed for his appearance." (2 Timothy 4:6-8).

What a prize it is that we run to attain! Truly, a "pearl of great price." Eternal glory with Jesus, which St. Paul felt assured he would attain as a result of his long years of "fighting the good fight to the end – of running the race to the finish." So, too, for us!

Unless we face death, we are not free. Death is the final barrier and the final liberation. We do not try to gloss over it as Christians, saying, "it's not real, it's an illusion." We do not say you should not grieve when someone dies. It is terrible. It is tragic. However, we need to distinguish between tragedy and catastrophe.

A catastrophe is something that is unredeemable. It is an unmitigated disaster. What Christ came to say is that there really, ultimately is no such thing. There is tragedy. There is pain, horror, and terror; but tragedy? Human tragedy is the prelude to the beginning of the divine comedy. All human tragedy culminates in divine comedy – the resurrection. So long as we are willing to stand at the center of our humility – the foundational virtue of our faith – and realize that the resurrection is a precious gift. Divine love is sheer gift. Transformation in Christ is a remarkable revelation. All we can do in our poverty is say, "Yes."

Jesus instructs us that we need a moral/spiritual compass in our lives for direction and in order to reach our goal of eternal life.

Jordan D. Peterson observes in his book, *Twelve Rules for Life*, that in today's culture many people suffer from intellectual and moral neglect by devaluing years of human knowledge about how to acquire virtue, dismissing virtue as passé, not relevant or worse oppressive. The very word virtue sounds out of date, and anyone who uses the word is moralistic and self-righteous.[47]

Natural birth, spiritual birth, and vocational birth guarantee a good dose of suffering. The question becomes, "am I willing to suffer in love, like Jesus, in order to reduce the suffering in the world rooted in fear, hatred, hostility, violence, racism, sin?"

Msgr. Murray was a master at helping me become more mentally disciplined and more spiritually reflective. Chaos is everything unknown to us and any unexplored territory that we need to traverse, be it in the world outside or the soul within.

Dr. Norman Doidge, author of *The Brain That Changes Itself*, postulates that raising children is difficult and requires sacrifice and suffering on the part of parents. Aging, sickness, and death are challenging. Without the benefit of a loving relationship between spouses, a spiritual director, wisdom and insights from previous ages, the challenges of aging, sickness and death are all the more demanding.

Doidge follows the teachings of Peterson (*Maps of Meaning*), and says the current culture presents us with major obstacles. One obstacle is ideology. Ideologies are simple ideas disguised as science or philosophy, that purport to explain the complexity of the world and offer remedies that will improve the human condition. Ideologues are people who pretend they know how to "make the world a better place" before they have taken care of their own chaos within. [48]

That's hubris, of course, and one of the most important teachings of Jesus is "to remove the plank from your own eye, before you remove the speck from another person's eye." (Matthew 7:5). Good, sound, solid, practical spiritual advice.

All four of the births outlined in the pages of this book are inseparable. The lessons you learn in each can be experienced from one to the next with just a tweak of a new angle of understanding. There is great reciprocity between natural birth, spiritual birth, vocational birth, and birth into eternal life. All four are intimately related.

The more we relate them to each other, the stronger the rope that ties your life together becomes. The more detached we become from each birth, the more chaos and confusion comes. With more chaos and confusion come many unanswered questions, and we often find ourselves hanging by a thread.

You can have your natural, spiritual, and vocational lives all in place, but you are always going to be stymied by death. It never comes on time. It always catches you off guard. You can be prepared for anything except death. I knew my mom was going to die. She was dying for five years, but the moment she did die, I was still caught off guard.

Each loss that we suffer in life can go in two different directions. We can either mourn too long and become inconsolable, keeping it alive in a negative way; or, we can learn from grief, sadness, and loss, and grow in light of the way that those people who have died lived their lives, keeping them present in a positive way, through faith, memory, and love! We will conclude this book with lessons in life from five people. But, first, a prayer – one you may know as the Prayer for Holy Rest by John Henry Newman:

O, Lord
Support us all the day long,
Until the shadows lengthen,
And the evening comes,
And the busy world is hushed
And the fever of life is over
And our work is done.

Then in thy mercy, grant us
A safe lodging and a holy rest,
And peace at the last.
Amen.

CHAPTER 36
Coping Methods

"I didn't see his hands, Master. The ancient Greeks claimed that death is only the separation of the soul from the body. After that the soul is pure and free. They said that men who fear death love the body, and probably power and prestige as well."

—Alan Lightman, "The Diagnosis" (2000)

Our journey through Birth Into Eternal Life may seem short as you read through to the conclusion of this work, and that is because I have experienced physical death. Not many people can say that they have and lived to tell. However, in the pages that follow, I will explain the lessons I have learned through the way in which others have lived. This is how we grow and prepare ourselves for life's greatest constant.

Death has held a firm grip on me since childhood. With the untimely death of my dad at 33 years of age, the mystery of death altered my worldview at the tender age of four-and-a-half years old. My fascination with death has absorbed much of my unconscious imagination from then into adulthood and throughout the journey of my priesthood. So much so, that shortly after my 33rd birthday I built my own coffin, which is presently stored in the basement of St. Mathew's rectory. It is a simple pine box with rope handles. I have often struggled with trying to make sense of what is often quite senseless: the nearly incomprehensible truth and reality involved in the pain of death and dying.

The loss of my father's physical presence as I was growing up became an overwhelming absence in my life. My mother, through story after story, brought my father's loving presence into our home, especially around the dinner table. The memories of love, laughter, and stories of my mom and dad's shared experiences in their 10 years together – memories such as their date at the Notre Dame-Navy game, their decision to open a store, vacations to the beach, raising children, and going to church – comforted my restlessness.

As you've learned, I channeled much of that restlessness into sports. I became a fierce competitor on the field and on the court. Religiously, I learned and committed to memory just about every sports statistic in every sport, knew the name and number of every collegiate star, every NFL player. I could recall, with uncanny ability, every Eagles game, just like a golfer recalls every shot in a round of golf. I dedicated these athletic endeavors into honoring my dad, who loved sports, but was too weak physically, due to his heart condition, to ever actively participate in the games.

So, I made it real. Friends often recall, many years later, my tenacity on the basketball court, on the tennis court, at the box ball field, and on the makeshift, pole-to-pole football field that became Hibberd Stadium, named for the street it was on. At the seminary, my reputation continued, and traveled into most every community in which I lived.

The first question asked by many who knew me growing up is always, "Are you still playing basketball?" Those who know me well recognize that my athletic intensity did not stop with basketball. At my own admission, I was a competitive overachiever. I outplayed bishops at tennis and virtually terrorized brother priests and seminarians at the St. Charles Annual Turkey Bowl football game. The game was friendly and fraternal, but winning was clearly my goal. In my competitive desire to honor my natural father, I took no prisoners.

Still, restlessness remained. My father's death would frequently haunt me. In Sacred Scripture, "to remember" is a holy act. It means to make events or happenings from the past come alive now. What events or happenings? All that Jesus did by way of example for us: helping the poor, healing the sick, forgiving the sinner, reaching out to the outcast. Whenever we come together as disciples of the Lord for the Eucharist, our faith tells us – assures us – that what we share is the risen body and blood of Jesus, Himself. We also share who we are for one another, that we are to be sustenance and support for one another. Paired with athletics, this is how I hoped to honor my father's life after his death.

We do not become a Christian community by sliding into a pew. Rather we become a Christian community by welcoming others, by reaching out beyond ourselves to stand in solidarity with the poor and the outcast, by encouraging the diversity within our community.

There are many kinds of hungers: physical, emotional, spiritual. Let's commit ourselves to find pockets of time to reflect first on how Jesus has satisfied our hungers by giving us His Body and Blood as food for our journey to heaven.

Let us also commit ourselves to satisfy the hungers of those around us by responding the first time someone calls, by praying for a friend and for an enemy, by writing the letter we so long avoided, by volunteering our time at school, a hospital, a soup kitchen, by mentoring a child, by meeting a person we have avoided. These are the ways my spiritual mentors acted, in good times and bad – my mother's gracious act of secretly delivering food to a neighbor; Father McNamara and my grandfather bringing joy to the world through humility, hilarity, hospitality, and holiness; Father Murray guiding a young seminarian not to seek the answers to his burning questions, but to instead seek the right questions.

Yes, let's work at it and discover new ways to feed others in our community, physically, spiritually, vocationally, and to the life beyond. Then will we be acting as Eucharistic people joined in a covenant sealed by the Blood of Christ. By doing this we make Christ's Body and Blood a most intimate part of ourselves. We become one with the Risen Lord and we become one with each other, truly the Body and Blood of Christ, Corpus Christi.

William James in his classic work, *The Varieties of Religious Experience*, attempted to articulate the complex, profound experiences that lie at the heart of so many people's lives, but too often go unattended. Some experiences defy expression and cannot be described adequately in words. James contends that these experiences achieve "insight into depths of truth beyond reason."

He adds, "ineffable" experiences are known as "illumination, revelations," and "full of personal meaning." They evoke an "enormous sense of inner authority and illumination," radically transforming the understanding of those who experience them, after calling forth a deep sense of being revelations of divine wisdom and truth. (James, op. cit.).

CHAPTER 37
'Go Right Past the Moon and Straight to Heaven'

"...the [Holy] Spirit too comes to the aid of our weakness; for we do not know how to pray as we ought, but the Spirit itself intercedes with inexpressible groanings."

—Romans 8:26

In April 2009, on the Monday of Holy Week, I visited the Pre-K class at St. Pius X in Broomall, Pa., and asked the 20-plus children, "What do we celebrate on Easter Sunday?" A little girl by the name of Madeline immediately volunteered her response with confidence.

"The Easter Bunny!" she exclaimed.

"Chocolate Easter eggs," another student named Maeve clarified.

"New shoes!" a boy named Nicholas shouted.

"A new dress!" followed Amanda.

But, an intuitive little one named Natalie settled the issue definitively when she stood up and said, "Father Heron, Easter celebrates when God got undeaded."

Seeing death through the eyes of a child can teach us a lot about ourselves – a lot about our eventual birth into eternal life.

In 1997, I received a call to respond to a family I knew as a teacher at Archbishop Kennedy. Married now, Lee and Lisa Famous had a son, four-year-old Shane, who was dying of leukemia.

On Dec. 26, 1994, Lisa and Lee gave birth to their son, and on March 26, 1995, Shane was anointed with the oil of salvation and given a new birth by water and the Holy Spirit. On the joyful occasion of Shane's baptism, the priest prayed that Lisa and Lee be the best teachers of their son in the ways of faith, bearing witness to the faith by what they say and do, in Christ Jesus, our Lord.

Little did Lisa and Lee know that it would be Shane who would teach them, not only about faith, but hope and love, as well. Early in the morning of Feb. 19, with the flame of faith burning brightly, with Lisa's guiding words, Shane went right past the moon to meet Jesus with all the saints in the heavenly kingdom. Shane was born into his eternal life on Feb. 19, 1997.

Lee and Lisa, along with the family gathered at St. Paul's church in East Norriton, Pa., to celebrate his birth into eternal life. I was the main celebrant and homilist. Shane's understanding of death came in phrases he shared with his parents.

- "I love you as high as the moon."
- "I love you with all of my heart."
- "Bless Daddy, Mommy, don't forget to bless Daddy."
- "Good night and God bless you."
- "Go right past the moon and straight to heaven."

This had a profound affect on my understanding of a passage from Isaiah the prophet, where it was written, "A child will lead us." My experience with Shane's death became a moment of revelation and insight into the mystery of God's prophetic word. A child will lead us right into eternal life.

Jesus himself said, "Unless you become like a little child you will not enter the Kingdom of God." A piece of my soul was forever marked with that deeper understanding.

We must always trust our Heavenly Father, even when we seek a reason why a four-year-old died. There is no simple answer, no satisfying explanation. As a family of faith we believe that God has printed upon all creation his own mysterious design. That design is the Paschal Mystery of which St. Paul reminds us, "There is no cross in Christ Jesus without a resurrection." There can be no real life in God without sacrifice, suffering and death. The cross is the great symbol of faith.

Some truths need to be told over and over again. Our Lord repeated certain truths about Himself, and used certain images of Himself, over and over again, like the rhyme in a song. Repetition not only instills an idea into our minds, hearts and soul, but it has the same power that rhythm has to make the idea part of us and dear to us, just as a Woody Wolfe (a favorite singer of Shane's) tune heard many times becomes a part of us and dear to us.

I advised Shane's family and friends to repeat the memorable quotes from Shane's life, over and over again, coupled with these quotes from the scriptures, as a way to connect to him.

- "A child will lead us."

- "Let the children come to me…"

- "Unless you become like a little child, you will not enter the Kingdom of God."

- "You shall love the Lord, your God, with all your heart, all your mind, all your strength, all your soul."

- "Do this in memory of me."

As we've learned through the way in which my mom kept my dad's presence familiar through faith, memory, and love, we too can learn from Shane to be connected to our loved ones by repeating quotes like these, and holding the essence in which our loved ones lived close to our hearts.

Shane knew the full measure of the greatest treasure we human beings possess, the simple purity of human love, the greatest gift we can give to one another. Shane brought tremendous joy to his mom and dad, his grandparents, his aunts and uncles, and so many countless others, from the day he was born and all through his long stay at the Children's Hospital of Philadelphia.

When you're at a young age, like teenagers, or even kids who are four to eight years old, how can you get a mature understanding of death? Shane Famous knew – because he was going to the hospital and asking questions – that his health was fragile. In the image that his mother used for him, when he would come home late from the hospital and get out of the car after sleeping on the ride home, he would see the moon and be fascinated by it. His mother encouraged him. "See past the moon, and that's where you're going to be." That became a symbol that there's something beyond the moon for him to live his life.

From just a physical level, you would think the space beyond the moon is just darkness. Do we have the faith vision to see even in the darkness? On this side of heaven, there's always going to be some darkness that we have to navigate. The battle between light and darkness is universal for everybody. I also think when you think of death, there is a major paradox of Jesus' teaching of the Gospel – that in order to live abundantly, you have to come to terms with your death, with limitation, with finiteness.

If you are still fearful of death, that will diminish the quality of your life. That's why baptism is so important. You are immersed into the Paschal mystery, into living life abundantly, but knowing that no one escapes this world without suffering. How you develop a Gospel disposition toward suffering is a key understanding: "I'm willing to suffer in love in order to avoid the suffering in the world that's rooted in sin."

Four years old ... I think the great lesson is, it's not quantity of life, it's quality of life on which we must always focus. No one knows how many years they're given, but what we all have to do is try to live each day, as Jesus said in St. John's Gospel, abundantly. Live it full tilt.

How does all of that translate into an every day level? How do people immerse themselves in life, suffering and death, and enjoy the promise of eternal life? To the degree that we can do that, life has rich meaning.

There's a diminishment of fear and anxiety that seems to be another pervasive force in the world. This little four-year-old, with his big, brown eyes, always had adults surrounding him. I never saw him in a context with kids his own age. Some kids were at the hospital, sure, but usually when I was there, it was all adults. He had the ability to teach all of those adults a lesson that they either avoided or were not taught in other life experiences that they had, no matter their age, experience, or wisdom. That was the lesson that my mother taught me. She was still in love with her husband even though she missed his physical presence greatly. She did come to terms with his death and that enabled her to live life more fully.

Loving Shane brought out the best in everyone alive. He touched and deeply affected many people's lives. He possessed an angelic wisdom beyond his years. He taught, with his big, gentle, brown eyes, to set our hearts and eyes on the higher realms, on the things that matter most. He taught many to stand back and take a long, loving look at the beauty of a Christmas tree.

Shane taught his aunt Linda not to fear death. He taught his uncle Tony to gaze at the splendid beauty of the moon. He taught many people that the finish line in life is the union with God – Father, Son, and Holy Spirit.

Looking into Shane's eyes connected people to their own souls. He was a true gift from God. The innocence of his life, the beauty of his soul, was a treasure to those who knew him.

Aside from memories and quotes, how do we express grief and thanksgiving during the mourning of such a young person? St. Paul says in the eighth chapter of Romans that we must trust God. This holds true, even when we are seeking the reason for why this had to happen. As a family of faith, we believe that God has printed upon all creation his own mysterious design. This is where the cross, our greatest symbol of faith, comes into play.

Someone who stood by that cross was Jesus' mother, Mary. She was no stranger to Shane, even when he was just two years old. Amazingly, he gave honor to Mary by praying the rosary. The rosary concludes with the Hail, Holy Queen. We beg Mary, our Heavenly Mother, and most gracious advocate, to turn her eyes of mercy toward us. I am sure that is exactly what Mary had done at the hour of Shane's death.

When those we love are taken from us far sooner than we expect, let us dwell on that love and that blessing, and try to never allow grief, nagging doubt, or any resentment or anger to shape our lives, because if we do that, we deny our faith and we deny all that Shane teaches us. We must be still before the ageless, awesome mysteries of birth, life, love, suffering, death, and resurrection. In that stillness, God will speak, and heal us again and again, with the living and loving memory of Jesus, our Savior, and the living and loving memory of inspiring teachers like Shane Famous.

In honor of Shane's life, I think it's appropriate to quote the Irish singing group, Celtic Thunder:

"The moonlight dances among the trees,

The campfire glows in the autumn breze

And I am lost in my thoughts of you

Remember me, recuerda me.

"A comrade strums on a sad guirtar

My mind is drifting to where you are

I'm holding you as I used to do

remember me, recuerda me, mi amor!

"So long ago, so far away, each night I pray

'volvero los dias passoados'

I promise you that come what may

Those days will stay ever in my memory

"In all this world I could never find, the love that I had to leave behind

But duty calls, so whate'er befalls

remember me, recuerda me, mi amor

"God only knows what tomorrow brings

You're in my hearts so my spirit sings

and I'll be strong just as long as you remember me,

recuerda me, mi amor!"[49]

CHAPTER 38

'I'm Putting Myself at the Foot of the Cross, and Let's Go to Lunch'

"The greatest things are accomplished in silence- not in the clamor and display of superficial eventfulness, but in the deep clarity of inner vision; in the almost imperceptible start of decision, I quiet overcoming and hidden sacrifice. Spiritual birth happens when the heart is quickened by love, and the free well stirs to action. The silent forces are the strong forces. Let us turn now to the stillest event of all, stillest because it came from the remoteness beyond the noise of any possible intrusion – from God."

–Romano Guardini, "The Lord" (1937)

In 40 years of being a priest, I have never witnessed this spiritual reality of *kenosis* (emptiness) and *pleroma* (fullness) as I had when I visited a woman named Karen Purcell to bring her Holy Communion. Karen had been suffering intensely from cancer. It had ravaged her. Yet, when I sat beside her bed and prayed with her in preparation for receiving the Eucharist, her eyes and face radiated profound peace, inexpressible joy, remarkable hope and love. Karen was a living witness to me and her family and the nurses who cared for her of not allowing excruciating suffering to distract her from putting on the mind of Christ.

She had accepted, in faith, the terrible emptiness caused by cancer. This woman reminded me of a profound life lesson: blessed are the pure of heart for they shall see God. Her gaze had enabled everyone around her bedside to see beyond suffering and experience human and divine love.

The Gospels are written from a faith deeply rooted in people's experience of the eternal. Therefore, it is important to listen and read sacred scripture with the creative powers of your soul – imagination, wonder, and love – all guided by the Holy Spirit.

Karen was a loving wife to Mike and a doting mother of four children: Chris, Jaclyn, Brendan, and Leanne. For me, meeting Karen for the first time on a rainy Saturday afternoon, Sept. 6, 2008, at Bryn Mawr Hospital, the first thing I noticed was that she embodied the mystery of the cross – the place of unimaginable suffering, which can also be the place of new life; a life that comes in surprising and unexpected ways.

Mike and her daughter, Jaclyn, were on either side of Karen's hospital bed. The conversation was lively and humorous.

Mike was floored by that and later told me that was the best she had been in many months. Laughter was more evident than silent suffering for her on that day.

I remember at the end of the conversation, asking Karen to pray for me.

She said, "Why?"

I said, "I have this trouble with Celiac disease."

She replied, "Wait a second, I'll call the nurses now, have them bring a bed, and the two of us will get better together!"

I had been recently assigned to St Pius X Parish in Broomall and the members of the Purcell family were active members. The following morning at Sunday Mass, with the Purcell family present, and Karen on my mind, I asked the congregation to pray for her and the family in a moment of silence.

Later, in silent reflection, I pondered the mix of emotions I felt. Ripped open by her impending tragic death – a woman full of life and grace – caused me once again to explore life's big questions:

- "Why am I here?"
- "Where am I going?"
- "How will I be remembered?"

These questions strike a deep chord in my soul. They connect me to a deeper yearning to know myself better and to know the Blessed Trinity – Father, Son, and Holy Spirit – better. Karen, somehow, lying on her deathbed, directed her fixed gaze into my soul, and encouraged me to look at the Paschal Mystery differently. Instead of birth, life, suffering, death, and resurrection, I shuffled them around – birth, life, resurrection, suffering, and death.

I believe Karen was blessed to be enlightened by the mystery and meaning of the Resurrection. I was blessed to have met her in her final days on Earth. Karen intuited that by letting go of this present way of life, then and only then, she would discover a deeper divine life awaiting her.

Jesus tried to help His disciples understand that following Him looks like loss, but is really a gain. This new way of thinking emphasizes following the Father's will, no matter the consequences. Karen strove to follow St. Benedict's principle: "May the Holy Cross be my light into eternity."

St. Paul is the New Testament expert on the Risen Body. He shows a fascination for a resurrected order of living. He writes about the personal longing for it. St. Paul surely had grasped the key to what Jesus taught during His life on earth. Karen, like St. Paul, possessed the kind of incandescent good will that made ministering to her a blessing.

My mom and my grandfather put flesh onto this abstract word: resurrection. Karen put words into that: in order to experience eternal life, "I need to place myself at the foot of the cross." I need to embrace suffering-in-love, rather than fighting it tenaciously and causing self-focus to be a consuming concern.

Karen was deeply in love with her husband and four children, and yet she was ravaged by cancer. After the doctors informed Karen, with Mike at her side, that there was nothing more they could do, they've exhausted all the medical means to help her, they got in the car, and Mike asked, "What now?" To which she responded, "I'm going to put myself at the foot of the cross, and let's go to lunch."

Somehow, she found the strength that she wasn't going to be healed, but in being able to trust in her Lord and Savior, even with that bleak diagnosis, she could still do something as ordinary as going to lunch. She didn't fully understand why, at 51 years old, this cancer had ravaged her, but she found strength in the symbol of the cross to enable her to face her sickness and continue to do ordinary things.

She recognized she had no control over certain aspects of life. She was consumed by disease and eventual death, and she knew she could do nothing about it. Whatever was to come was in God's hands. So, she could let go of trying to control that, which made room for her to be able to continue living her life. She abandoned full control, accepted the present, and continued to live as fully as she could. She embraced the idea that when things are not normal, we must do something normal and feel normal, once again.

Karen didn't give up, which is remarkable given the devastating news that she received. She understood there was still meaning and purpose, even to her death, to living life in an ordinary manner and not ignoring the fact that the window was short. She took full advantage of every moment of life that she had and embraced it even in its pain and diminishment.

Karen said that iconic statement to her husband, and I retell it, but her children were fascinated by that quote. She liked going to lunch! You were meant to enjoy it. It's the epitome of the proverb: "God will hold us accountable for every joy we do not experience."

Each component of the paschal mystery is a mystery unto itself. Death will always be a mystery. That means we want to continue to probe and come to a newer, deeper, richer, fuller understanding of the mystery of death. We will never come to any satisfactory answer this side of heaven.

I talked to a woman in her late 50s burying her mother, a gentle and good soul. She asked, why did she have to lose her husband 11 years into their marriage, why did she have to get dementia? Those questions are still burning in this daughter's mind. At least in my 40 years of dealing with questions like this, I think the most honest and best response I can give is that there is no satisfactory answer.

The questions are still going to be raised in your mind. That's a good thing, because that can help you come to terms with your own death down the line. If you're willing to probe that, but you're also willing to recognize that you don't have an actual need for an answer, then you will find comfort in your loss. The demand for an answer can blind you to a fuller truth about the person whose death you are presently grieving and about your own death. Rilke's words are insightful when you come face to face with the death of someone you love, "Be patient toward all that is unsolved in your life, and try to love the questions themselves".

Karen's Birth Into Eternal Life

On Monday, Sept. 22, 2008, I visited the Purcell home in the afternoon of the first full day of autumn. The cool, crisp air and the bright light of the sun reminded me of the poetic wisdom of Lin Yutang.

"I like spring, but it is too young. I like summer, but it is too proud. So, I like best of all autumn, because its leaves are a little yellow, its tone mellower, its colors richer, and it is tinged a little with sorrow. Its golden richness speaks not of the innocence of spring, not of the power of summer, but of the mellowness and kindly wisdom of approaching age. It knows the limitations of life and is content."[50]

Mike greeted me at the front door. He tearfully told me that his wife moves in and out of consciousness. Karen was lying in a hospital bed in the living room. Mike's parents, Patrick and Maryanne, were at the foot of Karen's bed. I sat in a chair on the right side of the bed. Cancer deprived Karen of speaking with her mouth. Instead, Karen spoke to me with her eyes. She cast her gaze toward me. Her look was steady, gentle, and loving. I gave Karen Holy Communion. I anointed her forehead with the oil of salvation. She fell asleep, at peace.

That sunny, autumn day as I left the Purcell home, I had a vague awareness that something extraordinary just happened during that sacramental exchange. I returned to the rectory at St. Pius X and went directly to the adoration chapel. Only one person was there, Nina Bowdler. I told her that I was just with Karen Purcell.

"Pray, Nina, pray," I implored her.

On Tuesday, Sept. 23, I returned to the Purcell home for my second visit. This time, Karen was in a deep sleep. I sat at her bedside in silence and prayed. Suddenly, Karen awoke and looked at me with a penetrating gaze.

"Karen can see through me," I thought.

At first blush, she was contemplating my face. On further reflection, Karen was focusing on my soul. I gave her Holy Communion the second day and I was conscious that a creation story was spiritually and dramatically unfolding. Karen fell asleep again and I returned to the adoration chapel again for silence, stillness, solitude, and solidarity with the Risen Lord, the Eucharistic Lord, and solidarity with Karen Purcell, a suffering servant of Jesus.

Wednesday, Sept. 24, for the third straight day, I visited Karen. Each day was different from the previous visit. Karen opened her eyes and I detected an internal tug of war. Agitation replaced the deep serenity of the day prior. Reading Karen's eyes on this day was like praying Psalm 42.

"Like a deer that yearns

For running streams,

So my soul is yearning

For you, my God.

My soul is thirsting for God,

The God of my life;

When Can I enter and see

The face of God?

"Why are you cast down , my soul,

Why groan within me?

Hope in God; I will praise him still,

My savior and my God.

"My soul is cast down within me"

I think of Mike, Chris, Jaclyn, Brandon and Leanne

"As I pour out my soul I shall remember

My husband and my four children

How can I lead them rejoicing

Into the house of God,

Amid cries of gladness and thanksgiving

Wild with Joy."

Deeply bonded families experience love for and attachment to one another. When a family experiences separation, there is pain and anguish. Karen knew she was near death. She loved her husband and four children, and was not yet ready to let go. She was not prepared to be physically separated from her family.

I awoke early on Thursday, Sept. 25, 2008. I was unsettled and restless. Why? I am not sure. Perhaps the answer will be revealed later in the day. I prayed before the Blessed Sacrament in an adoration chapel in the rectory of Sacred Heart parish.

I prayed to the Father for wisdom. I prayed to Jesus for compassion. I prayed to the Holy Spirit for peace and gentleness.

"Come, Holy Spirit, Come. Calm my restlessness. Help me to be present to everyone I meet today."

I left the adoration chapel to get ready to exercise and swim at LA Fitness.

I celebrated mass at St. Pius X and gave a homily on the five unskippable steps of the spiritual life. I visited the classrooms in the school. The children energize me and challenge me to be creative, to be real, to be a priest they can easily approach and relate. On my way back to the rectory some children were playing in the schoolyard.

A first grader shouted, "Hey, Fr. Heron, how is it going?!"

What a wonderful, simple question and greeting. Her voice and words gave me the peace and calm I was seeking. "Unless we become like little children we cannot enter the Kingdom of Heaven." (Matthew 18:2-5).

After lunch, I drove to the Purcell home to visit and bring Holy Communion to Karen. This encounter revealed to me that Karen mystically made a decision to surrender in faith.

"Into your hands O, Lord, I hand over my life and my love to you."

There are three descriptions of faith in the New Testament. Jesus tells Peter he has little faith (Matthew 14:31). Jesus announces boldly to the Syrophoenician woman that she possesses great faith (Mark 7:25-30). Jesus recognizes in Nicodemus that his faith is weak despite all his natural intelligence and acquired wisdom from life experiences. Nicodemus, still afraid, comes to see Jesus at night. John the Evangelist tells us, Nicodemus fails to grasp, to understand the importance in being born again in water and fire of the Holy Spirit.

Whether our faith is weak, little, or great, we are still personally, passionately and profoundly loved. Jesus teaches that if our faith is the size of a mustard seed (Matthew 13:31-33), great things will happen in our lives.

After giving Holy Communion to Karen on Thursday with her family gathered around her, everyone sensed death was near. Mike walked me to the door, expressing heartfelt thankfulness. Before leaving, I gave Mike my cellphone number.

I said, "Call me anytime, I shall be keeping the night watch." I received Mike's call around 9:25 p.m., and returned to be with the Purcell family.

We can be prepared for anything in life except the death of a loved one. Death never comes on time. It is too early, as in Karen's case or too late, when people linger a long time before dying.

Meeting Karen Purcell plunged me deeper into the Paschal mystery. Remembering Karen Purcell prevents me from becoming shallow and superficial. Her spirit sustains me in the depths of the spiritual life. When I think of Karen, tears still occasionally come to my eyes, but great joy wells up in my heart every time.

I am grateful to have met a holy, noble woman of faith, if only for a brief visit in a hospital room and five home visits in four days.

What is a Saint?

I once visited a third grade class and I asked the children, "What is a saint?" Several hands were waving in the air and I picked a girl named Rachael. She told me that a saint is "someone who follows Jesus and tries to live like Him." Great, great description!

I asked the third graders, "What did St. Paul mean when he said 'put on the mind of Christ?'" One student told me, "That's easy. It means to think like Jesus." I soon realized that the third graders were teaching me rather than me teaching them.

I went on to explain how important it is to put on the mind of Christ because when we think like Jesus then we can speak like Him and act like Him. I then asked them what a disciple is. No one was really sure about this question, so I told them that a disciple is a lifelong student of Jesus. A disciple comes to Jesus every day in prayer. A disciple comes to listen to Jesus, to learn from Jesus, to gather strength from Jesus, to rest with Him when life gets weary, and to come and be nourished by Jesus, the Bread of Life at Mass.

I then told them that not only do we need to be disciples but we also need to be apostles. Apostles go in His name. Apostles go and proclaim His living word. Apostles preach, teach, baptize, and heal.

Everyone who claims to be a follower of Jesus – not just third graders – needs to get into the rhythm of coming to Him and going in His Name.

St. Paul, in his letter to the Philippians, instructed us that Jesus did not cling to His divinity but rather emptied Himself in order to save us. Saint Paul goes on to say that we, too, must empty ourselves—kenosis—in order to create space for the Holy Spirit to fill us with divine love—pleroma.

A mystical experience with Karen Purcell began in a one, 15-minute conversation. This spiritual bond was born in contemplative silence. This relationship continues to grow in silence, holy silence, grace-filled silence, mystical silence.

The silence into which cancer had plunged Karen allowed her to enter more deeply into the truth and beauty of love suffering. Silence enveloped our souls. Karen Purcell continues to be the watch-keeper of my inner life: my mind, heart, will, and soul. Karen was buried on Tuesday, Sept. 30, 2008.

Her daughter, Jackie, ever by her mom's side, caring for her with the gentle and exquisite skill of a loving daughter and nurse gave Karen her final release. The battle is over. The race is won. The victory is hers.

Because we believe in the Resurrection, we buried Karen's body but not her spirit. We buried her hands but not her good works. We buried her heart but not her love.

The last four days of Karen's life continued to make me reflect on the fragility of all our lives and the importance of looking beyond. It became increasingly important to understand that diminishment as well as growth was a vital part of the spiritual life. John the Baptist captured this when he said, "He must increase, I must decrease." Death is not the end. Life continues into eternal life.

With an amazing leap of intuition, I realized that Shane Famous and Karen Purcell, despite their suffering spoke a mystical language with their eyes. Hope, joy, peace, and love from a place beyond transformed my mind and began to heal my restless soul. As I grew in spiritual maturity, the experience of Karen Purcell's death enabled me to experience a taste of resurrection, which gave me hope to face the future.

The Holy Spirit Makes Us Disciples

Karen, in her own words, put herself at the foot of the cross. What does this mean?

Some years ago, an archbishop spoke on the meaning of the cross. He chose two texts from the bible. The first was from the first chapter of Genesis: "And God said, let there be light, and there was light." The archbishop pointed out how easy it was for God to create the universe.

The second text he chose was from the gospel account of Jesus praying in the Garden of Gethsemane on the night before He was crucified.

"His sweat became like great drops of blood." Creating the world was easy, the archbishop said, but recreating humanity made God sweat blood, perhaps His greatest suffering of all. What an arduous task it is to live each day by God's will, Jesus' light, the Holy Spirit's love.

This reminds me of another story that can shed some light on discipleship in the darkness. In her mid-40s, Ellen moved into a new house. As she decided what to keep and what to throw away, she came across several letters her mother had written to Ellen as a teenager. At that time Ellen wasn't sure she would ever understand her mother or if it was even worth the effort.

Ellen's mother had died about 15 years after writing those letters. As she reread them, middle-aged Ellen finally understood her mother in a way impossible 30 years before. In fact, Ellen realized that in some ways she was becoming her mother. And that was not such a bad thing after all.

The seventeenth chapter of St. John's gospel tells us of Jesus' farewell discourse at the Last Supper. The apostles physically heard what Jesus said but they understood very little. They felt very sure that they knew what Jesus needed to say and do in order to succeed.

As disciples, we sometimes fear that Jesus may be asking too much of us, that being his disciples might cost too much.

Jesus had told the apostles that the Holy Spirit would guide them to all truth. If spreading the Good News had depended completely on the talent and courage of the apostles, the Good News would not have seen the one-year anniversary of Jesus' resurrection. The apostles would have found the resistance to it overwhelming. According to the first chapter of the Acts of the Apostles, the apostles stayed in Jerusalem after Jesus' ascension. They and the earliest Christian community remained in prayer, asking for guidance. Their prayers are answered in an unsettling way at Pentecost. It will take years to "unpack" that experience and its consequences.

They must keep the spirit of prayer and openness to God's grace, evident among the apostles between Jesus' ascension and Pentecost.

They must learn to accept Jesus' standards of success and failure instead of their usual way of calculating those. Often they must challenge "what everybody knows." The apostles were in for a big surprise when they realized that some Gentiles followed Jesus just as eagerly as they did. "They" were becoming part of "us," and it didn't feel very good at first. If the Good News of Jesus does not stretch us and challenge us, then it is a cheap imitation – not the real thing. Peter's First Epistle says that Jesus' followers will share in His sufferings.

When the Holy Spirit rushed upon the apostles at Pentecost, it was time to go out and face the people, to testify openly to Jesus and invite them to be baptized. The Good News of Jesus spread quickly, from one end of the Mediterranean world to the other, eventually across all levels of society. Faith in Jesus helped the apostles deal with the great variety of people who were becoming disciples of Jesus.

Once upon a time, there were no followers of Jesus where we now live. Disciples spread the faith and witnessed to it, not only by their words, but especially by their actions. That faith took root and grew.

Are we ready to live the Good News that makes us disciples, that is, lifelong students of His way, His truth?

CHAPTER 39
The Relationship Between
a Mother and Her Child

"I have read many books and learned many things that you [his parents] could not have taught me. But what I have learned from you remains the most precious and important, and it sustains and gives life to the many other things I learned later in so many years of study and teaching."

—Pope John XXIII's Journal

They were on the road – Jesus, Peter, James, and John – making their way up the mountain. The disciples were asking themselves, "Why do we have to climb this mountain? Why now?" Maybe Jesus wanted a secluded place to pray; they knew that He loved to pray at uncustomary times and in out-of-the-way places. And mountaintops have long been special places to meet God.

At nightfall, the clouds hovered around the top of the mountain. But somehow, tonight, the clouds were different, more present than usual, almost transparent with the divine. The tired disciples drifted off to sleep; not even their sore feet could keep them awake. But they were shocked out of their slumber by the surprise of their lives - there was Jesus, clothed in the glory of brightness that could only be from God, intensely engaged in conversation with Moses and Elijah.

Later Peter, James, and John came to understand why they had to make that long, tiring, difficult climb up the mountain with Jesus. God the Father had intended it to be the place of transfiguration for His beloved Son but also for them. For in that place, at that time, they would have all their expectations about God's Messiah changed. Salvation would not come to God's people through a military victory over their enemies; rather, it would come through the paschal mystery, God the Father's Easter plan in the dying and rising of His beloved Son.

We make this climb annually during the Easter season. Why? Why do we need to fast, pray, and help the needy? The answer is that Lent is the way to our personal and communal transfiguration at Easter. Maybe we are willing to observe Lent if we expect it to be a straightforward, if rather long, time of our usual Lenten practices: the predictable things, the customary practices, the good intentions that go into making a moderately good and not-too-painful preparation for Easter.

Lent might be God's best time for reminding us of this truth: God's love and forgiveness must be our surest strength and only hope throughout our life and at the moment of our death. My mother realized that.

There are ambiguous feelings that are connected with physical death. You're relieved the person you love is no longer suffering or in pain, yet you are also recognizing that an adjustment has to be made in that it's change, but it's not ended. So, that's why the time of death is always a time of faith. It is a radical, courageous trust, a radical risk, and ultimate surrender.

Two weeks before Easter Sunday, the Liturgy bids us reflect on death and life. Lent is a time for soul searching and spiritual housecleaning. Death faces us in the story of Lazarus. The sobering lesson is that being a friend of Jesus did not protect us from pain and suffering or from heartbreaking experiences.

Just consider Martha and Mary, friends of Jesus. They thought of Jesus as the miracle worker. He had raised Jairus' daughter from the dead, but He did not come to them in their hour of need. They were angry because Jesus did not seem to care enough to come when they sent for Him; when their brother Lazarus was still alive, while there was still some hope.

The death of someone you love is always a painful experience. Martha and Mary loved their brother Lazarus and were now learning the painful truth that, even though they were friends of Jesus, they could still experience a broken heart.

But Jesus had a plan – He had a purpose in delaying – to show the mighty power God has over death. Jesus grieved and wept over the death of His friend. He mourned this loss and then consoled Martha and Mary, assuring them that death is not final. He then restored Lazarus to life with the words: "Lazarus come forth!"

But John's Gospel is also about life. It addresses the longing all of us have for receiving life in the face of death or meaningless existence.

The prophet Ezekiel is famous for the image of a valley of dry bones – a windswept battlefield where soldiers once engaged in mortal conflict. All that is left are the skeletal remains of those who have fallen in battle.

Lives are sometimes like that. Lives get broken. Friendships die and wither. Unrealized dreams of youth fade away. Marriages break apart. Children are abused. Nations wage war.

There is a feeling of death and gloom. Dead bones. People speak of a kind of deadness beneath the surface of their lives. They spend their lives feverishly trying to get to the top of the ladder. They are burned out, fed up, done in, stressed out, and overwhelmed. Who will bring new life to this valley of dead bones?

What are left are shells of broken people with broken hearts, broken dreams, and broken promises. Just as Ezekiel's vision sees the dry bones coming to life, so, too, we can come to new life in Christ, through the Spirit of Christ living in us. How?

We have to hear Jesus call us forth from the tombs we have made for ourselves by:

- Letting go of a tenaciously held idea which we know is wrong and inappropriate

- Relinquishing what we know is an impossible dream

- Allowing a child to become an adult

- Leaving unsaid a wounding remark

Every time we let go of these things we are in the process of turning our lives around; we are coming out of those tombs with a new start on life; we are being converted.

Lent is a time for waking up – a time to shake off the fog from our minds, to get the sand out of our eyes, so that we can sit up and see clearly the spiritual condition of our souls.

Lent is our call to let go of what the secular and unbelieving world sees as important.

- We don't want wealth by any means

- We don't want honor by compromising integrity

- We don't want to destroy by word or deed

- We want to forgive the wrongs done to us

- We want the mind of Christ

- We want the heart of Christ

Jesus says to us what He said to Lazarus -- come forth! Begin to live life anew. Be truly alive in these last two weeks of Lent. Let Him heal your brokenness. Let Him put His spirit in you that you may live. My mother was a shining example of allowing Jesus to heal her soul.

Because she believed in eternal life, she was able to transform my father's physical absence into a real presence. Again, that language doesn't register for people who don't have faith. It doesn't register for people who don't believe that death is never the final word in anyone's life. It is a transition. Part of life is sadness, grief and loss, but how you deal with that, not in isolation where you become inconsolable and you're always focused on "he's not here anymore" can cause you a lot more grief than you realize. You can compound grief when it is only dealt with in isolation, but you can understand the human reality of sadness, loss, and grief when it's placed in a bigger context. Everybody grieves differently. Why? Because everybody's relationship with the deceased is unique and different. There's no standard that in three weeks you have to be over this. That can be mechanical and robotic. There's ebb and flow to it. You can sit around at the table and talk about the person and share memories and stories and laugh, and you can really enjoy that sharing that can be a part of the healing process, and enable us to expand our horizon beyond the physical dimension of life. That is such an important lesson to learn.

Physical dying is one thing, but you have to die to other things in life, too. Relationships are one example. However, that's not the final word. You can learn and grow and be richer in character when you experience that death in a bigger context: in the context of eternal life, faith, resurrection, and the cross. Most people can look at the cross without the eyes of faith and see ugliness and destruction. With the eyes of faith, it's victory. Same symbol, but the way you interpret the symbol and understand the symbol can radically change the meaning of this universal experience of death.

The fourth Gospel is often called the Gospel of Love. When you read especially chapters 13 through 17, you can easily see why.

The relationship between a believer, a true disciple, and Jesus is very intimate. There is no relationship on earth more intimate than the relationship of a mother and her child.

Dan Rather's book, *The Camera Never Blinks Twice*, speaks of a tour he made in 1965 on a hospital ship near South Vietnam.

Guides took him below deck to a very large room filled with soldiers recovering from amputations. Rather describes the horror he felt as he observed row upon row of young men bandaged, in pain, crying out constantly. The one name they cried out – "Mother."

When their suffering was so great as to be unbearable, they didn't call for a doctor or a nurse. In their worst moments when they were most desperate for comfort they turned to the first love they ever knew – that of their mothers.[51]

It is good that we should have this day to celebrate when we hear Our Lord tell us that this world was designed for love, for family, for relationships that last.

We should meditate on the value of our homes and families. There are a number of things we learn in the home and in our families:

1. It is there that our identity is established. We learn who we are— that we are persons of worth, of value; that we are bright, capable, persons of promise, loved by God and given many talents by Him.

2. It is in the family and in the home that we learn what is expected of us. This is where our Christian characters are formed; Christian virtues, instilled in us. We learn right from wrong, good from bad. We learn obedience, love for brothers and sisters, for parents.

3. It is there that we learn that our home and families are places of security in this uncertain world. A place to which we can always return.

We were created out of love. We were created for love. The ties that bind us together as individuals, as families, and as the family of Christ, are sacred ties that should never be severed.

Children can make all kinds of major mistakes in life, but they need to know that there is one place where they can always receive forgiveness, support, and love. This is at home.

It is part of the responsibility of mothers and fathers to create such a home.

That is why Jesus told a parable about a young man who went off to a far country and came back home defeated and in disgrace. But his father welcomed him with open arms.

That is how much God loves us. That is how we should love one another. Jesus asks His Father to give us the Holy Spirit to help us do this.

As we thank our mothers, let's not forget to thank God who gives us our true identity: His children. He tells us what He expects of us: keep the commandments and love one another. And He welcomes us home no matter how far we stray.

The Four Births of Dot Heron	
Natural Birth	April 13, 1921
Spiritual Birth (Baptism)	April 30, 1921
Vocational Birth	Oct. 15, 1949
Birth Into Eternal Life	Nov. 19, 2003

Dot Heron was born into eternal life on Nov. 19, 2003. She was 82 years old. Thank you, mom, for feeding me, physically and spiritually. Good night and God bless you. I love you very much.

CHAPTER 40
Death Never Comes on Time, Always Too Early or Too Late

"Lord, Jesus, may I know myself and may I know You."

—St. Augustine (354 – 430)

These untimely deaths – a 33-year-old father, a 51-year-old mother, and four-year-old child – mysteriously and ultimately gave me clarity. Death never comes on time, always too early or too late. All three deaths were preparing me for the great loss of my spiritual mentor, teacher, spiritual father, and close friend of 44 years, Msgr. Daniel A. Murray.

Death has a way of surprising us, even when "expected," because we are never fully ready to let go of the physical presence of the one we love, never fully ready for what seems to be a final farewell on Earth. I learned an early lesson around the family dinner table from the stories of my dad, and his words to me, "Tom, I want you to be my business partner," which became a way to understand the sting of death ... "Do this in memory of Me."

There is real presence. There is life after death. I had grown into understanding the nearly incomprehensible truth of the Paschal Mystery and then touched it. In Shane Famous, Karen Purcell, my mom, and now Dan's dying, I believed and could share this hope in the promise of the Kingdom of God. For anyone who seeks first the Kingdom of God, the promise of sharing in eternal life is real and sustaining.

Aug. 16, 2013, Dan and I had gone to the shore for a much-needed vacation. Both pastors now of thriving parishes, we were in need of some time in an out-of-the-way place. Our friendship, spanning 43 years, included many Fridays where an exchange of homily ideas, spiritual direction, and long walks on the boardwalk in Ocean City, N.J., inspired and uplifted both of us. So too, did our many vacations to the Jersey Shore for rest, relaxation, and renewal.

But, in August 2013, such was not to be the case. We traveled to the shore on a Sunday afternoon. By Tuesday, Dan's failing heart condition had so deteriorated that I finally called his cardiologist, who instructed me to get Dan to the emergency ward of Lankenau Hospital as quickly as possible. Dan reluctantly agreed.

I raced at breakneck speed to Lankenau Hospital, concerned that at any moment I might need to pull over and administer the Anointing of the Sick. Dan had only agreed to return to the hospital if I promised not to stay there, but to return to the shore.

He was admitted to the emergency room. I saw he was in good hands, and returned to the shore, just as Dan had requested. This emergency trip to the hospital began a steady, unrelenting, and descending spiral in Dan's health – only 11 months away from celebrating 50 years as a priest. Dan would live to celebrate that hallmark with his parish, St. Rose of Lima, in North Wales, Pa., the following Pentecost, June 8, 2014, but not the actual celebration of the date of his ordination, July 12, 1964.

I remembered a note that I had written to Bishop Michael Burbidge the previous September in which I conveyed my gratitude for a phone call he made to Dan.

"He still speaks with a whisper voice," I wrote, " when you are in his company as opposed to speaking with him on the phone. His voice is much stronger on the phone. I don't know why that is. His appetite is good, but the spark that is usually present is nowhere to be found. Please continue to keep him in your daily prayers."

His loss of weight, strength, and stamina became increasingly a concern for me, but also Dan's brothers, Marty and Kevin, and his sister, Maureen.

By January 2014, Dan began several stays in and out of hospitals and in rehabilitation facilities. When I visited Dan about five days before he died I spoke with Kevin, who is also a priest. We both recognized that the end was coming for Dan, and he did, too. So, we both decided to celebrate the sacrament of the anointing of the sick. Usually one priest does it, but we both anointed him.

Dan's response to that was, "Is there something you know that I don't know?"

Known as an intellectual, Dan informed Kevin and I that if anybody asks for his final musings to tell them this:

"Mairzy doats and dozy dotas and liddle lamzy divey" – words from the novelty song, "Mairzy Doats."

The ability to have humor is so vital in these critical moments. My mom said, after the priest went in and anointed my dad, she was brought back in and they laughed and they cried. The last thing my dad said to my mom, he whispered into her ear, "Pray hard, Dot, I'll always be with you." Those words echoed into her heart and soul until the day she took her last breath.

Being able to let go of life as we know it now and trust that something richer and fuller awaits us is the ultimate awareness in the hour of our death.

When we hear Jesus pray the High Priestly Prayer found in chapter 17 of St. John's Gospel, we read that He prays for His disciples, because He knows He will not be with them much longer. In this prayer He sounds a bit like a worried mother.

He is going to return to His Heavenly Father and is leaving His disciples in the world. He is worried about their safety. He sees how life creates divisions among people. He prays not only that they will be protected but for their unity—that they may be one. In chapter 15 of St. John's Gospel, Jesus prays intently for His disciples to, "Remain in My love."

Jesus doesn't ask God to take them out of the world; nor does He ask that they be given special immunity to the realities of the world. He asks that they may be safeguarded from the evil one.

In this lengthy prayer, Jesus is praying that His disciples may not be fully at home in this world. He asks His Father to empower them to say "No." He is hoping that they will refuse to adjust or adapt too fully to this world, which is not their true home.

This might seem strange to us today because we have been taught the value of making adjustments, of adapting to changing times. We are told that one sign of maturity is the ability to make adjustments. In fact, John Henry Newman says, "To live is to change and to be [holy], and to be [holy] is to have changed often."

"Adapt or perish," said H.G. Wells, "is Nature's imperative."

Yet, Jesus prays that His disciples will refuse to adjust or adapt. How are we to understand this?

To live with integrity, to be whole, to be healthy spiritually, we must know where the outer limits of our souls are. We can become so adaptable that we end up with no spiritual identity, no place to take a stand. Indiscriminate adjusting can be deadly.

Life as a Christian involves a delicate balance between being in this world but not of it. This is no easy task. Too often, we fall off the fence on one side or the other.

We live in a world of alienation. Break-up is pervasive. Families become seedbeds of estrangement and victimization. Many ask: "What's in it for me?" We don't know whom to trust. Money is "power" and brings "happiness." It is easy to see why Jesus prays that we be empowered to say "No" to such a life.

Dan died of heart failure. He was being sustained by a medicine. It had an adverse effect on all of his organs. Food was revolting. There was a collapse of his organs. He was born into eternal life on June 26, 2014, at age 76.

The Four Births of Msgr. Dan Murray	
Natural Birth	Nov. 27, 1937
Spiritual Birth (Baptism)	Dec. 19, 1937
Vocational Birth	June 12, 1964
Birth Into Eternal Life	June 26, 2014

We all grope. No one has such pure faith. Dan experienced intense anxiety, and yet he could inject humor into that, too. How well have you immersed yourself? That's what baptism is, and it is so important in the cyclical nature of our lives. Immerse yourself into this vision and philosophy of life that Jesus taught, and ask yourself, "How well have I come to absorb that, assimilate it, and make it my own?"

Dan was a tremendous teacher. The best teachers give away everything they know. In doing so, like Dan, they are generous of heart. Sacred Scripture depicts the teacher's knowledge as a lamp full of oil – its flame driving out the darkness. The light of this flame draws the student in and if the student pays attention, he or she will leave enlightened and changed.

Jesus is a Master Teacher. Israel and Nicodemus were His students. The book of Chronicles teaches us about the varnished truth of Israel's disregard for God's offer of love. The rulers, the priests, the entire people "added infidelity to infidelity, practicing all the abominations of the pagans and polluting the Lord's temple." Israel chose blissful ignorance and sloppy lifestyles over God's loving efforts to save them. In a word, they chose darkness over light.

Now, generally, people prefer light over darkness, except when it comes to sin or the challenge of conversion, changing our lifestyles so as to live in light.

We meet Nicodemus in the third chapter of John's Gospel. He is fearful and confused. He is tired of facing his own darkness and so seeks out Jesus – but he does so in the darkness of the night. Nicodemus listens as Jesus speaks at length about the cost and cause of our salvation. The cause is God's love for the world. The cost is the crucifixion and death of God's only Son – who is sitting right there, facing Nicodemus.

T.S. Eliot, in the third of his *Four Quartets*, said, "We had the experience, but missed the meaning."[52] Eliot is, of course, referring to the struggle we have to grasp the significance of what happens in life, particularly in those important moments that have the potential for making a huge difference.

Wasn't that true of Nicodemus? Isn't it true of us? There was old Nicodemus, sitting in the dark of night, staring in the face of the Light of the World – and he missed the meaning. We know that surrender to the new, to what challenges us, is a hard thing.

We know intuitively how difficult it is to gain the kind of knowledge that requires change and conversion. We know that ignorance is bliss, that non-engagement is easier – duller, but easier.

Like the Israelites of old and like Nicodemus, we too avoid the Good News of God's love. We prefer to sit in darkness. Jesus invites us to look on His body nailed to a cross in meditative silence. That's the experience – don't miss the meaning, because the meaning is for everyone – personal, passionate, and profound.

That body, nailed to that cross, accomplished the triumph of light over darkness, good over evil, which Jesus came into the world as the true Light. But, He does not make a forced entry into our lives. He does not impose Himself on us. The choice is ours.

Can we believe in God as much as God believes in us? The battle between light and darkness is played out in each of our souls. Most people want no part of this battle. They are tired and bored. They have no energy, no incentive, and no interest in anything. What do they do? They sit like zombies before television sets. They rearrange furniture every week. They buy new clothes. They purchase a new car. They play on their cellphones. What they are really choosing is darkness over light. Anyone who is not satisfied with his or her life should stop rearranging furniture, stop exercising their thumbs, and start rearranging their lives.

St. Paul implores us to rejoice in the Lord. The greatest rejoicing happens when we look on the body nailed to that cross and capture the meaning of what happened on that first Good Friday.

I say again, the choice is ours: remain in the darkness, or come out and live in the Light of Christ.

In the movie, *Saving Private Ryan*, a young soldier is rescued, but most of the men in the squadron, including the captain, died in the rescue attempt. As he lay dying, the captain's last words to Private Ryan are, "earn this."

Years later, Private Ryan, now an old man, visits the grave of his captain at Normandy. He kneels down and says, "Not a day goes by I don't think about what happened, and I just want you to know, I have tried, tried to live my life the best I could. I didn't invent anything. I didn't cure any diseases. I worked on a farm, raised a family, lived a life. I only hope, in your eyes, at least, I earned what you did for me."

Look at Jesus on the cross and hear Him say, "Earn this, be worthy of this." The choice is ours. Wouldn't it be a blessing if each of us could say at the hour of our death, "Lord, I hope in your eyes, I earned what You did for me"?

Msgr. Dan Murray, in my eyes, earned every drop of blood that came from the body of Christ for him, for us. Thank you, Dan, for guiding me to a greater, richer understanding of the spiritual life. May you rest in peace, and through the memories we have of you, continue to guide us all to ask the better questions.

CHAPTER 41

The Fine Line Between Tears of Sadness and Tears of Laughter

"May the road rise up to meet you. May the wind be always at your back. May the sun shine warm upon your face, the rains fall soft upon your fields and, until we meet again, may God hold you in the palm of His hand."

—Traditional Gaelic Blessing

William Blake once wrote, "And we are put on earth a little space, that we may learn to bear the beams of love." The beams he was referring to are the cross.

The memento of the Carmelite cross on the cover of this book is a symbol of the victory over sin and death, which Jesus wants to share with all of us. We must bear the beams of suffering all of divinity, which means living according to His way, His truth and His life. That allows us to live an upright life.

"Pati Humani," means that like Jesus, we are to stretch out our arms and love to family, friends, strangers, and enemies, alike. No one is to be excluded. Yet, we all fail in both of those beams. Jesus invites us again and again to come to Him when we fail, when we find life weary and burdensome, and he will refresh us, give us a new start and help us bear the beams of love with nobility and dignity, and recognizing we consciously choose to suffer in love to try to reduce the suffering in the world that is rooted in sin. The goal is eternal life. We have to keep our eyes fixed on the goal. There's also a means to achieve the goal. We have to be willing to buy into that.

"*Pati Divina,*" is to love in accordance with Jesus: "I am the way and the truth and the life. No one comes to the Father except through me." (John 14:6).

e.e. cummings writes, "We can never be born enough. We are human beings for whom birth is a supremely welcome mystery, the mystery of growing, which happens only and whenever we are faithful to ourselves."

The mystery of natural birth (your birthday) and the mystery of spiritual birth (when you become a son or daughter of the Blessed Trinity, so now you have human and divine love to surround and embrace you), allow you to discern your vocational birth. What role do you play in the plan of salvation history? Vocational birth is when you believe you have a role to play, and in playing that role, you make a positive difference in the world. Those three births prepare us for birth into eternal life. The degree that we are faithful to natural birth, spiritual birth, and vocational birth, transition into birth into eternal life will allow us to see it not in isolation, but in continuum.

When tasked with celebrating Mass of Christian Burial, I commonly recite the Hilaire Belloc quote, "Wherever the Catholic sun does shine, there is music, laughter, and good red wine. At least I've always found it so. Benedicamus Domino!" The sun in the poem is the radiant light of the glorious resurrection, not the solar system's sun. When that light breaks in, it sheds a whole new understanding of suffering and death, and then you can focus on not sadness, loss and grief, but focus on music, laughter, and good red wine, which are symbols of faith, memory, and love. When you have that, you can bless the Lord for the entirety of someone's life and the memories that we have of sharing life with him or her.

They are really important beliefs and truths to help us. We are all called to heaven. How we face dying and recognize that as a part of life – not fleeing from it – that enables us to live life more abundantly. When we come face to face with the death of someone we love and who has loved us, we experience fight or flight. We can try to deny it, fight it, and flee from it, or we can face it with confidence, courage, and compassion. Death powerfully teach us at least three important lessons:

The gift of time and how we use it, the gift of faith and how we practice it, and the gift of love and how we generously share it.

The prophet Isaiah has a great passage where he says, "On this mountain, the Lord of hosts will provide for all peoples a feast of rich food and choice wines, juicy rich food and pure, choice wines. On this mountain he will destroy the veil that veils all peoples, the web that is woven over all nations. He will destroy death forever." (Isaiah 25:6-8). In both testaments, throughout the entire Bible, the mountain was a symbol of a sacred meeting place between God and all of us. He would come down, we would go up. He would raise us up, we would ascend.

The altar in St. Matthew's church, and in many churches, is usually at a very high point. The altar becomes the new mountain place. At the altar, bread and wine are transformed into the Risen Body and Blood of Jesus and He provides spiritual nourishment every step of the journey in life on Earth. The altar is where, through the liturgy, the veil is opened up. If you believe Jesus came, suffered, died, and rose again, the Mass is meant to reenact the Paschal Mystery – his life, death, and resurrection. He died on Mt. Calvary. Some people would say it's a hill, but his death opens the gates to heaven and enables people to see beyond suffering and death, a glimpse of heaven. Isaiah goes on in that passage to say, "The Lord will wipe away the tears from all faces." He's not just elusive or aloof. He wants to be with us in our sadness, loss, and grief. He doesn't delegate someone else wiping the tears from our faces. He doesn't abandon us, but accompanies us through that, so that we can see beyond our sadness, loss, and grief. He reassures us that something greater awaits us.

The absence of a developing or maturing faith causes the fear of death. The absence of not understanding the story of Jesus of Nazareth, not grasping, allows us to embrace the darkness, rather than turning toward the light. The Paschal Mystery is birth and life, suffering, death, and resurrection. Most people want to bypass the suffering and death and just experience the life we have now, and then jump right into eternal life. That is, to me, selective and not really a mature approach to allowing Jesus to be the Master Teacher of your life.

There is a fine line between authentic faith and fanatical faith. We must exhibit the ability to walk that fine line and remain authentic in our faith. That's what "earthy mysticism" is about. You can't reject your humanity. God didn't create you to be an angel. He created you to be a flesh and blood man or woman, made in his image and likeness.

The first thing we would look to is, "what does it mean to be remade from this lowly body?" How do we turn flesh and blood into a glorified body, or a resurrected body. What does a resurrected order of living look like? No one completely knows. What happens is speculation occurs. Do we believe that we will be reunited with those who have already died? Yes. It's almost theology by exclusion. We believe there will be no more suffering, no more pain, no more hunger, no more poverty. All those things will be gone.

How long can you gaze at the beatific vision? That would be kind of boring. It would be relational. It will be filled with wisdom. There will be release from many limitations. Physical limitations, intellectual limitations, moral limitations. We'll know whether climate change is a hoax or a reality! You have to get it into those practical terms, but there will be some connection to this lowly body. Yet, it will also be a transformed, glorified body. Does that mean it will be the best body I had when I was whatever age I was? No, but you'll be completely at peace. You'll have joy. You won't need hope anymore because you've arrived.

There's an element of surprise. Who will be up there and who won't be up there? There's a lot of people who say everybody will be saved. There are some problems with that statement. Matthew's 25th chapter talks about separating the sheep from the goats. If we believe we have free will, we can make a conscious choice to reject sharing in the victory over sin and death. There are some mystics of recent vintage who believe that before anybody dies, Jesus comes and visits them, because mercy is of paramount importance in our relationship with the Risen Lord.

Justice will be eliminated in heaven. Thank goodness for that. The good thief at the end of the Passion story asks Jesus to remember him. We must live in His way, which is not our way. Are there benefits to living according to His way for an extended period of time in your life? Yes, there are benefits to that, but no one merits heaven. It is a free gift. So, people of fanatical faith think that they are putting in all of their spiritual practices into their spiritual bank account and trying to earn it. They expect it in return. Pride is not part of heaven.

Relationships play a vital role. They'll be purified and healthy. Even going back to the Baltimore Catechism: why did God make me? He made me to know Him, to love Him, and to serve Him in this world, and to be happy with Him in the next world – in eternal life. That's a very antiseptic but accurate truth in what we believe awaits us. Justice and mercy are products of the world, but they are not needed in heaven. These things cause anguish in people's lives, which is another part of fanaticism.

All those mindsets that we cling to tenaciously will be purified or liberated in heaven. We will not carry our sense of justice that we think is the best to heaven. Some people claim that this is the idea of purgatory. It purifies poor patterns of living and wrongheaded patterns of thinking that do not match up. "I can't forgive somebody boundlessly, I'd be a milk toast. I'd let people walk all over me." So, life is more from a Gospel view paradox than it is strict legalism. It constantly challenges us and knocks us off balance. You have to live through the discomfort of being off balance until you surrender in faith and establish a balance.

Why do people allow the negative emotions to dominate? It is because they are allowing their ego to respond to situations in life. That's where we all need grace to understand this life that is given as a gift. You always hear the saying from the book of Job, "The Lord gives and the lord takes away." Once we can create some space for God – the mystery of divine love – to help us in our seeking out the meaning of this, we are slightly freed from getting really tied up in the Ego Spirit.

There are people who are inconsolable. They cling tenaciously to these grieving emotions. The church believes that when you fall in love, you become attached. When there's detachment and separation, there's grief, pain, sadness, and loss. That's just part of the way we are all wired. To the degree that you love the person and are loved by that person, that can intensify the grief, sadness, pain, and loss. How do you process that? What are the methods? There is no blueprint and timeline for anybody. When a Mass of Christian Burial is celebrated, you can't ignore grief, pain, sadness, and loss. That has to be experienced. You have to come up with a way to inject hope that maybe not during the celebration of this liturgy four days after this person has died, but that there is hope on the horizon. What will stir that hope into a real-life experience is faith, memory, and love. The thread of grace always works through faith, memory, and love.

In sacred scripture, to remember is a holy act. Why? Because it can bring things from the past into the present and give new meaning. Simply showing up and being present can speak greater than trying to fumble with words. That's why when human words fail us, we depend on the Living Word of God to give us comfort, strength, and consolation. That makes a lot of sense to me, because you're recognizing the limitations of trying to grasp this mystery of death.

The psalmists have it right in that our allotted time on earth is about 70 years; 80 if we're strong. That's going back 2,500 to 3,000 years. I'm sure the life expectancy wasn't 70 years back then, but there it is, written. Some cultures might have experienced it at the time. That's why 33 years, four years, 51 years, really knocks us off balance. It's almost like we're owed a minimum of 60 years, and then it can be negotiated.

Laughter is a good thing. it tells us we don't have the whole ball of wax. No one does. Yet, you can still negotiate without having all the pieces of the puzzle. If we can cope in faith, memory, and love, we can miraculously transform tears of sadness into tears of joy and laughter. That is an amazing skill in the darkness of loss.

I'll close this work with a story about a man who passed away in 2017. He was 94 years old, and a very active member of the Scouts. Everybody in the church had a scout uniform on – even a lawyer, who gave the words of remembrance.

His son told me a story that solidified the idea that we're all creatures of habit. This 94-year-old man liked his pew at church. Toward the end of his life, when he was walking into church with his walker, if someone was in his pew, he would eventually take another seat, but before he would do that, he would stare down the occupants of his pew. The last time he attended church, there was a family in his pew with a newborn infant. As he made his way to another pew, it was almost as if he was passing the torch. He was moving out, and this newborn baby was moving in.

The Ladder of Imperatives

Paul Michael Gallagher, in his book, *Faith Maps,* intellectually describes the work of Bernard Lonergan. After years of intent study, Lonergan came to a paradoxical discovery: genuine objectivity is the fruit of authentic subjectivity. In other words, we arrive at truth through fidelity to the ladder of imperatives – present in our ordinary self-transcending question.[53] That ladder can be expressed briefly in this way:

- Be in Love

- Be Responsible

- Be Reasonable

- Be Intelligent

- Be Attentive

We are all called to climb this ladder, leading to our eventual births into eternal life. I end this book with a map of my own four births in this life of a priest. I leave the rest in God's hands. I put myself at the foot of the cross. Is it lunchtime yet?

The Four Births of Fr. Tom Heron	
Natural Birth	Nov. 14, 1952
Spiritual Birth (Baptism)	Nov. 30, 1952
Vocational Birth	May 20, 1978
Birth Into Eternal Life	TBD by Father, Son, and Holy Spirit*

*My coffin is ready, in the basement of the rectory, for my final birth

EPILOGUE

Checking Out
of the Mediocre Inn

"All my words come back to me in shades of mediocrity."

– "Homeward Bound" by Paul Simon

Dom Columba Marmion, a respected spiritual writer, once said, "The difference between the saints and the rest of us is, the saints plunge themselves into the consumed fire of Divine love. They come out burned, but magnificently transfigured." The rest of us put our little finger in, get burned, and spend the rest of our lives circling the fire, far enough never to be burned again and close enough to be warmed by it. This act can be defined as lukewarm, or in simpler terms, mediocrity. That's how too many people live their lives.

Mediocrity is compromise worked out into a system, and the system seemingly works. In other words, we never lose our reputation, but we don't go storming into heaven nor do we change the world.

My grandfather's words of wisdom continue to echo my soul. "Tommy, lad, be steadfast, be stouthearted." I did not understand the meaning of these words when he first spoke them to me as a 5-year-old. I knew he was giving me advice that would last a lifetime by the way he inflected his "Irish brogue." Later, I discovered my grandfather was quoting the psalmist.

Father John Simons, offered similar sage words as my grandfather. He taught me a course in the Romantic poets, in 1972. I always remember his wisdom: "mediocrity as a goal is deplorable, as an achievement is commendable."

I began this book with a legend. I end it with a fable.

On the way to the top of the highest peak in the French Alps, there is a small inn. It provides rest and respite for the mountain climbers. It's called the Mediocre Inn, which in French simply means "halfway."

The climbers experience the icy, windy conditions of the Alps. The cold seeps into their bones. They are exhausted, every muscle aches.

At the Mediocre Inn, the climbers find a hot meal and a warm bed. They begin to relax, put their feet up, and get comfortable. Who wouldn't like that?

But success is not found in rest and comfort. Success is reaching the top of the mountain and it requires going back out into the cold and wind. It requires stretching and straining - working toward the goal.

About 80 percent of the climbers never go any farther than the Mediocre Inn. Once they've had a day or two of rest and comfort, they turn around and go back down the mountain, never reaching the goal of their climb: the Alps' Highest Peak. They lose the determination to achieve what they set out to do.

Well, truth be told, we've all spent time in the Mediocre Inn, haven't we? Not the one in the Alps, but in our very own Mediocre Inn. Most are not too happy about that.

That's why heroes are so important. We like hearing about people who pick up where the rest of us leave off. We like stories of heroes who make it the rest of the way to the top of the mountain.

That kind of determination is what it takes to be successful in this world, whether you're building a career, a family, or a life. The basic question is, "Am I willing to give my all to achieve my goal?"

This brings us to some words of Jesus in the Gospel: "Whoever loves his life loses it, and whoever hates his life in this world will preserve it for eternal life." (John 12:25).

Deep down in our bones, we realize that Jesus is talking about a way of life that doesn't stop at the Mediocre Inn.

We all prefer a life of excellence. We want to give our strength to the weak, our substance to the poor, our sympathy to the suffering, and our hearts to Father, Son, and Holy Spirit.

To do this we cannot live forever in the Mediocre Inn. We want our lives to make a difference, to be remembered for our life in Christ. We want to be able to stand unashamed before God.

One of the reasons we come to church is to be inspired and to hear about the heroes of the Bible. We want to hear the challenging words of the prophets and of St. Paul. Most of all, we want to hear the words of Jesus Christ, who is the Way, the Truth, and the Life.

We come to give thanks and ask for His help in living an abundant, holy life. We need His help to leave the Mediocre Inn and answer Jesus' call to live a life of service.

Our commitment to holiness begins with a commitment to Jesus. That's the only way to escape the Mediocre Inn and find a joy that this world cannot know or provide.

The Gospels warn us about living a shallow, superficial lifestyle. Jesus continually invites us to go higher, to go to the top of the mountain, to go to that place of encounter – that sacred meeting place – and be transfigured into a contemporary Christ-man, a contemporary Christ-woman.

There is a story about a student who asked his teacher to explain the meaning of the word "soul" to him. Upon hearing the question, the teacher remained silent.

The student repeated the question two or three more times, without receiving a single word in reply. Finally, the teacher opens his mouth and says, "I am instructing you now, but you are not listening."

The answer, of course, is "silence."

The host of the Eucharist is the incarnate language of human and divine silence.

Are you listening?

Are you seeing?

Are you receiving?

ACKNOWLEDGMENTS

Miracles do happen. Sometimes the miracles even exceed expectations. Publishing my first book is a miracle. Without the help and encouragement of many people, this hope would still be unfulfilled.

I can think of no greater tribute to Dan Murray, my spiritual director of 44 years, than to say that he helped me to know myself, both the weeds and wheat of my personality. Painstakingly, Dan Murray led me from "naïve realism" to "critical realism" and that conversion has made and continues to make a profound difference in my life.

Two people made this book happen: Mary Kay McKenna and Kevin Haslam. Mary Kay wanted to do whatever she could to complete this dream of mine and make it available to readers. Mary Kay bore nobly on her shoulders the heavy burden of details and final organization of this book, which freed me to attend to the pastoral responsibilities of the care of the people of St. Matthews Parish. Her sensitivity to the subject matter and her creativity in connecting the dots between Natural Birth, Spiritual Birth, Vocational Birth and Birth into Eternal Life is a testimony to her friendship to me. I am most grateful to her.

I met Kevin Haslam in the latter part of 2016. Kevin came to the rectory seeking a letter of eligibility to be a godparent for the baptism of his good friend's first baby. He was also looking to volunteer his time with the church as a new resident in the area. We asked each other a few questions and discovered common interests, such as fitness training and writing. Kevin told me he wrote and published a book. I told him that I am writing a book, and I asked if I could show him my effort so far to see what he thought. Three weeks later, Kevin told me he would be interested in collaborating in my dream to publish a memoir/autobiography on the occasion of my 40th anniversary as a priest. His full investment, his outstanding editorial skills, his background in publishing and marketing, and his commitment to meet with me several times, mostly, early in the morning, enabled me to talk my way through the book and all its various parts.

I am forever grateful to Kevin and Mary Kay, both.

I am most grateful to my friend, Sara Lessard, who graciously spent much time reading, writing, and editing the section on Vocational Birth. This aided greatly in making that particular section an authentic reflection of that period of my priesthood.

To my siblings: Suzanne Stephan (husband, Jack), Joe Heron, and Mary Lafferty (husband, Chal). I would not change a thing growing up together at 500 Lafayette Ave., Collingdale, also famously known as Dot's Deli.

To my neices and nephews – First generation: Kevin, Courtney, Jill, Colleen, Kristen, Dennis, Dan, and Amy; second generation: Wesley and Nate.

To my cousins who have been a steady source of loving support and encouragement: Benene family, Christensen family, Fee family, Gallagher family, Gallen family, McKeaney family, Reilly families.

To my staff at St. Matthews: Deacon Joe Carr, Val DiGiovanni, Marie and John Baranowski, Bill McAvoy, Drew and Paulette Trainer, Helene Clegg, Claire Wiszclo, Sr. St. Herman SSJ, Alicia Fabrizio, Carol and Tim Kearney, and Barbara Zydzik. Your patience, understanding, and kindness I shall always cherish.

To my favorite elementary school teachers: Mrs. Carr, Mrs. Hoover, Ms. McCafferty, Sr. Ann Martin IHM, Sr. Stella Marie IHM, Sr. Noreen Joseph IHM.

To my favorite high school teachers: Fr. John Melton, OSA, Fr. Joe Jordan OSA, Mr. Rich Bulley, Mr. Vince Donahue, Mr. Ralph Celadonia, Mr. Jim McGrath, Mr. Bill Engblom.

To my favorite college professors: Msgr. Fran Carbine, Msgr. Vince Burns, Msgr. Jim McBribe, Fr. Sid Bourgoyne, Fr. John Simons, John Cardinal Foley.

To my favorite theology professors: Msgr. Dan Murray, Msgr. Fran Meehan, Fr. Mike Chabach, Msgr. John Miller, Fr. Jim Collins.

To my friends: Bill and Denise Mattia, Fr. Kevin Murray, Sr. Maureen Murray RSM, Caroline Murray, Jim and Tina Gula, Jeff and Mary Ann Bond, Chris and Alicia Bond, Pierce McKenna, Lindsay and Persephone, Mike and Mary Garvin, George DeFrehn family, Flounders family, Matthews family, Feehery family, McCormick family, Lorenz family, Joe Dempsey family, Bishop Bob Morneau, Bishop Mike Burbidge, Fr. Jim Sherlock, Msgr. John Jagodzinski, Fr. John Large, Fr. John Ames, Msgr. Phil Ricci, Msgr. Tom Owens, Fr. Joe Ryan OSA , Fr. Jim McKeaney, Fr. Christopher Cooke, Bishop Tim Senior, Shura and Joe Sullivan, Mary Ann Pruskowski, Mary Ann Cook, Bud Reilly, Ann Casavecchia, McKendry family, Lynch family, Cusack family, Woodland family, James "Moon" Mullen, Pat and Lori Getzfread, Ed Pluccinek, Chris Ruck family, Jonathan Smith family, Brian McGrath family, Eileen Baranowski, Margie and John MacDonald, Mr. John Lewis, Esq., Dr. Peter and Jennifer Lewis, Mark and Jennifer Lewis, Anna Dougherty, Patti Connor, Maryellen Smith, Nick and Peg Sciortino, Kim, Josh and Will Hannum, Alice O'Connor, Pat Ratoskey, Charles Mascio, Tony and Mary Dunleavy, Minnick family, McGroarity family, Pat Kelley and family, Eustace Wolfington, Purcell family, Boston family, Mullen family, DiCampli family, Berridge family, Butera family, Donnelly family, Clark family, Bowdler family, Wellman family, Williamson family, Sara Bacza, Hannon family, Jim and Mary Jo Danella, Chuck Hemcher and Great American Pub, Barry and Steve Marino with the Lucky Dog Saloon, Flocco Family, especially Donald, Jennifer, Carmen and +Sunny Marie, Priscilla and +Joe Littio, Guy Matthews, Trish Taggert, Julian Miraglia, Rachael Mattioni and family, Bob Manning, Denny Brown, Alex and Dave Piermani of Father and Son Beer Distributors, Lisa Gruchacz, Fazio family, Phinn family, McElwee family, Tom and Patricia Belmont, Regina Cunningham, Jeff and Eunice Prendergast, Carol Mancini, Marian D'Amora, Bob and Janet Cahill, Pat and Drew Hanna, Ann and Al Augunas, Mike and Barbara Olivieri, John and Cornelia Fruncillo, Tom and Marlene Waldron, Carol Ann and Paul Smith, Donald Moore Funeral Home, Adam and Bob Moore Funeral Home, Ciavarelli Funeral Home, Joyce and Ed Kelly, Maryellen Smith, Oliver St. Clair Franklin.

To those who carefully read the drafts and contributed invaluable comments: Jim Gula, Tony and Mary Dunleavy, George DeFrehn, Patrick McCaskey.

I wish it were possible to personally identify all of the people who touched my heart and soul over the years. It is not, but you know who you are, and I hope you appreciate the important role you have played in my life. Thank you! I am grateful.

ABOUT THE AUTHOR

John Thomas Heron was born on Nov. 14, 1952, the second child of four to Jack and Dorothy (Reilly) Heron. Raised in Collingdale, Pa., Heron's father died of a heart attack on Aug. 26, 1957, at the age of 33. Heron's mother went on to raise her four children (Suzanne, Tom, Joe, and Mary) by operating a corner convenience store. Heron remembers his mother as a woman of remarkable faith – one handed down to all of her children.

Faced with the task of raising four children alone, Heron's mother found salvation in a remembered love, constantly converting the pain of her husband's absence into a deeper understanding of his lasting presence. Heron recalls this as his fondest childhood memory – the poetic ability of his mother sharing the memories of his father. Even though Jack Heron was physically absent, Dot kept him alive in memory and in love.

Another key figure in Heron's life was his grandfather, John Joseph Heron. One of the most joyful people he's ever encountered, Heron recalls his grandfather' zeal for living life to its fullest. Throughout his childhood years, the family was often entertained by John's stories of Ireland – their common denominator being John's knack for making himself the hero each and every time. With a sparkle in his eyes and his calloused hands, Heron recalls his grandfather running his hand across his head and encouraging him to be modest, be generous, and not to let anyone take advantage of him.

Monsignor Daniel Murray played an influential role in Heron's adult life. They met in September 1970 when Murray was a professor of sacred scripture at St. Charles Borromeo Seminary in Wynnewood, Pa. Sharing a common interested in sports (especially basketball and tennis), the two bonded over Heron's pondering of life's unanswered questions – ones burning since his high school years. Msgr. Murray engaged Heron's questions, but raised many more. Even in death, Murray continues to serve as Heron's spiritual director and close friend.

Heron attended Catholic elementary grade school prior to enrolling in Monsignor Bonner High School from 1966 to 1970. Upon graduation, he entered St. Charles Borromeo Seminary's college division. He graduated with a B.A. in philosophy in May 1974 and began studying theology at St. Charles the following September. He was ordained a priest on May 20, 1978 for service in the Archdiocese of Philadelphia.

In 1978, Heron received a Master of Divinity degree, followed by a Master of Arts degree in religious studies in 1982 – both from St. Charles.

Following his ordination, Heron served in various assignments, including parochial vicar at St. Michael the Archangel (Levittown, 1978-82), professor at Archbishop Kennedy High School (Conshohocken, 1982-86), school minister at Bishop McDevitt High School (Wyncote, 1986-89), Formation Faculty at St. Charles Borromeo Seminary (1989-96), parochial vicar at Saint Cyril (East Lansdowne, 1996-97), pastor at Good Shepherd Parish (Philadelphia, 1998-2003), pastor at St. Gabriel's (Norwood, 2003-07), parochial vicar at St. Pius X (Broomall, 2008-09), pastor at St. James (Elkins Park, 2009-10), parochial vicar at St. Coleman's (Ardmore, 2010-11), and parochial administrator at St. Matthew (Conshohocken, 2011-12), pastor at St. Matthew (Conshohocken, 2012-14).

Heron has served as pastor of the newly formed St. Matthew Parish since 2014. *We Are All Called* is his first book.

WORKS CITED

1. James, William. "The Religion of Healthy-Mindedness." *The Varieties of Religious Experience: A Study in Human Nature. Being the Gifford Lectures on Natural Religion, Delivered at Edinburgh in 1901-1902.* (1902).

2. McNamara, William. *Earthy Mysticism: Contemplation and the Life of Passionate Presence* (New York: The Crossroad Publishing Company, 1983).

3. John, Elton. *The Greatest Discovery.* London: DMJ Records, 1970.

4. Wikipedia contributors, "Maximilian Kolbe," *Wikipedia, The Free Encyclopedia,* https://en.wikipedia.org/w/index.php?title=Maximilian_Kolbe&oldid=864868542 (accessed March 4, 2018).

5. Wikipedia contributors, "Dietrich Bonhoeffer," *Wikipedia, The Free Encyclopedia,* https://en.wikipedia.org/w/index.php?title=Dietrich_Bonhoeffer&oldid=864496711 (accessed March 4, 2018).

6. Peterson, Eugene H. *Holy Bible: The Message* (the Bible in contemporary language). (Colorado Springs, CO: NavPress, 2005), Matthew 9:36.

7. Kelber, Werner H. *The Kingdom in Mark: A New Place and a New Time* (Philadelphia: Fortress Press, 1974).

8. Ambrogic, Aloysius. *The Hidden Kingdom, CBQ Monograph Series, No. 2* (Washington D.C., 1972); Keck, Leander, "The Introduction to Mark's Gospel," NTS 12 (1966).

9. Robinson, James M. *The Problem of History in Mark, Studies in Biblical Theology, No. 21* (London: SCM Press, 1957).

10. Weeden, Theodore J. *Mark: Traditions in Conflict* (Philadelphia: Fortress Press, 1972).

11. Delling, G. *TDNT, Vol. III* (1965), pp. 455-64.

12. Schmidt, K.L. *TDNT, Vol. I.* (1964), pp. 479-90.

13. Behm, J. *TDNT, Vol. IV* (1967), pp 975-1006.

14. Bultmann, R. *TDNT, Vol. VI* (1969), pp 175-228.

15. Murray, Daniel. *Discipleship: A New Testament Perspective* (1972).

16. Oepke, A. *TDNT, Vol. V* (1968), pp 636-54.

17. Best, Ernest. *Following Jesus, Journal for the Study of the New Testament, supplement series No. 4* (England: Sheffield Academic Press, 1981).

18. Lonergan, Bernard. *A Second Collection* (Philadelphia: Westminster Press, 1974).

19. Tracy, David. *The Achievement of Bernard Lonergan* (New York: Herder and Herder, 1970).

20. Lonergan, Bernard. *Method in Theology* (New York: Herder and Herder, 1972).

21. Otto, Rudolf. *The Idea of the Holy* (London: Oxford: University Press, 1923).

22. McFague, Sallie. "Conversion: Life on the Edge of the Raft," *Interpretation, July 1978 Vol. XXXII No. 3*, pp 255-268.

23. Moore, Sebastian. "Created, Alienated, Redeemed." Speech, Boston College, June 1981.

24. Fitzmyer, Joseph. "Pauline Theology," *The Jerome Biblical Commentary* (Englewood Cliffs, N.J.: Prentice-Hall, 1968), pp 800-805.

25. Campbell, J.M. & McGuire, M.R.P. *The Confessions of St. Augustine* (Englewood Cliffs, N.J.: Prentice-Hall, 1961).

26. Lonergan, Bernard. "Cognitional Structure" and "Existenz and Aggiornamento," *Collection* (New York: Herder and Herder, 1967), pp 221-39 and 240-251).

27. Day, Dorothy. *The Long Loneliness, An Autobiography* (San Francisco: Harper & Row, 1981).

28. Berrigan, Daniel. "Introduction," *The Long Loneliness, An Autobiography* (San Francisco: Harper & Row, 1981).

29. Day, Dorothy. *Therese, A Life of Therese of Lisieux.* (Notre Dame: Ind.: Fides Publishers Association, 1960).

30. Day, Dorothy. "41st Eucharistic Congress," Speech, Philadelphia, Aug. 6, 1976.

31. *The Catholic Worker*, June 1946, pp 5.

32. Blum, Christopher O. & Hochschild, Joshua P. *A Mind at Peace: Reclaiming an Ordered Soul in the Age of Distraction* (Manchester, N.H.: Sophia Institute Press, 2017).

33. Turkle, Sherry. *Alone Together: Why We Expect More from Tech and Less from Each Other* (New York: Basic Books, 2012).

34. Gazzaley, Adam & Rosen, Larry D. *The Distracted Mind: Ancient Brains in a High-Tech World* (Cambridge/London: MIT Press, 2016).

35. Kazantzakis, Nikos. *Report to Greco* (Simon and Schuster, Inc., 1965).

36. O'Connor, Flannery. *The Complete Stories* (New York: Farrar, Straus and Giroux, 1971).

37. Shmoop Editorial Team. "Exploration Quotes: The Hobbit, or, There and Back Again Page 1." *Shmoop University, Inc.* Last modified November 11, 2008. Accessed April 9, 2018. https://www.shmoop.com/hobbit/exploration-quotes.html.

38. Nouwen, Henri J.M. *Here and Now: Living in the Spirit* (Darton, Longman and Todd, 1994).

39. Carfagna, Rosemarie. *Divine Designs: Exercises for Spiritual Growth* (Kansas City: Sheed & Ward, 1996).

40. Solzhenitsyn, Aleksandr I. *The Gulag Archipelago* (New York: HarperCollins Publishers, 1973).

41. Kunitz, Daniel. Short List derived from "What Is Fitness?" (Glassman, Greg, 2002).

42. Leiva-Merikakis, Erasmo. *Fire of Mercy, Heart of the Word* (Ignatius Press, 1996).

43. Douthat, Ross. *To Change the Church: Pope Francis and the Future of Catholicism* (Simon & Schuster, 2018).

44. "Black Saints: Martín de Porres." Accessed June 30, 2018. https://www.ncronline.org/blogs/ncr-today/black-saints-mart-n-de-porres

45. Vatican Council. 1965. *Dogmatic constitution on the Church: Lumen gentium, solemnly promulgated by His Holiness, Pope Paul VI on November 21, 1964.* Boston: St. Paul Editions.

46. Shaw, Russell. *American Church: The Remarkable Rise, meteoric Fall, and Uncertain Future of Catholicism in America* (Ignatius Press, 2013).

47. Peterson, Jordan D. *Twelve Rules for Life: An Antidote to Chaos* (Random House Canada, 2018).

48. Doidge, Dr. Norman. *The Brain That Changes Itself: Stories of Personal Triumph from the Frontiers of Brain Science* (Viking Press, 2007).

49. Celtic Thunder. *The Show.* 2008.

50. Yutang, Lin. *My Country and My People* (London: William Heineman Ltd., 1948).

51. Rather, Dan. *The Camera Never Blinks Twice: The Further Adventures of a Television Journalist* (New York: William Morrow & Co., 1994).

52. Eliot, T.S. *Four Quartets* (Orlando: Harcout, Inc.: 1943).

53. Gallagher, Paul Michael. *Faith Maps: Ten Religious Explorers from Newman to Joseph Ratzinger* (London: Darton, Longman and Todd Ltd., 2010).

APPENDIX A
The Art of Shooting a Basketball

1. Coordination
2. Consistency
3. Concentration
4. Confidence

Coordination and consistency are physical elements, while concentration and confidence are mental attributes. All four are necessary on every shot in order to achieve the result of putting the ball in the basket.

Commonly Repeated Mistakes

1. Players tend to shoot out instead of shooting up.

2. Reverse spin on the ball is fundamental to becoming a good shooter.

3. Players are inattentive when they miss a shot, and therefore do not know how to make a necessary adjustment the next time they shoot.

4. Many players lack the ability to focus and be one with what they are doing. This is evident when shooting a foul shot.

5. Correct form and proper technique are often neglected and ignored.

The Philosophy of Shooting

1. Be attentive to your experience of playing basketball.

2. Be intelligent in your understanding of the game.

3. Be reasonable in order to make good judgments regarding dribbling, passing, shooting, playing defense.

4. Be decisive with your eyes, hands, feet, and the ball.

Practical Tips

1. Tilt your shoulders slightly forward. Imagine when you shoot, not only is the ball going through the basket, but so is your entire body.

2. **Always** shoot to the back of the rim, no matter what angle you take on the court.

3. If you want to avoid a shooting drought, and enjoy a flood of 3-pointers (college or NBA), employ Heron's arc, and there will be a rainbow at the end of your game, like Noah's Ark.

4. A basketball shot is much like a golf swing, a baseball swing, and a tennis swing:

   a. As little movement as possible

   b. Bring the basketball up on a straight plane

   c. Exaggerate the snap of the wrist for distance

   d. Exaggerate the follow-through for accuracy

Drills

1. Bill Bradley Drill – 10 spots on the floor. Make three of four shots before moving to the next spot.

2. Dan Murray Drill – 10 spots on the floor very close to the basket. Make 10 straight shots from these designated spots.

3. Tom Heron Drill – 5 spots around the NBA 3-point line.

Remember to catch, square, jump, release, and splash!

For Coaches

1. Coaches must observe release points, balance, and the arc of each player's shot.

2. Good coaches should have the ability to change bricklayers (poor shooters) into sculptors (gifted shooters).

The Principle of Reciprocal Inhibition

Laughter releases endorphins, powerful brain chemicals (hormones) that relax the body, reduce stress, relieve feelings of frustration, and produce an overall feeling of wellbeing.

Laughter cleanses and inhibits the brain from releasing the stress hormone, cortisol, into the body.

1. The ball is an extension of your hand (physical).

2. I always expect the ball to go in the basket (mental).

3. If, for some reason, it does not go in the basket, I can easily make an adjustment on my next shot (mental).

4. Serving a tray of wine glasses (physical image).

5. Putting your hand in a pitcher (physical image).

6. A good shooter simply involves muscle memory.

7. A very good shooter combines muscle memory with confidence.

8. A clutch shooter adds hubris to muscle memory and confidence.

Final Thoughts

There is nothing more *practical* than good theory. Every time you shoot, in order to give the ball a chance to go in the basket, it is necessary to shoot to the back part of the rim so that the margin of error (the circumference of the rim that can fit two basketballs at once) is in front of you.

A well-constructed sentence, like any artful design – shooting a basketball, playing a musical instrument, performing a waltz – is the result of sound craftsmanship.

APPENDIX B

Father Tom Heron's
Spiritual Playbook

The spiritual life consists of five unskippable steps:

1. Mindfulness

2. Receptivity

3. Conversion

4. Discipleship

5. Apostleship

Step One: Be awake. Be attentive. Be alert. Be on guard. Be vigilant.

Step Two: Be receptive to the spiritual gifts and spiritual fruits of the Holy Spirit and the abundant graces for every situation and circumstance.

Step Three: Pick up your cross daily and follow in my footsteps (see front cover for visual representation of the Carmelite Cross).

Step Four: Come be a lifelong student of Jesus. Come and listen. Come and learn. Come and gather your strength. Come and be nourished at the table of the Lord.

Step Five: Go in the name of Jesus. Go and teach. Go and heal. Go and proclaim the word. Go and baptize.

The 4 H Club

1. Humility
2. Hilarity
3. Hospitality
4. Holiness

What is Your Game Plan?

"I have come that you may have life and have it in abundance." (John 10:10).

1. Physical
2. Intellectual
3. Emotional
4. Social
5. Spiritual

APPENDIX C

Homily Delivered at the First Mass of the Rev. J. Thomas Heron

Sunday, May 20, 1978, St. Joseph Church, Collingdale, Pa.

Homilist: Rev. Daniel A. Murray

The Universal Church celebrates one of her central feasts today, the feast of the Most Holy Trinity. The Church of Philadelphia celebrates today because she has ten new priests. I begin my reflection in honor of the Trinity: In the name of the Father, and of the Son, and of the Holy Spirit.

I'm sure everyone here feels like the mother in the advertisement who is seeing her son off to school for the first time and has the thought: The future always arrives before we're ready to give up the present. Young Tom Heron a Priest? My, how the years slip by.

The air of excitement and joy is so obviously present this afternoon that we have to celebrate. We celebrate to show that we cannot grasp the totality of God's gift of love. Celebration is a receptive attitude of mind which opens us to mystery, to a time of peace in the depths of the heart, to the realization that there is within each of us a place where beauty and the holy dwell. Every liturgy is celebration, because of its constant reminders of the meaning of all things: spring, summer, death, life, suffering, joy, words, music, woven together into a meaningful pattern.

When we want to understand ourselves to find out what is most precious in our lives we search our memories. There is much memory-searching today. The priests here remember their own day of ordination and first Mass. Everyone here remembers something, some incident, conversation with Tom. Many of you remember him as the young kid who ate and slept basketball, and who seemed to have a loud speaker attached to his voice box. Others remember being thrown out of a game by a demanding, over-zealous, would-be coach. I remember him when all he knew was the name and number of every professional and collegiate athlete in the country. But he's changed a lot since then. His teachers at Bonner will be pleased at that. His Mass book reveals the names of some of his new friends: Augustine, E. Browning, B. Lonergan, Leo, V. Frankel, M. Rilke , philosophers, theologians, saints. Not bad company. But all these are passing memories.

We have another kind: living memories. Sometimes people and events so enter our lives, and become so meaningful that we never forget them. We remember them always. I have to mention Father Andy Lavin here. The Pastor of this parish is living history; one of the few priests whose appointment came from Cardinal Dougherty. Father Lavin was pastor here when Tom was born, and has watched his growth and progress, sometimes with exasperation, but mostly with pride. Tom has many vivid memories of Father Lavin: playing in the surf with him, serving his Masses, ringing the parish bell to announce the death of Father Tim Lavin. The lives of Father Lavin and Father Heron have been closely entwined for 25 years.

I want to tell you the story of three tables in the life of Father Tom Heron, and the living memories associated with them. The story of the first table began some 2000 years ago. A young Jesus of Nazareth sat around a table with his friends: try to capture the mood of that meal when faced with His own death. During the course of that meal He blessed bread and wine and gave it to them, telling them it was His Body and Blood: and then He added: "Whenever you do this, remember Me." He wanted to be remembered. He tells his closest friends that only in memory will real intimacy with Him be possible; only in memory will they experience the full meaning of what He has done and been for them. They understood what He meant. In the Old Testament, remembering is never simply looking back nostalgically at past events. To remember is to bring those events into the present and celebrate them here and now. To remember is to participate in and have an intimate encounter with the real acts of God's love. Through memory, a gulf is spanned. That's why they remembered Abraham, Isaac, Jacob; that's why they remembered the Exodus every year. To remember is to recapture the original vision. The first words of Genesis indicate this: "In the beginning... The entire Bible can be summed up in one word: "Remember!"

And so when Jesus says, "Do this in memory of Me", He wants His friends to make all they have experienced, and will experience with Him a present reality; He wants them to remember so as to participate in and celebrate His life, death and resurrection; He wants them to remember so as to capture the original vision. Jesus' friends did not forget. In fact they state that their first obligation to the people is to make them remember what they have received and already know. Peter says: "I consider it my duty to keep refreshing your memory as long as I live, even though you already know and are firmly rooted in the truth you possess." Paul tells the Romans that he has no doubt of their goodness; nevertheless he writes to refresh their memory, and writes somewhat boldly at times, because he considers it his priestly duty to do so. John tells us that Jesus promised the Spirit who will remind us of all He taught and more besides.

This brings me to the story of the second table: the Eucharistic table in this Church. The act of remembering is fundamental to what we do here. When we read the Word of God, we remember. God, Himself insists on this: "Take my words and engrave them on your hearts; drill them into your children; speak them at home, abroad; bind them to your wrist, a pendant on your forehead; write them on the door posts of your houses and gates; let them become your flesh and blood." When in the Eucharistic prayer the priest repeats the words of Jesus: "Do this in memory of Me", he is asking God to remember. In doing this the priest brings something before God, the Father : the entire life-death-resurrection of His Son, Jesus. The priest asks the Father to remember this and act once again on our behalf. The priest asks the Father to effect something, create something here in this liturgy. "Do this that God may remember me."

At this table the priest prays that God will remember those who offer this sacrifice of praise, that He will act on their behalf today; that they become sharers in this sacred action; participants in this mystery. The priest prays that we remember Jesus, passion, resurrection, ascension and so recapture the original vision once again. In the same way the priest asks God to remember those who have died. In all this the priest becomes the living reminder of God to his community as Peter, Paul, John were to theirs. An awesome task! The Priest hears, sees, touches and tastes so intimately the Word, Who is Life. How can he be other than a living reminder that all we hear, see, touch, and taste reminds us of God, of the origin and purpose of our lives? This, then, is an important Table in Tom, s life. Tom, as priest, you are to reveal the connection between our sufferings, and the story of God's suffering in Jesus. You are to reveal the connection between our life, and the life of God within us. As priest you are the living reminder that our faith is the achievement of ages, an effort accumulated over the centuries; you are the living reminder that if we cut off our rich past, we paralyze our future. You are the living reminder that the true test of character is not whether we follow the daily fashion, but whether the past is alive in our present.

Tom, God's people need a poet; someone to make sacraments for them from the substance of the earth; someone to help them feel life again, touch it, sense its goodness, perceive its intrinsic and undying value, someone to remind them that the secret of wisdom is never to get lost in a momentary mood or passion; never to forget the friendship of God or one another because of a momentary grievance; never to lose sight of lasting values because of a transitory episode; someone to show them that remembering is a holy act; that they sanctify the present by remembering the past. I know you are a priest and poet, that you will seek the Lord and remember Him, and know that His goodness and mercy are enough for you.

To a noble person it is a holy joy to remember, an overwhelming thrill to be grateful; while to a person whose character is neither rich nor strong, gratitude is a most painful sensation and the present is all he has. I know Tom well enough to say that he is rich and strong in character, and his moods today are joy and gratitude. This is due in no small part to the story of the third table, the kitchen table in the Heron home. A modern songwriter has written that the home is a wounded heart : an apt image to describe the Heron home: the heart, symbol of much love, affection, and warmth; but wounded some 21 years ago when Jack Heron died. The wounds were healed by memory, and Dot Heron was the doctor here. The kitchen table in her home is a very sacred place, a source of physical nourishment, and of shared memories. Dot made sure her children remembered their father. Faced with the task of raising four children, all at first seemed dark and she saw no exits. Dot Heron found salvation in a remembered love, and she constantly converted the pain of her husband's absence into a deeper understanding of his presence. There is a lesson in this for all of us. The memory of a friend can sustain us in the midst of agony and struggle; the memory of love can nurture us in our day-to-day struggles. Such memories are living, they connect us with our past and keep us alive in the present.

Dot, among the best things you gave your children were good memories - kind words, signs of affection, gestures of sympathy, peaceful silences, joyful celebrations. I'm sure there were times when childish ignorance blinded Sue, Tom, Joe and Mary to the decisions you had to make, and the cares and anxieties you nobly bore. But the clouds of childish blindness have lifted, and what you have been and are to them, becomes clearer with each passing day. I know how alive in Tom are the memories of trust, love, acceptance, forgiveness, confidence, and hope that you instilled in him. You've taught him more about giving than he'll ever need to know. In many long conversations he has testified to his heartfelt appreciation of your tender care, and the many acts of self-denial for your children. He has many memories of his childhood, of you, of his father. These memories are living ones; they connect him with his past, and all of you should know that it is these memories that give bounce to his walk; joy to his life; keep the smile on his face.

Dot Heron fits the description of the ideal wife-mother in Proverbs who has unsuspected resources of moral strength and love; she is an unfailing prize clothed with strength and dignity, opening her mouth in wisdom, and on her tongue kindly counsel. Dot, the memory of your husband is so alive that everyone here can rightly congratulate you and Jack. We all share with you two the joy you must feel today as Tom's mother and father.

Yesterday at the Cathedral everyone applauded when the names of the new priests were read out. I know all of you will want to acknowledge the good things God has done in this noble woman, and will do in her priest-son by your applause here today."

APPENDIX D
The Poetry and Writings of John Joseph Heron

Tommy's Birthday (November 1963)

A little boy went into church and up the aisle he walked

He knelt down at the altar rail; to the crucifix he talked.

'Say do you really love me, God? My mother says you do.

Then, how much do you love me God if y what she says is true;

Do you love me more than a penny's worth or more than a dollar can buy;

Could it be a hundred dollars worth? I guess that's going too high.'

The little fellow listened then; He wanted to hear God's voice, and God

Just had to answer him; He had no other choice.

'Oh, yes, I love you Tommy lad, what your mother says is true;

and more than all the world's great wealth is the love I have for you.

And, you know, I'd like to reach my hands And clasp you up to me.

But I can't – because of love for you, the've nailed Me to this cross-shaped tree.

So never forget I love you, boy.

May I ask one thing of you.

Because I love you, Tommy Lad,

won't you try to love me, too?'

Untitled Poem (April 1978)

He was no angel. Just our ordinary boy.

His childish pranks, filled my heart with Joy,

and from a toddler, my

Little boy Tom, to daily Mass he loved to go.

As he grew older I blessed the day

His mother encouraged his vocation and sent him away.

He went to college and after studious years

He was ordained: through joy I shed many tears.

With God's help we will see him some day

In Mass vestments clad

A priest of God, my own Little Lad,

Thomas Heron.

Christmas Eve at St. Mary's

[Twas Christmas Eve at St. Mary's and the Pastor, Father Heron, was watching Michael, the sexton, as he carefully fixed the crib.]

The sheep and the oxen were standing guard

The straw was nearly piled;

And Mary and Joseph were kneeling

Admiring their tender Child.

The star that guided the Magis

Flooded the stable with light.

'Tis beautiful, Michael' the Pastor said,

'It looks like that First Holy Night.'

'Ah, faith and I think it is terrible,'

The sexton replied with a frown;

'The way our Saviour had to be born,

In that miserable pagan town.'

'Sure there isn't an Irishman living,
Much less is there one in the grave,
From County Derry down to Donegal
That'd let him be born in a cave.'

'If the Irish were living in Bethlehem,
Joseph need not have knocked.
Sure, Mary and he could have walked right in
For our doors were never locked.'

'And if they had come to my cottage,
They'd have found the door full wide –
'caed mile failte' I'd say to them
God bless ye and step inside.'

'I'd shake up the old turf fire,
And make them as warm as could be,
And I'd have my wife, God rest her,
Make them a pot of tea.'

'And if the soldiers of Herod
Came after the Baby, the fakes,
Me and the neighbors would rout them,
Like Patrick drove out the snakes.'

'Tis a pity, Father, I tell ye,
without a word of a lie,
That there wasn't an Irishman living,
When Mary and Joseph passed by.'

Untitled Poem

I am a jolly old Junker

my name is John you know

when I get up in the morning

it's Junking I do go. I Junk

All day until night, happy as

Can be. Let nixon have the

White House. a Junker I will be.

Happy Birthday Tommy

Stick to your school

The Old Man and the Winter Sky

Reflection by Fr. Tom Heron

I brought out the wood cut print by Bob McGovern entitled "Old Man and the Winter Sky." This print was a profile of my grandfather. I unveiled the print was a profile of my grandfather. I unveiled the print and asked him what he thought. He looked at it for a while and stated: "I'm better looking than him." Followed by a big smile and a hearty laugh. He kept looking at it and said, "I would take him in. A fellow like this you'll have no trouble with. He's a good one. A real crackerjack. I've seen him over in Ireland. Oh, yeah."

A great man for taking *care* of things. He takes *care*. He's willing to talk to anybody, very simple, good plain person. I had to straighten him out a few times. But I had a good time with him. I'm telling you, any person coming in and seeing that man, they'd say "he's from *some place*."

He told me five stories during this visit. He was the hero of each story. Getting this man out of trouble and that man out of trouble.

His thoughts then turned to my hair. "I wouldn't clip it anymore. A little water not too heavy. You are a good, clean-cut fella. I wouldn't have to throw any water on you, thank God!"

His steady advice to me was to be modest, be generous, don't let anybody take advantage of you, don't give up – keep trying.

I said "Pop, you have big, strong hands!" He lifted his hands with pride and said "that's right. Not like some dainty jackasses I know!"

"Pop, that's a nice hat you have." His response to my compliment was "do you want to take this one? I can get another."

Gulf Gas

This poem was sent to Gulf Gas and the author received a radio prize.

As a user of Gulf gas I want you to know

I don't have to worry wherever I go

My motor does hum

My valves they go free

My engine is singing sweet Mother Machree

Our nation's power as is to control

As our auto needs Gulf gas

to pull out of a hole.

So you radio listeners

take a trip from a click

Fill your crank case with Gulf pride

your valves will not stick.

A Message From Santa Claus to Ann, Alice, Dad

I'm taking this chance to inform you

that misfortune has taken away

the things that I need for my visit

my presents, my reindeer, my sleigh.

Now I'm making my rounds on a donkey

Who's old and feeble and slow.

So if you don't see me this Christmas

You'll know I'm out on my ass in the snow.

My Dear Mary

I am sitting on the porch steps, Mary
Where we sat side by side
On a bright May morning long ago
When first you were my Bride.

The grass was springing fresh and green
The birds sang loud on high.
The red was on your lips, Mary
The love light in your eye.

The place is so much changed, Mary.
The day not bright as then.
The bird's loud song is in my ears
The grass is green again.

I miss the soft clasp of your hand
Your breath warm on my cheek
I still keep listening for the words
Although you never speak.

It's but a step down Darby
Where the little Church stands near
Where we were wed, Mary.
I can see the spire from here.

The graveyard lies above, Mary
Where your body is laid to rest
Though your soul is up in heaven
With your son you loved the best.

My Mother's Rosary

I'm only an old Irish mother
And I haven't much leisure for prayer,
But the beads I take out of my pocket
When I have a moment to spare,
And I try to forget all my worries
The cattle, the crops and the weeds,
As I talk to my Mother in Heaven
In doing the round of my beads
I pray for the priests that are working
In faraway lands and at home,
I pray for the shepherds, the bishops
I pray for our Father in Rome;
I beg their sweet mother to guard them
And succor them all in their needs,
And I feel that she'll heed an old woman
That's doing the round of her beads.
Her help I implore for the tempted
For those who have gone far away
From the house and the home of their Father
For those who are going astray.
I call her the Refuge of sinners,
And I know in my heart that she pleads
With her Son for her wandering children
As I'm doing the round of my beads.

Rosary Time

'Tis Rosary time in Ireland
and looking across the years
A picture unfolds before me

'Tis dimmed with a mist of tears

For sure it lacks gorgeous setting
no wealth of color does it boast.
But Rosary time in Ireland
is envied by angel hosts.

Ah! never was rank or station
or fame of glorious deeds
As dear as the scene in Ireland
when Mother took down the beads.

And readily would I barter the trophies
that through the years I've won
To kneel by that hallowed fireside
When the day's rough task is done.

I care not for stately temples
or glamor of service grand
I'd rather one prayer in Ireland
For isn't it God's own land?

The smell of the turf for incense
And love for the sacred light.
Ah! Rosary time in Ireland
My heart is with you tonight.

The Streets of Philadelphia

The streets of Philadelphia originated by Billy Penn when he took
Philadelphia over. He moved Germantown Avenue further back and
made Market Street Center City of Philadelphia. All trolleys and buses and

wagons left Market Street going to their destination going up town. I went ot the Market. Passed through the arch to see the race which was to take place on Vine Street. I told them I would climb Callowhill go through the Willow, which I thought it a noble way to Buttonwood. Through Spring Garden they called me Green. But Wallace on Fairmount Avenue told his neighbor of it. He lived in same parish and was very popular. John got on car past Girard Avenue. The conductor yelled out Thompson. I said what is it, master? I spoke to my brother Jefferson who was a graduate of Oxford. He sang Hail Columbia. Then I traveled past Berks and Montgomery until I met Morris. He told me he found a diamond on the banks of Susquehanna. He sold it to a chump from Dauphin. He took the money, went to York and Cumberland where there was a little Huntingdon. He made a fool of himself by dabbling in Lehigh stock. He turned a complete somersault [Somerset] which landed him all the way from Cambria to Indiana. But form there he had a clear field all the way up to Allegheny. I thought I had gone far enough uptown. I went back to the same Market, picked up a Chestnut feeling strong as Sansom I cracked a Walnut. There was a policeman nearby who had a Locust club. He told me to Spruce up and not Pine away. Then I met a colored man by the name of Lombard. He was from the south, formerly a slave owned by two men named Bainbridge and Fitzwater. He had his wife with him. A perfect queen and a good Christian. She had him settle down and work at his trade which was Carpenter. Then he heard of Washington and Ellsworth who was Colonel in the warmy of the Rebellion. He hired with a man by the name of Wharton. He taught him to Reed. He was giving a few lessongs by Emily Dickinson. He would have asked her more but was afraid of Mifflin her feelings. Then he met McKern who was full of bad stuff which he got when Snyder of law and order found Himself, down in the neck.

The Beautiful Hands of a Priest

To my grandson, Tom Heron

The beautiful hands of a priest.

We need them in life's early morning.

We need them again at its close.

We need their warm clasp of true friendship.

We need them when seeking life's woes.

When we come into this world we are sinful.

The greatest as well as the least.

The hands that will bless and unite us

Are the beautiful hands of a priest.

APPENDIX E
Risen Jesus

—Pope Francis

A holy card sent to Fr. Tom Heron from Pope Francis.

"Let the risen Jesus enter your life, welcome him as a friend, with trust: He is life! If up till now you have kept him at a distance, step forward. He will receive you with open arms. If you have been indifferent, take a risk: you won't be disappointed. If following Him seems difficult, don't be afraid, trust Him, be confident that He is close to you, He is with you and He will give you the peace you are looking for and the strength to live as He would have you do."

Made in the USA
Coppell, TX
30 November 2019